The Real World of the Public Schools

It is impossible for us adequately to conceive the boldness of the measure which aimed at universal education through the establishment of free schools. As a fact, it had no precedent in the world's history; and, as a theory, it could have been refuted and silenced by a more formidable array of argument and experience than was ever marshalled against any other institution of human origin. But time has ratified its soundness. Two centuries of successful operation now proclaimed it to be as wise as it was courageous, and as beneficent as it was disinterested. Every community in the civilized world awards it the meed of praise; and states at home and nations abroad, in the order of their intelligence, are copying the bright example.

—HORACE MANN
Tenth Annual Report as Secretary of the
Massachusetts State Board of Education, 1846

Moral egotism begets the faith in education. Everybody believes in it—Catholics and Protestants, individualists and socialists, capitalists and communists, despots and anarchists, conservatives and radicals. . . . Why has not education long ago removed our social ills? . . . Parents are notoriously bad educators of their children and the sons of psychologists seem to be no better off than the sons of Pericles. . . . The school asks for children better trained at home and the home asks for children better trained at school.

—F. J. E. WOODBRIDGE, *The Son of Apollo*, 1929

HARRY S. BROUDY

The Real World of
the Public Schools

HARCOURT BRACE JOVANOVICH, INC.

NEW YORK

Paperbound ISBN 0-15-575846-2
Hardbound ISBN 0-15-175965-0
Library of Congress Catalog Card Number: 72-78456

Printed in the United States of America
B C D E

To Dorothy and Richard

CONTENTS

PREFACE

If one can be certain of anything, it is that this book will be tabbed as a defense of the public school establishment by an educationist. It may astonish the reader, therefore, to find far more serious criticisms of our educational system in this volume than most of the shrill critics have leveled against it. Indeed, the great danger of the current abuse of the public school is that it will draw attention away from its more serious shortcomings.

Inasmuch as most of the criticism of the public schools is based on impressionistic visitations to selected schools and anecdotal reports, it is virtually impossible to counter it on a factual basis. Indeed, if there were really reliable relevant data and reliable methods of interpreting them, many of the issues in education would no longer be controversial. Most of the controversy in education is still in the domain of values, pseudoscientific claims to the contrary notwithstanding. This should hardly be surprising in view of the fact that education, unlike some highly abstracted forms of conditioning, is a general concept, like health and social welfare.

I point this out because I know of no factual way of deciding, for example, whether "the schools are oppressive" or what "oppressive" is supposed to mean. This being the case, I have no choice but to rely on an analysis of what seems to me the most cogent aspects of the school in American society, in order to assess its successes and failures. In doing so I have neither sought nor received help from any foundation or government agency. Indeed, I have deliberately refrained—with one exception—from asking my colleagues to examine the manuscript and to give me their advice. I am sure that this would have been a better and more balanced book if I had done so; on the other hand, it might have expanded into an endless seminar and not been written at all. The work, therefore, should not be construed as representing any organization or institution officially, educationist or otherwise. Yet the book does, I believe, voice what many competent and dedicated school people—teachers and administrators—would want to say to parents and citizens everywhere.

Because the book is intended primarily for the general public, technical matters and references to them have been kept to a minimum. Although I owe much to the writings of many people in many fields, I have written this book on the assumption that the reader's view of the schools has been formed more by accounts in the press and in books highly publicized by the press than by the more technical literature on education.

I am indebted to Professor Fred D. Carver, at the University of Illinois College of Education, for his reading of the chapter on public school finance, although he is not to be held responsible for its contents, and I am grateful to Mrs. Christiana M. Smith for her generous and skillful help with the bibliography and the index.

The Real World of the Public Schools

CHAPTER I

Oxen and Axes

Talk about children in general, and their schooling in particular, is not automatically popular. Listening to recitals about other people's children is a test of courtesy and character; to refrain from talking about one's own offspring is a test of self-control. Parents cannot seem to understand that "How's your boy, Jamie?" like "Hello, how are you?" is a form of phatic communion—a ritual of greeting rather than a request for information.

I have watched with amazement my sophisticated friends at a P-TA meeting. They listen attentively to routine descriptions of school procedures; they examine children's drawings with more concern than the latest exhibition at the Museum of Modern Art; every word of the teacher about their Jane or Dick is carefully noted. To anyone not a parent the discourse is about as engrossing as a lecture on diaper rash.

So much for the difference in attitude toward education occasioned by those who have children and those who do not. But there is another peculiarity about educational discourse. Almost everybody wants to talk about education, but virtually nobody has anything good to say about it.

As a topic for general conversation, education has its points. It can be discussed in mixed groups, although caution is advised if there is a color mix. Furthermore, everyone has had direct

3

experience with education, or at least with schooling of some sort. It is better than religion, because nowadays so few people know enough about religion to argue about it. Moreover, so long as the search for God in the pharmacy, in the commune, in the gutter, or in the morgue continues, controversy over religion in the traditional categories is, as the saying goes, irrelevant. As a field in which one can have strong convictions with a minimum of knowledge, education is rivaled only by politics. Unlike controversy on other topics, in which one side defends a view that the other attacks, discussion of education is pretty much a debate as to *what is really* wrong with it. All parties affirm the negative. Have you ever encountered anyone who is contented with his local school system? Enthusiasm for a particular teacher, possibly; for a particular school, occasionally; but for the system as a whole, no. Even its staunchest friends preface the defense with such remarks as, "Nobody realizes better than I the shortcomings of our schools and our teachers." As for the defense itself, what does it come to? Is it any more than a plea that the system, despite its shortcomings, is better than one has a right to expect?

Any survey of a fair sampling of articles, letters to the editor, and books on the subject will disclose a long inventory of complaints, with emotional overtones ranging from mild derision to outright hostility. There are a number of reasons why this is the case. For one thing, the dramatic interest of a well-managed, smoothly functioning institution is low; well-managed institutions create a minimum of surprise, suspense, and climax. Whatever charm helter-skelter may have, we do not welcome it in our hospitals, banks, or transportation systems, any more than in our own households. Households in which meals are irregular, housekeeping is sporadic, and life is one improvisation after another are amusing in fiction, but not in our homes.

What is one to say about schools when, and if, they ever do function properly? One could, of course, describe the procedures, the routines, the incidents that never really disrupt, the characters that mildly amuse, the slow progress from day to day. When the school is properly run, even internal strife is modulated. Sören Kierkegaard, the mid-nineteenth-century existentialist theologian from Copenhagen, remarked that nothing is so aesthetically impoverished as eternal bliss. And while smoothly functioning schools do not compete with eternal bliss in philosophical significance, they share its poverty of dramatic interest. The positive in education makes for dull reading. As a consequence, interest perks up only when the schools malfunction. To those who are directly involved with schooling—as producers, consumers, managers—the positive aspects are important, and so is information about them. Newspapers carry this information on an inside page, as they do the community calendar. For teachers and parents, information about programs and procedures, calendars and timetables, daily routines and routine triumphs are "interesting reading," but not to the uninvolved citizen, and certainly not to the editor of the front page of the daily newspaper. For the latter, only crisis, failure, charges, and countercharges of villainy warrant a headline. As one TV personality put it, "You don't have to announce daily that the mail is going through or that the firemen are on duty."

Perhaps a more fundamental reason for the negative tone pervading educational writing is that for most people discontent is the normal state. The moments of contentment—not to be confused with moments of ineffable joy or ecstasy—are brief interludes between the struggles to achieve it. Perhaps this is inevitable; perhaps it is even a definition of what it means to be human, but, in any event, discontent with life goes hand in hand with discontent with schools.

Education, thought of as a means to a better life, is judged to be as successful as life itself happens to be. And it makes no difference what "better" is taken to mean. Fagin's school for pickpockets and a young ladies' seminary both expect "improvement" by virtue of the instruction they impart. If the expected success fails to blossom, the seeds and cultivation are blamed. If one thinks of the seeds as inherited intelligence, it is clear why parents tend to apportion most of the blame to cultivation—especially to the cultivators appointed by school authorities—rather than to genetics.

Although discontent with the schools is ubiquitous, the forms it takes are as varied and numerous as the shapes of frustration itself. The mother of a young girl whom the boys ignore is bitter about the school's neglect of social adjustment; the father of the girl whom the boys like too much thunders against the permissiveness of the schools and latitude of visiting privileges in college dormitories. Every evil in individual life and in society, with a little thought, can be traced to education.

This observation is of some importance because, if sound, it helps form a proper attitude toward criticism of the schools. For one thing, such criticism should be regarded as a symptom of the critic's total attitude toward life. This, in turn, means that although the specific complaints are not to be brushed aside as hypochondriac manifestations of mankind's malaise, they are not to be treated directly. The analogy to treatment of symptoms in physical disease needs no elaboration, but it does need some emphasis, because the reluctance of school systems to treat symptoms is branded as "unresponsiveness." However, that education is no better than the social order permits it to be is no excuse for abandoning efforts to correct its purely "educational" inadequacies. Unfortunately, when the volume of criticism is large and uttered in many tongues, it is not easy to sort out symptoms from causes, direct from incidental effects. As a result, school systems, as social institutions, tend to react to attacks with improvised innovations or by token changes in form, while bureaucratic inertia leaves the substance unchanged. For evidence of the first type of response, the reader is referred to the celebrations of educational innovations in such magazines as *Time* and *Saturday Review* and to the advertisements of the education industries that now offer for sale prepackaged "innovations" to the bureaucracies. For evidence of the power of bureaucratic inertia, one need only appraise the total effect of the innovations of the last decade. Where are the innovations of yesteryear?

One could make a career of investigating the mice brought forth by the mountainous labors of some of the recent educational innovators. The innovators blame the educational establishment for dragging its feet, for hostility to change, and, above all, for defending the *status quo*. Less often do the innovators, or the resisters to innovation for that matter, ask whether the new development was consistent with the social reality in which the school was to operate, or whether it was a response to dissatisfaction with the culture. For example, how many of the current complaints about the unresponsiveness of the schools to the psychological needs of black children are really symptoms of the profound collective guilt of which we are trying to rid ourselves? How many of the demands for "humanness" in schooling, for encounters and "relating," are symptoms of a hope that the new culture will find us returning to a pastoral state in which simple face-to-face relationships will be the units of social intercourse? Open classrooms, it is broadly hinted, will produce an open society—this borders on faith in magic.

An example of another type of myopia is the inability of the innovators to overcome widespread resistance to "teaching machines," televised college instruction, and other technological "boons" to schooling. The resistance has little to do with whether the innovations are good educationally—as I believe, within well-defined limits, they are—but, rather, whether they pose a threat to a venerated conviction about the role of the teacher. Apparently it never occurred to the bright, young, eager technologists to ask: how does a man who has spent twenty years of his life teaching introductory French feel when told that a machine could do it better? The resistance of this teacher is not to be explained by the fear of losing his job; he probably could have a job tending the machine or writing programs for the machine. It is to be explained, rather, by the challenge to devaluate his career and thus himself as a person. How would the salesman of the teaching machine feel if told that selling machines could be done by machine? Why the bright innovators are not bright enough to know that an offensive against a life work, against a cultural role, against personal significance will engender a defense is hard to understand.

Some of the disappointing results of the reform effort must be traced to the fact that educational criticism and educational proposals for change are a kind of political action. Politicians routinely disclaim political motivations for what they say and do, but a politician does not really expect to be believed. It is enough that members of his constituency vote for him. The case is somewhat different with pronouncements about education. When a charge is made against this or that aspect of schooling, it contains two parts: one is an allegedly *objective* description of a state of affairs that is judged to be bad; the other is a prediction that the proposed change will be opposed by the bureaucracy for *noneducational* reasons, because, presumably, it has a vested interest in the *status quo.* The reformer disclaims ulterior motives for himself, but he never fails to attribute them to the opposition.

This familiar ploy "poisons the wells," because any answer the opposition can make is falsified in advance, just as every denial a patient undergoing psychoanalytic treatment makes that he is suppressing illicit desires can be interpreted as evidence of both the desires and their suppression. Inevitably there buds a suspicion that the reformers are not without their own axes to grind; hidden axes, to be sure, but axes nevertheless.* Once the argument has become thoroughly *ad hominem,* with one side impugning the motives of the other, the educational merits are obscured in the fog of the resulting suspicion.

Well, one might ask, do the reformers have pure hearts, or is it cricket to raise the question of motives in educational controversies? After all, it is not cricket to do so in scientific controversies, although, in the stories of scientific discoveries (James D. Watson's *The Double Helix,* for example), some interesting nonscientific information about the scientists involved reveals how all too human scientists are.

To charge that a school system is miseducating the young, that it is stifling the creativity and even the humanity of children, is not the same sort of judgment as, "The weather in the Midwest is dismal." The weather continues on its errant way regardless of our condemnation, and, aside from cloud seeders, nobody really is doing too much to change it. Complaints about education, by contrast, are calls to action. Actions have consequences; these consequences affect people as well as practices, and some people more than others. If wishes for power are at stake in educational controversies, then it is always pertinent to ask whose oxen are being gored or fed.

When, for example, the unhappy parent of the unpopular girl complains that the schools spend more time on teaching algebra than in making young girls happy, he has his facts straight enough, but the facts derive their import from his predicament.

---

* *The Ax-Grinders,* by Mary Anne Raywid (New York: Macmillan Co., 1962), is worth reading for a survey of the broad array of those who do have noneducational motives for influencing educational institutions.

He would like the school to change the facts, and the reason for such a change is that he would like his daughter to be popular. This is a perfectly good reason, but not an educational one. Or consider the steady drumfire of criticism that emanated from the Council for Basic Education in the fifties and early sixties. The facts presumably were that high school graduates were ignorant of the disciplines that the critics thought it important everyone master. The inference was that this situation was deplorable. The blame was placed on teachers colleges, which allegedly substituted courses in "education" for study of the disciplines. The proposed remedy was to take the training of teachers away from the teachers colleges, to give it to the liberal arts faculties, and to interdict all prospective teachers from reading the works of John Dewey.

Despite numerous efforts to get the facts "straight," the criticisms were reiterated again and again, as if no rebuttal had ever been made. For example, the critics repeated time and again the charge that the teachers colleges were responsible for the ignorance of high school teachers even after it was pointed out to them—many times—that the bulk of secondary school teachers had been trained in liberal arts colleges and not in teachers colleges. With perfectly straight faces the critics asserted (1) that education courses were vacuous and silly, and (2) that eight or ten semester hours of such coursework had the power to corrupt the seven and a half semesters of study in the liberal arts program. This kind of persistence is characteristic of a neurotic-paranoid reaction and prompts the conjecture that the real purpose of the criticism was not the intellectual salvation of the young and their teachers but rather the wresting of control of teacher education from the professors of education.

And so one wonders whether the plaintiff is coming into the court of equity with clean hands, and whether, when one party accuses the other of vested, noneducational interests, it does not open itself to the same charge.

Consider the possible motives stirring the breasts of professors of botany, English, and history in the fifties as students arrived on campus for the summer session. Thousands, most of them schoolteachers, flocked to register in the accursed education courses. Instead of enrolling for a master's degree in botany or English or history, they were candidates for the master's degree in education. Why teachers did this is a long and complicated story. For one thing, the courses in the academic subject fields were not always available in summer; some academic departments—perhaps most of them—did not regard the need of teachers-in-service as a legitimate claim on their resources. Then there was the matter of usefulness. There may come a time when the teacher needs educational courses more than further study in his field. Sometimes, although such situations would be rare, nonprofessional courses did not count toward salary raises. But, to return to motivation: would the fact that the education faculty were earning extra money for the summer session, while many liberal arts professors had no opportunity to do so, have anything to do with the contempt for education courses and Colleges of Education?

A fairly amusing illustration of this melancholy thesis was the fact that during the sixties some of the most vitriolic criticism of the public schools came from wives and mothers who had taken an A.B. degree from a "good" college in one of the standard disciplines—a major in history from Radcliffe, a major in English from Smith or Vassar or Wisconsin, Michigan, or Berkeley. In due course the children were enrolled in the public schools and brought home accounts of what went on in the classroom. It occurred to Mother that she could do much better than the teacher, who probably did not have a major in the subject from Smith, Vassar, Radcliffe, or even from a major state university. Later—especially when released from the chores of tending the children—she applied for a teaching position herself, but she was slowed down or blocked by certification requirements. Among these would be courses in education, which, of course, she had not only not taken, but also would not want her best friends to know if she had.

Mother's wrath can now easily be imagined. By an inductive leap she arrives at the conclusion that Shakespeare would not be allowed to teach English at the local high school, and Einstein would be barred from teaching mathematics there. Need anything further be said? Is not this the ultimate *reductio ad absurdum?* Her friends agree; her husband, whose academic background was no less immaculate, agrees; the local paper's editor finds the reasoning faultless.

This example is not to be construed as a generalization regarding female graduates of Smith, Vassar, and the other good schools. Some who wanted to teach did get certification through special arrangements with certain schools of education; some swallowed hard and dutifully took courses in educational psychology and history. Many, of course, did not try to teach, although their opinion of the local high school's staff was pretty low—they merely sent their children to good private schools. My example refers to those who tried, were turned aside, and did become vitriolic critics.

Then there is the motivation supplied by the desire for money and power. James B. Conant undoubtedly wielded more influence on public education in the fifties and sixties than any other single man. As ex-president of Harvard and a distinguished scientist in his own right, he hardly needed or wanted more power or money for himself. Yet he served as a key man for enterprises that generated enormous power and prestige and dollar rewards also for scores of men—the men who constituted the New Establishment in education during the sixties and extending into the seventies. The Educational Testing Service, the surveys and critiques of the high schools and of teacher training, the push to establish the Education Commission of the States— all were directly or indirectly accomplished through the Conant-Carnegie axis, later made even more powerful by an alliance with the U.S. Office of Education through Commissioners Francis Keppel and Harold Howe. This New Establishment had more of everything—money, prestige, influence—than the Old Establishment had, except numbers. When these numbers began to organize into militant unions, the high-riding New Establishment slowed down. Today the U.S. Office of Education does not trust the universities, the State Departments of Instruction, the school boards, or the unions; the unions trust nobody, and the universities spin their wheels taking contracts from anybody. Out of this battle royal may emerge two chief antagonists: the Education Commission of the States, an alliance of state governors and legislators, and the teachers' unions (including unions of college faculties), to fight the bitter battle for the distribution of tax monies.

Clean hands in controversies mean avoiding even the semblance of guilt; factual innocence is not enough, and this requirement is not confined to the candidates for the Supreme Court bench. One cannot, in good grace, condemn a fellow professor for running to Washington and playing the power game if one has never himself been invited to Washington; one must refrain from downgrading the author of a best seller if one's own books have not hit the jackpot. Objectively, a criticism may be just, and if it were, it would be just regardless of who made it. But the point in social controversy is not so much truth as credibility, for we act on the basis of motives and whether they are pure, and this we judge on the basis of the "impartial observer," who has no reason for not being objective and every reason for seeking the truth, for seeing things as they are. To qualify as an impartial critic of anything, one must first prove a lack of envy and self-seeking.

This leads to the impossible conclusion that legitimate social controversy can be properly carried on only by those who have no "interest" in the issues or only the most refined or sacrosanct interests—disembodied, intellectually nonvested interests. Since social controversy would probably never engage such pure spirits, the only course left to us is to take these ulterior motives into account or discount, and, please note, this makes them relevant.

Motives are relevant to educational discontent and controversy for still another reason. The extraordinary diversity in the expressions and targets of the discontent can be understood if one takes them to be the result of a variety of motives—that the shoe pinches different people in different places. In the early seventies, for example, there was much hard-nosed talk about making schools accountable in terms of results. "The fundamental weakness of the school must be remedied by a reward structure that is related to educational effectiveness," wrote one commentator. If one asks, "Success in what?" the examples given usually begin with "Reading" and end with " 'Rithmetic."

Yet in the same article an equally loud plea was made for not imposing middle-class values—presumably including the three Rs—on minorities, and for abandoning the "prejudice" that the urban minority child is somehow inferior to the middle-class child. In another article, equally bitter about the school system, the "book" was named as the prime villain, with the middle class foisting its own criterion of literacy on children who had other than "book" values and presumably better ones. How, pray, is one to reconcile the demand that school be held accountable for teaching reading and the charge that reading is the villain of the school system? Surely the liberal arts professors would not condemn the book. We find the new math lauded over the old math, but is new math any less middle class than the old?

Some critics would have the children learn all the standard disciplines in a straightforward way and become creative afterward. Others see no need to wait that long; let children create from the start, and the disciplines will take care of themselves, and if not, so what? Some publishers have done rather well in the late sixties and early seventies with books that called on children and parents to revolt against the schools because they destroyed the child's freedom, creativity, and personhood. In these accounts the blacks were subjugated and oppressed by middle-class white schoolteachers; the middle-class children were oppressed and depressed by middle-class values of middle-class teachers; the middle-class teachers were oppressed and depressed by middle-class administrators, who were part of a middle-class bureaucracy.

Now, for all I know, this is all true and just, but, if so, what is one to make of the charges that because of permissiveness, sloppy standards, and John Dewey's baleful influence, the young are now hung up on drugs, sex, riots, and anarchy? Or is one to construe dissatisfaction with drug addiction, campus violence, and the like as another middle-class prejudice exploited by one clutch of politicians against another?

Or take another puzzle. One hears pleas for diversification of schools to allow freedom of choice to parents, ethnic groups, religious groups, ideological groups. The Southern defenders of states' rights want diversification, and so do Northern liberals, but apparently for different reasons. Some blacks want decentralization of the school bureaucracy, and some private schools would like public monies to provide diversification and freedom of choice. The stated justifications are freedom of choice and the inherent goodness of variety, but the real reasons, the operating motives, are quite diverse. The upshot of which is that if ever these diverse reasons were given a chance to operate freely, we would have as lovely a chaos as could be imagined—enough to blow the mind of the most emancipated among us.

To deepen our confusion, the most vociferous advocates of privatism, decentralization, parochialism, and other variants of educational *laissez faire* are often the inveterate enemies of economic *laissez faire*. No longer has each party to the controversy one ox to be fed or protected from goring, but each has many oxen, and they are goring each other.

If the foregoing comments give the impression that the world of education is a political arena in which sinister figures struggle to gain control of the schools, it is not the impression I am trying to convey. To say that those who express their discontent with the schools have real as well as good reasons for their views is not to deny that some of these motives are neither hypocritical nor mean. On the contrary, for every individual who uses the schools to slake a thirst for power and prestige, there are dozens who scold the schools because they are unhappy with the value systems of the people around them. There are those who sincerely, honestly, and with some evidence believe, with Vilfredo Pareto, that a society cannot exist, much less be run decently, without an elite small enough and self-disciplined enough to rule. And there are those who, with no less sincerity and zeal, believe that all men really are created equal, and that only a perverted society renders them grossly unequal. The Platonic tradition that elevates theory to the top of the ladder of perfection is far from dead even in those who know it only by reputation; the impulse to rebel against this tradition has not been without its champions and certainly does not lack for any now.

Nevertheless, whether the motives be broad or narrow, selfish or altruistic, motives they are, so that when one runs across any allegation that this or that school system is good or bad, it is always in order to ask good or bad for whom and for what.

As a pretty fair working example of the almost inevitable politicization of academia, consider the activities of the private foundations. They have been called philanthropic in recognition of their chartered concern for the welfare of man and their mission to spread the benefits of large private fortunes to the public from which ultimately they were derived. The gifts of these foundations range from help to the aged to international amity and education. In 1966 the grants for welfare came to $80,512,-000; international affairs to $141,232,000. However, in recent years the charge has been made that a strong political bias pervaded the allotment of monies, and moves were made to make foundations subject to taxation on those of its activities that do not seem to comport with their tax-exempt status.

I am not here concerned with the justice or accuracy of the charges, and I welcome the activities of the foundations in behalf of liberal causes. But politics and personal or ideological preferences are what they are wherever they are, and foundations cannot qualify as Olympians merely by asserting in their charters that they intend to reside on the Mount. As one writer noted:

> With money you can promote an ideological perspective . . . or you can create a major institutional revolution within the university system and a whole new center of academic power, as was done with the institutes of international studies in the post-war period.*

In education, some of these foundations—especially Ford, Carnegie, and Kettering—have spent millions to "improve" education, to encourage innovation, to reform the training of teachers, to produce "better" curricula. One of the most persuasive arguments for this intervention was that the public school establishments, including State Departments of Instruction, teacher-training institutions, school boards, and teachers' organizations, were so self-serving—presumably to preserve their lucrative jobs —that they could not be trusted to reform themselves. To this was added a subtle but clear insult: even when their hearts were pure, their brains were meager and addled; and this for at least two reasons: one was that, coming from the lower socioeconomic classes, their native intelligence was not really first-rate; and the other that their training in inferior institutions, manned by inferior staff, merely compounded ignorance with innate deficiency.

Again, this is not the place to weigh the merits of these alle-

* David Horowitz, "Social Science or Ideology?" *Social Policy* 1, no. 3 (September-October 1970): 36.

gations. There are statistics, some of them furnished by studies done with Carnegie Foundation support, that to some extent confirm them. Nor is the point to justify the conditions that made the allegations plausible. No, the question is whether the motives actuating the foundation's efforts were themselves non-political; whether they did not also reflect the preferences and biases of a social class.

If a researcher designs a project so that it fits in with the "philosophy" of a foundation or with that of the reigning hierarchy in the U.S. Office of Education, is this project "politically pure"? Can this researcher honestly say that he does not really mind *who* carries it out and to whom the funds for doing so are allotted? This need not be his sole motive or even his primary one, but to the extent that it exists at all, it becomes a relevant factor in deciding the stance one is to take toward it. For, to this extent, it produces benefits selectively—it helps this researcher, not that one; this institution, not that one; this public, not that one; and, for this reason, the social consequences are properly considered in assessing the enterprise. Thus the intervention of the Ford Foundation to decentralize schools in New York City had to be evaluated on more than its directors' intent to help the ghetto residents achieve better education for their children, and of course the teachers' organizations took this into account in their evaluation.

Suppose a man points a gun at you with the exclamation: "See what a remarkable gun I have invented!" Here one confronts two issues: "Is it true that the gun is a remarkable gun?" and "Will he shoot the gun at me?" Philosophically these are two distinct issues and logically independent. But to a human being interested in staying alive, the second issue takes priority over the first, and you might very well destroy the gun and perhaps the gunner while muttering all the while, "Yes, it really was a remarkable gun." Why a foundation that launches an innovation that jeopardizes the security of established personnel should be puzzled about resistance to the innovation is a problem that some foundation ought to investigate. A just social reform distributes the benefits and risks fairly. The resistance to labor-saving machinery is justified not by the claim that the machinery is bad or that efficiency is bad, but rather by the fact that its initial impact is selective and unfair. And the unfairness is bad even though the efficiency is good. If a reform threatens such unfairness, resistance to it is justifiable.

The heart of the matter is whether "foundations can be the source of support for disinterested evaluation of government activities" or, one might add, educational activities or any other social activities, as they claim they can. I would dispute this claim, not because the men who head foundations are evil or unduly biased, but because they are men, and men not chosen at random from the population but from a very small stratum of society, and because their projects involve men and money and, inevitably, power and prestige. Short of putting Saint Peter and his Apostles on their Boards of Directors, I know of no way of convincing anyone that they have no axes to grind. It would be interesting to trace the overlapping memberships of the advisory boards of the major educational foundations and the powers in the U.S. Office of Education during the sixties. One Ford Foundation employee, for example, according to a General Accounting Office report, received $16,000 in consulting fees from HEW. The network of research grantees, consultants, advisory panels, and educational writers constitutes an educational establishment of which it pays to be a member. By comparison, the NEA (National Education Association) establishment is diffuse and sprawling, although large in numbers. The political threat posed by the New Establishment accelerated the conversion of teachers from the ideal of "professionalism" to the reality of collective bargaining. In the ensuing struggle between the establishments "the welfare of the child" will provide the pretext rather than the text for educational reform.

Those who have read Michael Polanyi's *Personal Knowledge* have probably been persuaded that pure objectivity is a fiction even in the work of the scientist. The scientist's passion for truth is a highly individual, personal matter: it leads him to find problems where others see none; it sustains him through long periods of doubt and skepticism. Only when reasoning and knowledge are electrified by passion does the effort have a chance of amounting to something important. So bias is nothing to be ashamed of, but the bias of science is for integrity of inquiry; whereas bias in foundation activities is likely to influence action as well as inquiry.

Grinding axes, however benign the motive, means accountability, and why the foundation as a source of political action is to be above accountability while insisting on it from all others is beyond understanding, unless, of course, Saint Peter really is on the Board of Directors. Again, to be without preferences is impossible, so to make believe one is, is not only hypocritical but silly. Revealing one's political goals is the only honest recourse, but this makes one accountable to those who have a valid concern for the way the consequences affect them.

Is one to conclude, therefore, that educational controversy is a waste of time? Is it a madhouse of bias and bureaucracy on which it would be wise to turn the key and relax with a good recording of the Bach suites for unaccompanied cello? Much controversy in this field is a waste of time. Discussions that ignore the massive logistics of a public school system in a country such as ours are indeed a waste of time. Not much more significant are the stock anecdotes about teachers. There are many contexts for the discussion of educational discontent—the economic, the intellectual, the personal, the societal—and each has its own constraints. When the contexts are confused or the constraints ignored, a good deal of nonsense is generated.

A few examples of confused controversy may be useful. Although figures can be made to tell a variety of stories, one does not have the liberty of seriously proposing a Summerhill type of school for 46 million school children or of prescribing that each be placed on the end of the log with a Mark Hopkins at the other. A pupil in front of a computer-aided teaching console is a more likely image.

Another example: some of the experiences in underdeveloped countries have been very satisfying to Peace Corpsmen and their hosts. If we regard the disadvantaged people in the ghetto as "underdeveloped countries," then schools should take the form of communities in which analogous corpsmen do the "teaching." The Salvation Army hostel, the storefront church, the settlement house, all have been put forward as models for the school in the ghetto. The criterion of "success" in these experiments is the "turning on" of the pupils. That one can fashion the real ghetto schools after this model is highly improbable once the differences in context are noted.

Still another example with a high potential for mischief is the spate of books on the destruction by the public school of the autonomy and creativity of the individual. Do schools destroy autonomy and creativity? I am sure they must limit them. Is this bad? To this one must make the most unsatisfactory of answers, 'That depends." School systems inevitably respond to the total network of demands that constitute the social order; parents quite naturally think about the life plans of their children; the pupils don't give much thought to either. Meshing these contexts is not made easier by ignoring the distinction between them. For example, the amount and kind of vocational training to be provided by the school is really not a community affair; it is part of a national strategy based on trends that hold for the nation. In the larger perspective, imaginative projects that allow nonbookish adolescents to "turn on" may not be so important as at first blush they might appear.

No matter what our biases may be, there are social facts upon which reasonable men can agree. And once we agree, for example, that in the next fifty years we shall not revert to a pastoral society, some imperatives for the school become noncontroversial.

So although much controversy about education is fruitless, some of it need not be. Indeed, there is no better way to find the oxen worthy of protection and the axes worth grinding. And there must be oxen, axes, and controversy, because in talk about education people reveal the hostages they have given to whatever it is they believe life ought to be. Education belongs to that strange class of puzzles that lures us back again and again, not because we hope to solve them but because we do not know what we would be without them.

CHAPTER II

Why the Schools Are Unresponsive

For more than a decade we have been hearing that the schools—the public schools and more recently the colleges and universities—are not responsive. Because the complaints come from men and women who have not succeeded in turning the schools in what they regard as the right direction, it would be futile and meaningless to deny the charge. The schools have been and are unresponsive insofar as individuals are dissatisfied with them. So to assess the import of the unresponsiveness, one needs to ascertain the identity of the plaintiff, the nature of his discomfort with the school, and why he believes a change in the school would relieve that discomfort.

In the early sixties the unresponsiveness was ostensibly to the defense needs of the country as defined by Admiral Hyman Rickover, but more directly the schools were blamed for being unresponsive to the advice of enlightened citizens on and off school boards. This was the theme of James B. Conant and other reformers who asserted that the good sense of the citizens was being kept from influencing the schools by the educational establishment, notably the National Education Association, school administrators, and professors of education.

By the mid-sixties the unresponsiveness of the schools was said to be toward the children of the city ghetto, then toward all poor children, and finally toward all children and youth. By the end of the sixties, the schools were alleged to be unresponsive to all social evils—poverty, racism, the war in Vietnam, and the pollution of the environment. In short, the schools at all levels were unresponsive to the Age of Aquarius. If one substituted for the school any other social institution, the indictment would remain the same. The volume of literature on this theme of unresponsiveness is so large that by now there is no need for extensive documentation. Furthermore, one hesitates to mention books and authors because it is hard to sort out the responsible writing from the silly and shrilly things that some publishers rush into print in order to take advantage of the market. The books that get the most promotion become the "standard" references, and inasmuch as size of readership may be an index of influence, this may be as good a standard as any in assessing the "importance" of the product.

I have already mentioned the speeches and writings of Admiral Rickover. The indignation of the Admiral with the low quality of scientific instruction in the schools was widely publicized and made hay for the Council for Basic Education and for Arthur E. Bestor, who had been fulminating against the educationists in the middle and late fifties. *Quackery in the Public Schools* by Albert Lynd was a typical attack on the public schools' unresponsiveness during that period.*

John Gardner made "excellence" a household word in education just as John F. Kennedy did in the mansions of political rhetoric. James B. Conant's *Slums and Suburbs* sounded an early warning about the unresponsiveness of schools to the problems of the ghetto, but a much more frenzied outcry came later from such writers as John Holt, Jonathan Kozol, and from Charles Silberman (*Crisis in Black and White*), the author who led the keening over the death of gaiety in *Crisis in the Classroom*. In the meantime, Paul Goodman, Edgar Z. Friedenberg, and a supporting coterie in the *Saturday Review* education section, the education department of the New York *Times,* and the *New York Review of Books* kept the public informed about the unresponsiveness of higher education to the needs of alienated youth.

---

* Also in the same mood were Mortimer Smith's *And Madly Teach* and *Diminished Mind;* Arthur E. Bestor's *Educational Wastelands;* and Hyman G. Rickover's *Education and Freedom.*

I repeat that this is but a tiny fraction of the writing on this theme.

These writings not only exposed the unresponsiveness, but they also shared similar hypotheses as to why the educational establishment was unresponsive. Again the refrain is by now so familiar that it will be sufficient to identify the villains most frequently mentioned.

First came bureaucratic rigidity. The establishment's arterial system was complicated and hardened; it was impossible for anything "innovative" to circulate within the system even after it had been injected into it. This theme, for example, is reiterated on virtually every page of *Community Control and the Urban School*, an account of the Ford Foundation's efforts to decentralize New York City schools, by Mario Fantini, Marilyn Gittell, and Richard Magat.

Second on the list was middle-class bias, a brew made up of WASP mentality, Puritan ethic, and capitalistic economics, laced with outsize portions of stupidity and hypocrisy.

Third was a lack of sensitivity and intelligence among teachers and administrators. They were portrayed as time-serving tenured civil servants of low academic quality seeking to rise above their lower-middle-class origins. This staff of about 2 million classroom teachers was characterized as not very bright, conforming, "uptight," and, at best, only half alive. The teachers' unions in the big cities were conceded to be alive, but their militancy was being exercised in behalf of deplorable causes.

Fourth was what Mr. Silberman referred to as the "mindlessness" of teacher-training institutions and the professors of education. Of all the causes of unresponsiveness, this one was and still is the one most frequently mentioned.

There is just enough truth in each of these allegations to render them plausible, but there is a good deal more reason to believe that even when taken together and given all the credibility they deserve, these hypotheses do not account for the unresponsiveness of the school. I submit that the instigators of reform, its major propellants, so to speak, by their approach, attitude, and methods made—and even now are making—sure that the reforms would not come about at all, or not to the extent that would justify the effort or the expense or the publicity drummed up in their behalf.

Imagine, if you will, an army of about 46 million troops engaged in a campaign under the direction of about 2 million assorted officers. Each of the soldiers serves anywhere from eight to twelve years in this army, so that there is a constant replacement of veterans by recruits. On a smaller scale there is constant renewal of the officers. The campaign plans were drawn and revised little by little over a period of 100 years. Imagine now what it will take to alter the campaign or the movement of the army in any significant way. Of this we can be certain: a simple command by any general—even the top one—will not effect a discernible change, at once. But the army we are talking about has no supreme general, and only by ignoring reality can it be compared to one army. The more realistic comparison is to thousands of herds of varying sizes, all moving more or less in the same general direction at differing speeds over a vast terrain.

Now imagine further that the horde or the army does begin to change direction, and then all of a sudden the command is sounded for the army to reverse itself. I suggest that even if every member of the officer force heard the command and were disposed to respond, nothing much would be discernible, except confusion. To a large extent this has been the story of educational reform in the last decade.

It will be recalled that Sputnik rose in 1957, and, before a year had passed, episodes such as the following were not unusual. One frosty morning, an elementary school teacher in an Illinois country school found a box of books on the school doorstep. They were books on science and the teaching of science. It turned out that the district superintendent felt it was a step toward meeting the demand that more and better science be taught to school children so that Admiral Rickover could build better atomic submarines and our rocketry could catch up with that of Russia.

The new math and physics programs got their initial thrust from "real" physicists and "real" mathematicians, who shouldered the "educationists" aside to demonstrate the "real" article. The National Science Foundation, dispensing huge amounts of money for research in science, made available funds for research and development in science education as well.

Almost overnight powerful forces were unleashed to promote and reform science education. Project Talent was typical. It was designed to identify youngsters with high intellectual potential. It was a really clever child who could evade this hunt. Merit Scholarships, all sorts of fellowships, and training grants for graduate study created an educational research and training complex that contributed as much as 40 to 50 per cent of the budgets of universities, including their Colleges of Education. Research-and-development centers, funded in the millions, acted as magnets to which were drawn eager young scholars, each hoping to become someday the founder of a research empire, or at least to rule over a good-sized colony.

The U. S. Office of Education, long a fairly pedestrian data-gathering and data-disseminating agency, became a funding source and thereby a maker of educational policy. It was staffed, whenever possible, by bright young men (noneducationist) who, like the physicists and mathematicians, were ready to show the educationists what could be done with brains, drive, and the Kennedy *élan*. The talk in academe—in every department—became indistinguishable from that at board meetings of General Motors, General Foods, or the Rand Corporation. One heard endless pronouncements of new verities: "Resources have to be concentrated to achieve a critical mass"; "Brains go where brains are, and money goes where brains are"; "We need to foster centers of excellence." It was "Good-bye, Mr. Chips" on the college campus.

The word "prestigious" became part of the academic lexicon. It came to mean institutions on the East and West coasts that were heavily funded for research in the sciences and in technology based on these sciences. One read much about the "best" five institutions or the "best" eight. Anyone who put out a rating could get it published, and administrators panted for these lists either as a source of self-congratulation and as a justification for grants and contracts or as a bludgeon with which to get more funds for their institutions from state legislatures.

The commodity-market approach was also taken toward staff appointments and promotions. At one meeting I was amazed to hear an influential academic propound the principle that salary increases should be allotted to persuade the people "we want" to stay. As for the faculty members who, in an earlier and less delirious era, had joined the academic profession for other than purely economic reasons and who did not relish the competitive ground rules of industry, it was agreed that only tenure could keep them on the staff. The swingers deplored the shelter afforded Mr. Chips by tenure, but with plenty of soft money available, all sorts of intellectuals could be hired for work in institutes, centers, and on projects without tenure. To the Cassandras who warned of a day of reckoning, the swingers turned an amused eye and a deaf ear. With all their creative imagination, of which the swingers were supposed to have more than a fair share, the empire builders could not imagine a day when the soft and hard money would run out.

Among the multifarious effects of the sudden growth of the academic money tree was the new professor freed for the first time from money troubles and able to make decisions on the basis of other than financial considerations. For it was a time when he could make considerable money, if he chose to do so. Many did so choose and founded glamor electronic and research industries on the East and West coasts. Ironically the most prestigious universities were harboring the very students who were soon to reject the military-industrial complex the universities had uncritically served and who in time were to disenchant the country with the aerospace industries. The ill-concealed arrogance of the scientific establishment preceded a great fall, as manifested in the doldrums of 1969–70. This arrogance short-circuited the sympathy that otherwise would have accrued to the unemployed scientific professionals, inside and outside academe, whose jobs evaporated as the NASA budget was cut, when the SST was in trouble, and when Pentagon and other federal research funds shrank.

But the important point of our discussion is the effect this all had on the responsiveness of public schools. The net effect was a commitment to Mr. Gardner's plea for excellence. In the early sixties this meant being the kind of young man or woman who could master academic subjects at a high level of intellectual sophistication. Being admitted into a prestigious college certified the individual as being a probable success, and it also certified the secondary school from which he was graduated as being the right kind of school. The curriculum suitable for such a good school was the good curriculum. "Structure of knowledge" became the key phrase in curriculum building; and understanding this structure, the goal of teaching. The most widely quoted book of this period was Jerome S. Bruner's *Process of Education,* which was a direct outcome of a conference devoted to the structure of knowledge and concept attainment—in short, intellectual excellence. Jean Piaget's genetic epistemology, with its stages of cognitive development, was "rediscovered."

In the rage for excellence during the sixties (before the "democracy boom") there lurked the danger of forgetting that in a democratic society excellence has to mean more than winning Merit Scholarships and getting a Ph.D. from a good university. It means the use of high-grade science and the humanities in behalf of all social and personal goals—and for everybody—as well as in the service of the military-industrial complex.

But the promulgation of this ideal would have had little impact in any event, because by then the schools were only beginning to respond to the demands of 1957; they and the intelligent laymen were in the grip of a scientific fever. Cautions about democracy and pleas for the humanities were useless; they were not even heard.

As a result of that fever, even the humanities faculties in the universities had to adopt the science talk about usefulness to the defense effort or to the cold war. I once jestingly congratulated a noted scholar of Byzantine culture on the irrelevance of his field to the war machine, and he informed me indignantly that he had just received a grant to study the effects of certain developments in his field on certain esoteric aspects of the cold war. It was a long time before any attention to the humanities in the curriculum of the public schools could be drawn. During the early sixties I walked up and down Madison Avenue begging for a small grant for the study of aesthetic education in the schools. But not one foundation on that street was interested. Although "creativity" and "imagination" were the watchwords of these geese that laid the golden eggs for academe, I could not persuade any of them that in the seventies the public schools of America might be as far behind in the aesthetic domains as they were in the scientific domains in 1960. As for democracy, in those days, talk of democracy did not sound well in the halls of excellence.

The point to be noted is that if a relatively small group of reformers cannot change its direction once it has the momentum of a devoted coterie, then how much more unrealistic is it to expect the vast agglomerate we refer to as the public school system to alter whatever course it happens to be embarked upon?

How was the mind of the public school teacher at the end of the fifties furnished? I dare say that by that time most of the working force of teachers in the elementary public schools were familiar with the theory and practice of projects, units, and core curricula as propounded by John Dewey and his disciples. Even schools with traditional curricula used some of the methods and many of the text materials that reflected this outlook on schooling. The general outlook on life was what today one would call liberalism—perhaps of the weary variety. It assumed that, given a chance, men would arrive at rational decisions about their lives and, in collaboration with their fellows, would progress gradually but steadily toward the humane community. The democratic society was held to be the instrument par excellence for achieving this end, and the school was the eminently appropriate institution to prepare individuals for participation in such a democracy. This was a far cry from the vision of a society led by a scientific elite who were to guide the young, the astronauts, and the government into paths of excellence.

What about the high schools? They, too, were not prepared to take the route of excellence proposed in the early sixties. On the one hand, the college-preparatory curriculum, which was still standard in most high schools, contained materials that had not kept up with the developments in the various disciplines. Professor Arthur Bestor blamed this situation on the influence of teachers colleges for having neglected the content of the sciences and concentrating instead on methods of teaching. In this charge he was somewhat less than half right. Most secondary school teachers at that time were graduates of liberal arts universities and not of teachers colleges, so that if they were teaching bad science, it was because of the inadequacy of their college science courses. To this day college courses in the sciences are not always models of excellence. Bestor's remedy—to take more science in college—was not the panacea he thought it to be.

On the other hand, the high schools had been jolted badly in the Depression of the thirties when the college-preparatory curricula baffled hosts of nonacademic youth who, lacking jobs, roosted in the high schools, to the discomfiture of themselves and their teachers.

Education for All American Youth, a popular report on secondary schools in the Depression, tried to map strategies for coping with the mass of nonacademic youth. So did a cluster of youth studies which concluded that secondary schooling of the college-preparatory type was not "relevant," and that for the majority of youth the high school ought to do something else: concentrate on occupational training.

Although the Dewey doctrine never made much headway in the secondary schools, its practical spin-offs did produce core curricula and a variety of schemes designed to make instruction more directly instrumental to vocation and the tasks of citizenship. Above all, the problem of "motivating" the nonbookish pupils to work at their studies became central. It was not surprising that, for many school people, the abolition of the formal study of the standard intellectual disciplines suggested itself as the only practical solution.

What the Council for Basic Education thinks now, when some of the best students at the prestigious colleges are turned off by "excellent" courses in the academic disciplines, I do not know. One would expect the Council to be embarrassed to hear its shining examples of excellence using language that is so reminiscent of the educationist life-adjustment jargon.

Consider, then, the task of turning the whole secondary school system—and, to no small extent, the elementary one as well—around to the vision of excellence. In the fall of 1959, there were 8,271,000 pupils in grades nine to twelve of the public schools, and by 1969 the figure had risen to 13,022,000. In 1959 there were 524,000 teachers in the public secondary schools; 906,000 ten years later. Special institutes were established to retrain instructors to teach the new math, physics, and biology, but how many could be reached by these institutes? How long would it take for the colleges to turn their own faculties around? One does not switch from old to new math by an act of will alone. The new math is a different way of conceptualizing quantitative relations and not merely a new method of computation. Every organized discipline is more than a body of facts; it is a mode of inquiry, with its own entities, relations, probems, and criteria of evidence. Specialists master this in their own disciplines, but we have not devised ways of teaching the concepts of a number of disciplines so that the student can use them to interpret his experience without becoming a specialist in each of them. We know even less—despite much talk about interdisciplinary studies—about teaching interdisciplinary cognitive patterns.

In somewhat less abstract language, all this means is that while we have been more or less successful in teaching "good" chemistry to prospective chemists, we have not solved the puzzle of how to teach the prospective lawyer, merchant, or housewife how to use chemical concepts and their relationships, physical concepts and their relationships, biological concepts and their relationships, linguistic concepts and their relationships, so that, as nonspecialists, they can use these categories in their reading and discussion as citizens and as human beings. High school science teachers, for the most part, had taken the first few steps toward a specialist's training in a science—an undergraduate major. It would take much more than this to enable the teacher to convey the "structure" of good physics or chemistry or history either to specialists or nonspecialists. For that matter, many of the college teachers were not ready for the new math, the new biology, and the new physics.

It is not an easy matter to convince the public—especially those who measure American secondary schools by Eton and Harrow, the German Gymnasium, or the French *lycée*—that in this country high school teachers are not scholars. A major in biology or history or any other subject is not the equivalent of a university degree in that subject from Oxbridge or from a French or German university. The social status of the secondary school teacher in the United States and in Germany or France cannot be compared without considerable embarrassment on the part of America. The call to academic excellence entailed a demand that secondary school teachers be what they were not and, indeed, what few of them had any intention of becoming. Teaching was probably not their first choice as an occupation, and, if they were male, perhaps not even their second.

Of course, this picture of high school teachers is overdrawn. Some of them do think of themselves as scholars, more closely related to college instructors than to teachers in the junior high school. In New York City, for example, the high school teachers, especially of the standard academic subjects, found it difficult to accept a single salary schedule—one that does not differentiate among the elementary, junior high, and senior high staffs—since it would deny the academic superiority that high school teachers claimed. The development of the junior college in recent years has provided a more appropriate notch on the academic totem pole for this grade of teacherdom than either the high school or the four-year college.

Similarly, one must soften the indictment that teaching is not popular even with teachers. Frequently there is commitment to the calling, but it is not, as a rule, the commitment of a scholar to the discovery or the dissemination of knowledge. Rather, a mildly messianic commitment is directed toward the realization of the American faith in education. These teachers, and the administrators who were once teachers themselves, believe in the redemptive power of schooling—as much of it for everybody as the nation can afford to give, and perhaps even a little more. Whether it was the second-generation immigrant child from the ghetto or the black or the poor child from the farm, schooling, it was believed, would elevate him on the economic, social, and moral scales. In the Puritan ethic is there any difference between these scales? However, the commitment to schooling was not necessarily a commitment to academic excellence, and one found among the most deeply committed schoolmen the strongest proponents of vocational education and the life-adjustment curriculum. The clarion call to excellence did not always elicit sympathetic vibrations from the dreamers of the democratic dream.

Let us now return to the early sixties, when the new curricula in the sciences and mathematics were being developed and urged upon the schools. If the profile I have drawn of the teaching personnel of that time is at all correct, then, of course, they were unprepared for the new math and the new science. The reformers muttered bitterly about foot dragging, but they were suffering from several illusions, or perhaps from one illusion with several aspects.

The major illusion was that instituting a change in education was like introducing a new product in agriculture or manufacturing. In the latter fields the mere demonstration of a superior product virtually guarantees the recognition of the superiority and a willingness to change from the old to the new product. What farmer, for example, could fail to see the advantages of the tractor over the mule, or hybrid corn over the older varieties, after several well-staged demonstrations? To be sure, the farmer would need new skills and understanding to shift from mules to tractors, gang plows, and hybrids, but, given good extension agents and market competition, such a transition could be accomplished in a relatively short time. For industry the problem is often more complex, but the logic is as compelling.

Between arithmetic as the practice of computation and the new math, and between science as a set of facts and the scientific mentality in the act of discovery, however, there is a breach in cognitive style. To know that $2 + 2 = 4$ and to prove it are quite different mental operations. It may seem foolish to want to prove such verities. The average teacher in the elementary school and perhaps in the high school was not taught to regard arithmetic and algebra as deductive systems; some, perhaps, were not too secure with this structure even in geometry, once the safety of proofs of the standard theorems was left behind. I am not saying that these teachers could not have understood all this had they been taught to do so in the first place, but most of them were not; nor were the textbooks to which they had become accustomed geared to thinking about their subjects the way a good mathematician, a good physicist, or a good biologist is accustomed to think. To the mathematician and scientist who had been so trained, the resistance of the schoolteacher appeared as unwillingness or inability to change; they were forgetting that these teachers did not have the benefit of their own long tuition. Indeed, the innovations proposed by the new curricula were not innovations to the proponents; the cognitive strain of change was not threatening them at all. In short, the reformers were demanding not merely that the farmer use a new plow or new seed but that he become a new type of farmer, and in a year or two.

The schools seemed unresponsive for the sorts of reasons already alluded to: bureaucratic rigidity, unwillingness to change old habits, and so on down the familiar litany of condescension. But the critics who cited these reasons badly underestimated the difficulties of changing the total cognitive structures of teachers, textbook writers, and the teachers of teachers. Not even huge infusions of money as incentives to this or that school system to innovate could hasten the process substantially; neither could exhortation and name calling. Such systemic changes require the change of the total blood supply of the organism, a new teaching generation—and such a generation is not much less than twenty years in forming.

Let us look at two kinds of innovation that have been urged on the schools since 1957. One was the shift to academic excellence, and that does not fit the dissemination model of a product or a process familiar in industry or the military, because it asks for a change in the total cognitive-affective make-up of thousands upon thousands of individuals.

Another type of innovation does resemble the model of industrial innovation. Some device or machine is manufactured to do more quickly and efficiently some of the things that teachers have to do. These products resemble the motorcar and electric refrigerator in their appeal to progress. The education industries, which were born in the early sixties, are still puzzled because their products were not snapped up as readily as the other labor-saving devices that have characterized the modern way of life.

The education industries bloomed brightly and vigorously in 1964 and 1965. Such sophisticates of electronics as IBM, Raytheon, and Xerox, in alliance with textbook houses, were about to revolutionize education with programmed instruction, computer-aided instruction, mechanical tutors, and other gadgetry. But as early as 1968 signs of disappointment were evident, and in 1971 Robert W. Locke, vice-president of McGraw-Hill Book Company, reiterated the disappointment and tried to account for its causes. He noted wistfully:

Perhaps the difficulty in 1970 was that much of the money had run out, and people who were willing to gamble with somebody else's funds were reluctant to gamble with their own.*

* "Has the Education Industry Lost Its Nerve?" *Saturday Review,* January 16, 1971.

How market researchers, who know so much about the psychology of the housewife on the supermarket prowl, can know so little about the psychology of teachers and parents is a mystery.

I happen to believe, as will be evident in later chapters, that educational technology does have a future—if the innovation enthusiasts don't strangle it prematurely. But if the merits of the hardware are so obvious, why does the very mention of teaching machines, computer-assisted instruction, and television lectures "turn off" so many teachers, students, and parents? The answer of the technologists usually is: "Fear of innovation, fear of losing one's job." This is a shallow answer, and its shallowness may itself be a cause of the failure to "sell" educational technology.

It is more likely that teachers are "turned off" because of their participation in the mystique of teaching. The mystique is that teaching is an encounter of persons in which some mysterious change is undergone by both the pupil and the teacher. The change may be from ignorance to knowledge or from folly to wisdom; from darkness to light; from fuzziness to clarity; from inhibition to freedom. Like all mystiques, this one is based on a doctrine of the transubstantiation of matter into spirit. The forms of the mystique are endless, but whoever shares this mystique is not going to believe that a machine, however subtle, can partake of it, and if, *mirabile dictu*, it could, he would regard it as monstrous, possibly satanic, but certainly not human.

Teachers who share in the encounter mystique are humiliated at the thought of being replaceable by buttons, tubes, and whirling tapes—even when they themselves control the machinery. It is not merely a job that is threatened, but a whole value system. It forces the teacher to devalue himself, for, despite the assurances that the machine is only an instrument, he realizes that our mechanical servants in time become our masters. It is a moot question, to extend this point, whether the automobile—and its allies in trucking, road building, and banking—is our servant or our master.

Parents want their children treated as individuals and persons and special persons at that. To their mind this means personal attention from another person. Machines can individualize instruction by adapting to the abilities and degree of achievement of the learner, but they can't personalize it. Students resent machine—even very good television—instruction because it symbolizes a lack of concern for them as persons. "The professor didn't care enough to come in person, so how much does he care about us?" "This is a recording" in response to a telephone call affects us in the same way. No matter how good recordings are, they do not replace the experience the personal appearance of the artist gives.

This attitude toward educational technology may be misguided, but it is understandable. There is a way to convince people that although there is a mystique of encounter in teaching and learning, not all learnings share equally in it, but the pushers of technology have not used this approach.

However, let us get back to the other shifts that the school system and its personnel were asked to make in the sixties.

Around the mid-sixties we rediscovered the poor, the blacks, and the other disadvantaged segments of our population. Toward the end of the decade the mood toward science, technology, machines, and efficiency had done an about-face. The American dream had turned out to be a nightmare, and many awoke shaking and sweating.

No doubt the Vietnam war lay at the root of the protest that swelled on the campus, but the war was construed as an evil thing for many reasons. It was bad because it was a sign of American imperialism; because it symbolized the domination of American life by the military-industrial complex, of which the university was a more or less willing ally; because it exploited the poor by taking money away from social reform; because it exploited unwilling youth through conscription; because it brutalized the Vietnamese people and our own soldiers; because it clarified and objectified the suppression of individual life in behalf of abstract causes for which the individuals who did the suffering had neither loyalty nor sympathy.

Nevertheless, we did renew our consciousness of racism and poverty, and felt a new urgency to deal with them. The civil rights movements dramatized the events sufficiently for the mass media to take notice of them, and the Kennedy and Johnson administrations put their rhetoric and some of their power behind social justice. The Supreme Court decision of 1954 ·on school desegregation gave them leverage. But no less important, although far less obvious, was the realization that for the economy to grow at a pace sufficiently rapid to keep the cycle up-right, we could not afford large populations of underconsumers. Mass production demands mass consumption at home and abroad. The oft-quoted remark of Donne about men not being islands applies most literally to mass production economic systems.

The poor create a demand for goods, to be sure, but it is a low-grade demand because they are not high-grade producers. Crime, drugs, and sickness flourish in the ghettos of the poor, whether in the city or country, and this increases the cost of public services in the form of welfare, added police, special pressure on education, and health and housing services. Relief recipients spend their checks within the local economy, but they do not create their share of goods and services.

Let us not be so cynical as to believe that our drive against discrimination and poverty was inspired only by our concern for economic growth, but let us not blink the fact that when humanitarian impulses happen to coincide with economic incentives, the principles of social justice are likely to become politically expedient.

So, in the mid-sixties, as the war in Vietnam escalated, as the writings of Michael Harrington and others became popular, as the work of Martin Luther King and other civil rights workers became newsworthy, the stage was set for another wave of school reform. Hardly had the schools shifted their direction toward Mr. Gardner's and Admiral Rickover's excellence than the order to reverse engines was sounded. The plight of the blacks, Puerto Ricans, Chicanos, Indians, delinquents, and drug addicts was caused, we were told, by inferior or inappropriate schooling. We were inundated by statistics on dropouts and their relation to the socioeconomic status of families. Segregated schooling was held to be responsible for the social inferiority of the blacks. I do not wish to rehash the volumes of literature that sounded, echoed, and re-echoed this theme. It is still being produced in quantity.

The cry was that the schools were unresponsive to the needs of the poor and the insulted in the inner city and the forgotten countryside, who needed education the most. The schools these unfortunates were forced to attend were inferior in physical

plant, equipment, and teachers. The last factor was properly regarded as the most important one. Teachers who were largely
white, Anglo-Saxon, and Protestant, obsessed with middle-class
values and ambitions, did not want to work in the ghetto
schools. If pressed into service there, they left as soon as possible
for the suburbs. These teachers, it was said, were not sympathetic to the ghetto children's handicaps or to the culture that
produced them. They simply didn't know how to cope with children who did not behave as middle-class children did, and they
were frightened by the lack of discipline and the prevalence of
violence, which on occasion was directed against them.

What to do? Clearly the thing was to turn the school around.
How does one do this? One can put black children into white
schools or white children into black ones. One can change the
curriculum in the black schools; one can take the control of the
black schools away from the white bureaucracy and give it to
the blacks; one can start storefront schools; one can stop insisting
on conventional literacy requirements and stop using tests that
work against disadvantaged pupils.

Overnight the new math and the new biology and the new
physics and the new language labs were pushed into the background. The research funds began to flow into schemes in which
elitist subjects and activities were "put down" so that poor children would be "turned on."

For the moment I am not interested in arguing the merits of
the shift in emphasis, or even in disputing the remedies proposed
by the reforming innovators. The point to be clear about, it
seems to me, is why the schools did not move as rapidly in the
new direction as the reformers wished. It is sufficient to note
once more that the foot-dragging, change-resisting, middle-class-
bias hypothesis will hold only so much water. Instead, the reformers displayed an amazing ignorance of what the changes
they proposed involved.

Just as the excellence of the early sixties called for a change
in the cognitive apparatus of millions of teachers, so the "humanism" of the late sixties called for a shift from schooling as an
induction into the traditions of Western culture to schooling as a
personal encounter that changes the quality of being and feeling
of persons. This proposed humanism, however, is not the classi-

cal humanism, but rather an existential humanism. It is not merely a new form of the classical *humanitas*. *Humanitas*, from Cicero on, meant the disciplining of thought and feeling through study of the products of human genius—the classics of literature, philosophy, history, and the fine arts. The mood of existential humanism is a rejection of these norms; on the contrary, no norm is authentic unless generated by the individual for the individual. It is hard to assimilate Marcuse, Norman Brown, Hesse, and Vonnegut with Plato, Aristotle, Cicero, Montaigne, and Matthew Arnold—even though, at the level of ultimate concern about the good life, there is more in common in these two camps than meets the eye or erupts in their rhetoric.

It is even more difficult to scrap a curriculum based on the notions of rational order in both thought and feeling and turn the school into revolutionary cells that deny these norms of order. The new humanism or existential humanism is a challenge to all formal schooling and not merely to a specific form of it. "Relating" and "touching" and "mind blowing" are simply not in the same stable with studying, comprehending, and formulating. Peter Marin wrote an enlightening article for the *New York Times Book Review* (February 21, 1971) in which he described a second-grade class creating poetry by scrambling the language every which way, scribbling over boards and paper, combining letters and words and images as the spirit moved them:

It was all fine until we came to the end of class. Now, said the teacher, let us read back to one another what we have written. So they stood in their various places and tried to make sense of what they had done. No couplets. No *moon* and *spoon*. Instead, a batch of unreadable scrawls that were socially useless—for they could not be read aloud. Some began to cry, and others turned to me with betrayed or angry faces, for they had broken free and now there was no way to express what they had done within the rituals of their given world.

And there you have the measure of the shift the schools were asked to make—right away. Are schools unresponsive? Yes, I am afraid they are. As institutions, they protect their functions and functionaries. To violent attacks upon them, they respond with confusion, hesitation, and *ad hoc* improvisations. They may even adopt the rhetoric of their attackers and identify with them.

These adaptations are transitory and superficial. Systemic and pervasive reform awaits changes in the success routes of an epoch and a change in the ideology of the dominant groups of the society. To the dominant groups of our time, the Puritan ethic and the values of classical humanism are still reality, not ideology. As long as this continues to be the case, schools may use the rhetoric of the counterculture or the rhetoric of the industrial corporation or the rhetoric of the think tanks, but they will be used as protective coloration.

For these reasons, it is incumbent upon educational statesmanship and leadership not to think of educational reform in terms of the pressures exerted on the schools by the foundations, the education industries, or the current regime in the U. S. Office of Education. For systemic reform the leadership has no choice but to guess as shrewdly as it can the shape of the world of the future. Shall we return to some form of preindustrial society? What ethic will replace the Puritan ethic? Will the new humanism replace the old? Can we continue to mature technologically and still remain divided into elites and masses? What sort of schooling will a technologically mature society require if that society wishes to retain some form of democracy? Can such a society find room within the interstices of its web of interdependence for individual freedom and identity? I propose to touch upon these questions in later chapters, but let us first turn to some other reasons for the unresponsiveness of the schools.

CHAPTER III

The Professional Teacher—
A Mischievous Illusion

The alleged unresponsiveness of the public schools to the wishes of parents, the needs of pupils, and the zeal of reformers has been blamed upon the inertia of bureaucracy, the conservatism of school administrators, and the prejudices of the middle class. However, most editorials, pronouncements of prestigious commissions, and orators at educational conventions sooner or later identify the ultimate, fundamental, basic obstacle to progress as the teacher. Critics who finally locate the sensitive nerve of education in the teacher, of course, are on the right diagnostic route but are led to the further question: why are the teachers of our public schools, both elementary and secondary, so nonadaptive when it comes to responding to justifiable calls for changes in education?

One way of getting at an answer to this question is to ask another: what sort of competence would teachers have if they were properly responsive to the demands made upon them?

One fairly sure way of getting nowhere with this question is to query teachers, parents, superintendents, supervisors, and pupils about the characteristics of a good teacher. A lot of time and money have been poured down the drain on this kind of research. Instead of providing objective measures of good teaching, the reported traits tell us more about the respondents' psychological history and educational ideology than about the teaching process. One supervisor likes orderly teachers; another is enchanted with enthusiastic ones. Some superintendents find it hard to believe that a pretty young thing can be a poor teacher, but some P-TA mothers find it just as hard to believe she can be a good one. Furthermore, two combinations of the same set of traits may not yield the same judgment.

Even more important than these factors is the psychological bias of the respondent. Invariably the answers indicate what a certain teacher in his own life did to make him feel good or bad about school. And what made him feel good about this teacher? Whatever satisfied some psychological need of the moment, and this satisfier could be anything from a pat on the back to a slap in the face; the "bias" could be anything from a crush on the teacher to hatred of her fiancé. Rarely is the pupil's learning used to measure the goodness of the teaching—even teachers rarely use this as a measure. More often the excitement, eagerness, and interest of the pupils are taken by the teacher as evidence that his teaching is good. This is not a wholly irrelevant way of judging the matter, because given excitement, eagerness, and interest, the chances that learning is going on are better than where there is apathy. But just what is being learned in the excitement, excitement alone does not tell us. Almost any break with school routine—singing popular songs, for example—will generate excitement in a class, but the educational value of rock-and-roll is not thereby established.

A somewhat cynical, but not untypical, way of measuring teaching effectiveness was stated with rare candor by one well-seasoned school superintendent of a small New England city a number of years ago. He put it this way: "Teachers about whom I hear bad things from parents, I rate as poor; they ought not be retained—if they do not already have tenure. Teachers about whom I hear fine things from all quarters, I rate as *C*. They may be potential troublemakers or bucking for the principal's job. If they get into the newspapers I get really worried." "Who, then," he was asked, "are the teachers you rate *A* and *B*, the best teachers?" "Why," he answered, "the teachers about whom I hear nothing."

The single outstanding fact about teachers—especially in American public schools—has been their docility. Until very recently it was tacitly understood that classroom teachers were to carry out policies and programs designed by administrators, principals, and supervisors. A large proportion of the elementary school teachers were female, and unabashed male chauvinism was taken for granted when it came to appointing superintendents and principals, not to speak of membership on school boards.

The superintendent was very much the rooster amid a clucking seraglio of school marms anxious to please him. Together they presented a reassuring example of civic probity and domestic virtue. High school teachers were a different lot. Many of them were male, so that the seraglio metaphor did not apply to them. Instead, they constituted a mildly resentful clutch of mercenaries kept at their posts by financial need, a need exacerbated by the economic law that kept wages down to the amounts that women would work for.

High school teachers of both sexes were somewhat more difficult to manage than their elementary school counterparts, because, as a rule, they held degrees with a major in some discipline. This gave them some sense of intellectual dignity, some of the pride of the specialist, who could look the principal or superintendent in the eye—and tell him that he knew nothing about mathematics or geography or whatever. Furthermore, the subject-matter specialists, for the most part, were preparing their charges for college, and a slight whiff of social superiority swirled around them. Nevertheless, not even these advantages were enough to stiffen their backbones when confronted by the administrative apparatus.

Accordingly, the teacher's role in making decisions was minuscule. Even when the revision of curricula by committees of teachers became customary, only by the greatest courtesy could it be said that *they* made the decisions. This is so because curriculum committees spend most of their time examining what is being done elsewhere and submitting their choices to other committees, which, in turn, consult with review committees, until something called a curriculum guide emerges from the State Department of Instruction or some other equally lofty level in the bureaucracy. This process of constructing curricula by consensus is a bow in the direction of democracy, a bow that becomes a full-fledged genuflection when the total citizenry is invited to participate. Neither the teachers nor the citizens participate because of their special knowledge about what needs to be taught. The citizens give the committee the benefit of their own experience or vent their dissatisfaction with the state of society by demanding that the school teach this or that: the evils of alcohol or the virtues of thrift. The teachers, for their part, bring to curriculum construction their experience and views about the teachability of specific items, and by teachability they do not always mean what can be taught. More often the "teachability" of certain learning tasks depends on whether the pupils, confronted with these tasks, will be "turned on" sufficiently to allow the maintenance of some semblance of order in the classroom. The substance or structure of what is to be taught, for most teachers, is either a matter of tradition or something to be determined by the writers of textbooks.

In short, like any other large system, the school lives by rules that are supposed to take care of standard cases. Because the standard school systems are organized by grades, content must be organized into graded sequences. Each grade depends on the one preceding it to "cover" prescribed bits of information or skills. The logistics of instruction require rules about attendance, time periods, and movements through the building. In most schools teachers are required to sign in and out; bulletins flow from the central office; reports are in transit in all directions, at all levels. It is easy to make fun of this routine—the other fellow's logistics are always ludicrously complicated—but obviously no system can do without these rules: a congeries of classrooms having no commerce with one another would not be a school system. I know of no formula by which to balance nicely the logistics and the outcomes to which they are instrumental, but a reliable symptom of imbalance is the preoccupation of administrators with rules and procedures. When their eyes glisten as they describe their command of process, a sound instinct tells the layman to intervene and remind the expert about means and ends.

School operation is so rule-ridden that the teacher's autonomy is restricted to trivialities. About all she can do on her own is make minor adaptations in the curriculum material, in the program of study, and in her own style of teaching. Major changes would almost certainly breed suspicion and brew trouble. Why are rules so important to the system? Because it has no other principle of order.

Lest this be taken as a dark saying or glib cynicism, let us ask what other factors control the activities of the school. For about half of the high school population, acquiring sufficient credits to enter college is a controlling principle—and this, too, is largely governed by rules. But for the other half, this is not an operative principle; even for the college-bound it may not be as definitive as it has been. Systematic study of the intellectual disciplines is under attack. Perhaps it is part of the attack on all existing institutions—social, political, moral. Perhaps it is a phase of the anti-intellectualism that intellectual rebels affect. Whatever the reason, the rational order by which the graded study of subjects articulated the school system is being challenged. Sensitivity to social issues, interdisciplinary approaches, mind blowing, and relevance are not yet adequate substitutes for the order they are challenging.

A science of education and a set of rules derived from it would constitute a rational order of instruction. This kind of intellectual frame maintains order in medicine, engineering, and law. But no such science exists—if by science is meant a set of generally accepted empirical theories. Teaching is not the application of scientifically validated theories. It is more like preparing meals in a restaurant; the menu is prescribed and so are the recipes. Neither the menus nor the recipes are grounded in a coherent theory of nutrition or anything else—except possibly the economics of restaurant keeping or the art of cookery. Accordingly, changes made by management, as well as by employees, can be justified only by success: the general satisfaction of the client. When we say schools have failed, we mean that some adults are unhappy, but their unhappiness may be caused by anything from bussing to achieve integration to a daughter joining a hippie commune.

This somewhat dreary but, I believe, not inaccurate delineation of the teacher's role makes it easy to understand why the pivot of the system is not a pivot at all, but rather a satellite moving in fairly steady and predictable orbits, according to rules determined by almost everyone but the teacher. However, the rhetoric persists. The "good" teacher is supposed to possess arcane knowledge and charisma which overcome all obstacles—economic, social, and psychological—that plague the pupil. The "bad" teacher presumably has neither the knowledge nor the charisma nor the love of children, which makes up for virtually all other lacks.

How far is the rhetoric about teachers from reality? If we take the rhetoric seriously, the teacher is expected to act *in loco parentis, in loco communitatis, in loco humanitatis,* that is, in place of the parent, the community, and the culture—and to do so as an expert in pedagogy.

As representing the parent, the teacher is in the odd position of having to be as concerned about twenty-five or thirty-five children as the natural parent is about one, two, or three children. And, unlike God, who is excused from being concerned about His children as far as their overshoes and temper tantrums go, the schoolteacher is expected to vibrate sympathetically with every child in concrete predicaments of this sort. The blithe idiocy with which we repeat the refrain "Treat every pupil as an individual" is revealed only when we ask how many people does anyone treat as an individual human person. A half dozen is about par for most of us; the modern novel, moreover, often has as its subject our failure to reach even this small number. Indeed, parents are indicted a thousand times a day for not treating their own children as individuals deserving the dignity of persons. Husbands are accused of not treating their wives as persons in their own right. Those who are reluctant to study the evidence of the sociologists and other academicians need only follow the newspaper columns of Dear Abby or Dr. Rose Franzblau for a week or two.

In loco parentis, if it means anything, means playing the role of an ideal parent. As such, the teacher is endowed with an infinite capacity to love all children but freed from the bias that the love of the natural parent is likely to suffer. Good rhetoric, no doubt, but psychologically nonsense. Taken literally, it would make a shambles of teaching, as it would of healing, practicing law, or any other of the humane professions. The mystical glow of the Froebelian kindergarten came from the metaphysical fires of Hegelian idealism; partakers of that mystique and any other have always been few. The image of the teacher as the surrogate of the loving, tender, understanding, wise parent is a tribute to fantasy and, when made a model for public school teaching, breeds a mischievous sentimentalism.

About all that can be said for this notion is that those who dislike young people or who do not want to understand them should not go into teaching. Furthermore, men and women who plan to teach young children over a long period of time had better resign themselves to speaking and perhaps thinking like children for a good part of their waking day. Elementary school teachers often complain that they have been infantilized by their work, an occupational hazard from which clever innovators, who do not work constantly with children, are free.

Perhaps this is why research, theorizing, and large-scale planning in education are not often undertaken by classroom teachers. Teaching may keep one young—if it does not produce premature aging—but it may also preserve immaturity and thereby make more intellectually demanding tasks uncongenial.

So the *in loco parentis* doctrine dribbles down to a legalism that permits teachers to chastise children (under very prescribed circumstances) and to admonish them for their own good without first receiving their consent.

There is, however, another interpretation of *in loco parentis*. Consider Miss F, who is adored by pupil P, because Miss F supplies the affection that his own mother denies him. Miss F might serve as a sister surrogate for some other pupils and for others as a love object. In other words, teachers can serve *in loco parentis* and of other members of the family, actual or potential. Whether or not this surrogation is psychologically healthy either for the teacher or the pupil is debatable.

Certainly teachers should not use pupils to make up for their own psychic deprivations; certainly they should not—like over-possessive mothers—make pupils overly dependent on them. At this stage, I think you will agree, the question "What should be the proper relation between pupil and teacher?" becomes hopelessly vague. When the question is modified so as to read: "What should be the relation between a teacher and each of thirty pupils?" the query becomes absurd. Thus much of the writing on this theme, it goes without saying, is absurd.

The peculiar relation between teacher and pupil is an old mystery. If it is not like that between parent and child, lover and the beloved, master and servant, what is it? The terms "guide" and "midwife" are only two of many suggested to describe the essence of the relationship, and in some situations, such as the Socratic dialogue or the great research man and his graduate students, these metaphors are apt. But young pupils are not on journeys and are not pregnant with the kinds of ideas that require a Socratic midwife—at least it takes quite a stretch of the imagination to think of children's gropings in this way. In our time, perhaps, the professional-to-client relationship is more suggestive of what many in the educational enterprise seek. Students appreciate a relationship with someone who is concerned about them as individuals, but who does not consider them as psychological burdens or crutches. The occupant of such a role, however, needs not only time to think of pupils as individuals but also a theoretical understanding that does not confuse concern with sentimental identification. If his teaching resembles therapy, it cures through knowledge and insight. But first and last the teacher is responsible for instruction.

Not much less confusing than the *in loco parentis* doctrine is that of *in loco communitatis*. This claims that the teacher represents the community mores and morals, which, presumably, the pupil is to make his own. The teacher is expected to discharge this role by being a model of community-approved behavior and, it is made plain, by inculcating communal expectations. She is somehow to reinforce these standards with appropriate praise and blame.

The first type of enactment is now less enforceable than once was the case. Not more than twenty-five years ago, schoolteachers were expected to stay out of bars, cocktail lounges, gambling halls, and places featuring erotic entertainment. The younger teachers, of course, resented these expectations more than the older ones; the latter more often than not had already absorbed the mores of the community and had no apparent trouble serving as sufficiently luminous exemplars of them. This was all the more understandable because teachers in the public schools were recruited neither from the upper classes nor from skid row —social strata in which the most deviant social behavior was likely to be found.

As to producing middle-class virtue, the public school teacher had neither qualms nor special efficacy. She or he merely reinforced by speech and attitude what the community had already made habitual. The teacher praised honesty, bravery, kindness, loyalty, patriotism, and hard work—as did the textbooks. If I have doubt about the teacher's special efficacy in moral education, it is because in those instances in which pupils had not been habituated by the family and the community, reformation rarely occurred. When in the sixties the younger generation defied its parents and the community elders by flaunting long hair and unconventional dress, the impotence of both the school and the family in enforcing the mores was revealed. In that moment of truth it became clear that *morality* had become identified in the minds of the community with middle-class *manners*, an identification that neither the young nor the courts would countenance.

If the teacher no longer acts *in loco communitatis* as regards the mores of dress, speech, and social sentiments, does it make any sense to speak of him as representing the community's value system in general? A little, but not much. Which of the numerous value schemata that now divide the community should the teacher represent? That of the WASPs of the upper, the middle, or the working class? The intellectuals of the left, middle, or right? The blacks militant or the blacks integrationist? The Chicanos, Puerto Ricans, Indians? America as a melting pot of cultural differences is no longer a popular notion. Some still hope for a savory stew in which diverse ingredients retain their identity while giving up enough of their essence to produce a pervasive flavor. Many reject even this much unity—so long as the capitalistic economy and its supervening establishments remain intact. Others fear that the unity of a Communist state would be worse than no unity at all.

Of all these doubts and questionings, the crack in the ideal of an American, New-World, democratic culture is the most serious. Cultural pluralism is nothing new in the world; neither is pluralism kept together by a conquering despot. The novelty of the American dream was a cultural unity chosen or accepted freely by people with a variety of ethnic origins—the unity of the American Creed as celebrated and worried over in the late 1940s by Gunnar Myrdal in *An American Dilemma*.

For the teacher to act *in loco communitatis* some such ideal must be accepted by all the divergent groups. Perhaps it is still accepted by a majority of Americans; repeated polls say so. Yet the minorities who reject the ideal are loud and powerful. They make the media, as well as the college campus and the intellectual journals, reverberate with their rejections of any unity. The old-fashioned liberals are not only tired but a little frightened as well. Just as the longer hair style captured even conservative middle-agers, so the liberal thinks a bit longer before risking the scorn of his more radical colleagues. A beard gives him a bit more courage and much more credibility when uttering his verities, but falling out of fashion kills a doctrine more surely than error. That the fashionmakers are not a majority of the people does not diminish the power of the fashions they set. As the decade of the seventies gets underway, there is no question as to what is fashionable: a cultural pluralism; a rejection of structure and of the established order and its norms. In such a climate, to speak of the teacher as representing the norms of the community is meaningless.

The third expectation that teachers are supposed to fulfill is that of serving *in loco humanitatis*. The humanities in their original sense signified the best that man had thought and wrought and said—*humanitas* was the opposite of *barbaritas*. The Greek and Latin classics were thought to make the difference between truly human beings and barbarians. With the help of Cicero this notion held sway for centuries in the Western world. The idea still whispers in the halls of the academy when the noise of the scientific machinery permits it to be heard; it still persuades people to buy the great books and visit the museums for a look at Greek statuary. The plays of Sophocles and Euripides are staged every so often, but the idea, as Cicero held it, and as it shaped the curriculum of schools up until, say, the beginning of this century, is quite dead; the motions we discern in it are induced by classicists, not by the classics. The teacher as the representative of the classical ideals of Greece and Rome, accordingly, is virtually nonexistent.

The classical ideal of *humanitas* has been displaced by the ideal of knowledge in a broader sense. Rather than regarding education as the absorption of a small set of ancient literary and philosophical masterpieces, standard humanistic education today looks to the mastery of the major intellectual disciplines to fashion the mind of man. To think the way the scientist does, to perceive and imagine as the artist and poet do—these are the contemporary goals of the humanities. The humanities may not stress technology, but they must never be maneuvered into the position of having to say that it is permissible for a humanist to think as witch doctors and astrologers do about physical events.

The authority of the classical writers is now vested in the *cognoscenti* of each of the disciplines and the arts; to be an educated man is to think and perceive and imagine and feel somewhat as they do. Education is the induction of the young into these ways of thinking and feeling. It is this version of the humanities that has guided what is loosely called the liberal arts and science curriculum in the colleges. Is this the *humanitas* that the teacher is supposed to represent?

In a way, yes. This was the point behind the movement to require teachers to have a good general education before undertaking more "professional" studies. The same motive is responsible for the requirement of some professional schools that at least the first two years of college be devoted to finishing up or polishing off general education. Insofar as teachers have increased their exposure to the disciplines, I believe they do begin to qualify as being *in loco humanitatis*. Insofar as this exposure has been narrow, specialized, and professional, they are probably not good examples of the all-round-educated person. If the exposure has not been successful, it is because it is virtually impossible to find on any "good" college campus very much study undertaken for what Aristotle would have called self-cultivation, or, better, the cultivation of one's human potentialities. Most of what is dubbed liberal arts and sciences in college catalogues is a sequence of courses taught by professionals to preprofessionals, or to imaginary preprofessionals called majors.

Nevertheless, until recently it has made sense to say that the teachers in our schools—at all levels—should represent the best that is being thought and said and felt in our culture. It meant approximating the forms of thought and feeling as embodied in the learned and wise of our time. These norms were held to be valid for man as man, not for whites alone or for the rich alone. They did presuppose leisure for self-cultivation but did not presuppose that all but a few would be denied that leisure. With secondary schooling becoming well-nigh universal in this country, and with more than half of the high school graduates giving higher education a try, this ideal, for the first time in history, began to be more than a mere ideal in a democratic society.

Yet, as this is being written in the early seventies, this version of humanism is also being challenged, and, to the degree that its validity is brought into question, the expectation that the teacher will serve *in loco humanitatis* also loses its meaning.

When C. P. Snow reactivated interest in the ancient rift between the scientific and literary cultures, he was talking about scientists versus literary people, philosophers, historians, and artists; between those who delved into the ways of things—and men as things—on the one hand, and those interested in the ways men coped with men—and things—on the other. Snow decided that the future was with the scientists; they could understand what literary men said, but what could literary people do with the language of science? He did not anticipate the dethronement of science in the hearts of the young rebels in the late sixties. They also thought of themselves as humanists and certainly as humanitarians. Yet they resembled the humanists whom Snow had in mind so little that the major cleavage in education today is not between scientific and humanistic studies, but rather between the old-line standard humanists and the new, or existential, humanists.

The infighting between them rages on the college campus and in the political arena, and it has now filtered down into the elementary and secondary schools. I know of no brief way to make the distinction between the standard and the existential humanists that will not oversimplify the issue and that will not draw protests from those who do not find themselves exclusively in one camp or the other. Yet a rough line of demarcation can be drawn on the basis of what each side takes to be the criterion of what is to be called "human."

The classical humanist finds the mark of humanity in man's conquest of the impulsive demands of his physiological drives.

The key to the human strategy from Plato on has been self-mastery, the control of commitment and action by reason. Reason to rule the appetites and emotion to reinforce the decrees of reason was and, I believe, still is the formula for liberal humanism—and it was to apply in all departments of life, private and public, individual and social; it acknowledged no cultural exceptions. The cosmos "followed" this law as inexorably as it "followed" the physical laws, even though, and perhaps precisely because, man was free to try to break that law.

Accordingly, the classical humanist looks to the masterworks of literature, philosophy, and art for the formulation of the law and men's experience with it. To induct the new generation into the community of men involves teaching the young to understand and cherish these monuments to the human adventure.

The human adventure is the story of how our biological needs and impulses have been transformed—almost beyond recognition. Take any activity in which we share our animality with other species—feeding, shelter seeking, fighting, reproducing, nurturing the young—and apply human consciousness (reason, memory, and imagination) to it. A peculiar and extraordinary change takes place. Feeding becomes dining, acquiring in the process aesthetic, religious, and social values. The houses we build, we hope, will provide adequate shelter, but how much of the cost of a dwelling is justified by its sheltering properties alone? As soon as they could, the pioneers added the amenities to the essentials of feeding and sheltering. Perhaps the greatest transformation of all has to do with the physiological act of sex. In other animals instinct and physiological mechanisms take care of most of this transaction; in humans surprisingly little sexual activity is explained by either instinct or physiological mechanism. Mostly, psychiatrists tell us, sex is "in the head," where imagination has lodged it. Fighting has been adorned, by imagination, with courage and heroism. It is an instrument of national policy, not merely a means to food and a mate.

These transformations are sublimations of animality, but the very same imagination, reason, and memory can transform biological drives into subanimal behavior. Eating can become gluttony; the *fear of hunger* can become an excuse for aggrandizement and unbridled cruelty. Man can devise forms of combat so frightful that even the thought of annihilation of the entire species does not deter him. Sex can become lust as well as love; it can be driven to the perverse and the bizarre, as imagination invents new forms of stimulation for jaded appetites.

It is this potentiality for the transformation of our nature to the superanimal and subanimal that gives dramatic tension to the human adventure. The direction in which man should go was clear to Plato and Aristotle, Vittorino da Feltre and Montaigne, to Emerson, Ruskin, Matthew Arnold, and the long array of writers who can be thought of as humanists in the classical sense of the word. Do the new humanists reject the classical answer to the human question? It is hard to say. When both sides talk about the kind of individual life and society they would regard as good and admirable, one finds them agreeing. Neither side can abide the injustice, cruelty, bestiality, and folly of men, but it is not easy to assimilate the writers listed above with Nietzsche, Sartre, Genet, Fanon, Marcuse, and their followers on the campus.

The difference is that the existential humanists do not want to wait for the cosmos to carry out its design, or for the second coming, or for whatever distant millennium. They do not regard the Platonic self-mastery through ordered thought and feeling as the glory of the human species; they prefer freedom from all preconceived restraints. This freedom creates a compelling need to commit oneself to a significant deed—one that will authenticate the self. One must change the evil situation now and not stop with the understanding of it. Too much understanding is a temptation to forgiveness, and to forgive the evil of the world is precisely the temptation to which the new militant humanists believe the classical humanist yields. The scholarly humanist, confronted by evil, goes back to his study to study some more (or he appoints a committee to study) while the poor become more wretched, the environment is ruined, and men wreak violence on each other and ultimately upon themselves. A neohumanist is a classical humanist gone berserk, and, freaked out in this frenzy, he may swing from superanimal to subanimal behavior to make his point. Freedom *from* the order of society and *from* the norms of the culture, and even *from* old ideals provide the sign that one is existing authentically, indeed, that one is existing at all as a human being. The regression from din-

ing to casual feeding; from marital fidelity to uninhibited serial
sex; from thinking to touching; from self-mastery to self-
expression—these, often allied with drugs to deaden inhibition
and deny limits, seem to be the signs of humanity for some of
the new militant humanists.

And where in this struggle are the scientists? They, too,
would like to be classed with the humanists, but with which
kind? Scientists can do one of two things: assert that their
knowledge is our most potent tool for humanization and thus
ally themselves with the classical humanists; or separate their
science from their human "being" and join the neohumanists in
action programs, which may or may not be directly related to
their roles as scientists.

In academe this struggle has taken the form of an attack on
and in defense of structured courses, structured curricula, and
the structured private life of students. The neohumanists urge us
to make the human problem the curriculum. To the classical humanists, who regard the living tradition of the intellectual and
artistic disciplines as the essence of achieved humanity, the rejection of the disciplines is a rejection of all order—of the very
norms of humanity and humanism. In politics—on the campus
and off—the struggle is between alternative ways of achieving
social change. In the elementary and secondary schools, the
struggle is between a curriculum based on academic disciplines
and a curriculum—if one can call it that—devoted to freeing
pupils from the demands of conformity to the establishment—
moral, economic, social, and political. Is the goal of schooling to
teach and learn biology, chemistry, literature, mathematics, history, and the like, or, in the argot of the moment, is it to become
an uninhibited, caring, sensitive person? The Holt-Kozol-
Friedenberg-Goodman writings on the schools, it seems to me,
leave little doubt as to the nature of the issue—and perhaps of
their answer as well.

The split between the old and the new humanism, accordingly, has made it difficult to say in what sense the teacher shall
act *in loco humanitatis,* but, as is usual in these matters, the
probable answer is that the teacher will be asked to represent
both the new and the old humanism and, as is also probable, will
succeed in doing neither.

We now have, I hope, a fairly clear summary of what we

expect from teachers. First, there is the over-all expectation that the teacher be an expert in teaching; second, that he represent the ideal parent; third, that he represent the community at its ideal best; fourth that he represent the human being at his best. But it is not at all clear just what these expectations demand in the way of competence and the sort of training that would reasonably insure such competence.

Roughly, the person envisioned by these demands is a good man skilled in teaching, to paraphrase Quintilian's formula for the orator as a "good man skilled in speaking." More concretely, the modern teacher is expected to be a person with a good general education (the old humanistic studies), acting as a professional, that is, applying what educators (or educationists) know to teaching the content of the disciplines he has mastered, and all the while acting as a warm, child-loving father-, mother-, brother-surrogate who "relates" to human beings (the new humanism). These three types of demands make up the bundle we call the ideal, professional teacher who should be in every classroom.

How realistic, then, is this ideal of the professional teacher for every classroom? What sort of teacher education would meet this ideal? How far does the education we now give to prospective teachers go toward meeting this ideal?

The argument for teachers being schooled to a professional level is based on the assumption that mere rule-following technicians will not be flexible enough to meet the complex and shifting demands of the learning situation. How can the modern teacher take account of the individual differences of his pupils and of the cultural and economic factors in the learning situation? How can he manage the vast increase in knowledge by mechanically following rules of practice? The standard answer is that he cannot.

If society's expectations of the school are to be taken seriously, then there is no alternative to a program of teacher education in which theory that enables the practitioner to be rational about rules plays a prominent part. But what sort of theory is available for this purpose?

When one speaks of "applying theory," one usually has in mind something like the use of chemical theory to guide the manufacture of synthetic fabrics or the science of mechanics to guide the work of the engineer. Let us call this *applicational* theory. In education, this might be illustrated by the application of the Skinnerian theory of operant conditioning to the designing of teaching machines or to the maintenance of discipline in the classroom. Or one might formulate rules of class management from the principles of developmental psychology or from group dynamics. Alas, the amount of empirical theory that can be "applied" to practice in education in this way is pitifully small, but whatever there is of it certainly belongs in a curriculum that has any pretensions to professional caliber. These constitute the behavioral foundations of teaching.

A really scientific theory of teaching will probably come—if it ever comes—from the neuropharmacologists. With brain surgery and drugs, social managers of the future should have no trouble, at least in principle, in teaching anybody anything. For example, drugs are already being used to sedate overactive children, and one must suppose that it is not impossible to invent a drug that will inspire pupils to love arithmetic and spelling. Since teachers now devote most of their time and ingenuity to teasing their charges into thinking they can master and thus like arithmetic and spelling, the use of drugs may render the resemblance of the teaching profession to the healing profession even closer than it already is. I doubt whether we really want teaching to become that efficient, and perhaps that is why the science of education has progressed so slowly. In other words, for us to accept the perfect teaching machine, we first need to invent a drug that will dispel the anxiety of losing our humanity altogether.

For the most part, however, the theory that one finds in the teacher-training curriculum is of another sort. Principles of education, philosophy of education, social foundations of education, psychology of education, and history of education are its more common titles. These studies purport to place the aims of education, the curriculum, the teaching-learning process, and the organization of the schools in a rational context, with the aid of concepts from the parent disciplines. Thus the problems of education can be placed in philosophical, sociological, historic, psychological, and other contexts. The rigor, order, and sophisti-

cation of these foundational studies vary over a great range—
from common-sense reflections on life to technical treatises. The
personnel who teach such studies as part of teacher education
also vary in their competence, but in recent years a very respectable cadre of specialists trained to the doctoral level have been
available for such instruction. Mr. Conant and other critics of
educationists in the liberal arts faculties generally charge that
this type of course is flaccid intellectually, because those who
teach it are not really historians, philosophers, or sociologists,
and consequently the course has no real content. Every attempt
to convince these critics that courses in the history of education
and philosophy of education do have a distinctive content has
failed largely because the critics never read the attempts to rebut
their far from self-evident criticism. By a strange twist of events,
these foundational studies make more sense to the "turned off"
students—even in the best colleges—than do the parent disciplines. This should not be surprising, because the cry for relevance, although misguided in many ways, nevertheless is the cry
to which foundational work in education and, indeed, in any
profession is a response.

However, from such humanistic foundational studies no rules
for pedagogical practice can be deduced. Consequently, their
usefulness for the teacher is questioned, especially by the prospective teacher. Some critics say that they should be eliminated
altogether, and that the teacher's general education will take
care of providing this sort of background. Others, who sense
some value in these studies, believe they can be postponed until
after the teacher has acquired some experience in the classroom
—postponed, so to speak, for in-service training. On this view,
the pupils taught by the beginning teacher presumably can
forgo whatever value these studies do have for the teacher.

The point, therefore, is whether these studies are useful in
some sense other than as a source of rules to be applied to practice. This is an issue in all general studies and in the role of
foundational studies in any professional curriculum. The most
plausible defense of them is to point out that they provide the
context of practice rather than the *rules for practice*. Thus, an
understanding of the sociology of poverty does not directly give
rules for healing the diseases of the poor, but the dietary pre-

scriptions that a physician might give to the poor will be more enlightened if he does understand the sociology of their condition. Knowledge of social context, therefore, affects the general strategy of education, of appraising the teaching situation in many dimensions, and for making decisions that take account of these dimensions. It is what Karl Mannheim meant by "correlational thinking," as distinguished from the linear thinking of the technician.

Now it may be—and one devoutly hopes that it will be soon —that the behavioral sciences of empirical psychology, sociology, anthropology, and the like will provide educationists with extensive applicational theory from which rules of procedure can be derived. This would provide us with a methodology and technology. But as matters now stand, the applicational theory is scant and not very significant, whereas the interpretive, context-building theory derived from the humanistic disciplines is plentiful but not applicational in the ordinary sense of the term.

There are no really satisfactory responses to this predicament. One might promise that the humanistic foundations (interpretive theories) can be applied, and that study of them will help the teacher in solving everyday problems. Such promises are the rule rather than the exception, but they merely embitter teachers when the promised help does not arrive. This bitterness is then reflected in the judgment that teachers pass on their teacher-training programs. In answer to questionnaires, they dismiss virtually all theory courses as a waste of time, because they gave no immediate help in keeping order in the classroom, in discovering what to do in impoverished school systems where materials recommended in courses were not available, in motivating children from homes in which what was learned in school was not highly esteemed.

There is the alternative of eliminating all theory and reducing the teacher-training curriculum to the practice of rules derived from experience. On this alternative, one might still claim that the training was professional or candidly admit that it was not. Either of the latter choices, I believe, is an abandonment of the professional ideal, but the latter is more honest.

The preferable response is to admit that we must rely pretty heavily on interpretive theory, but to stress the usefulness of such theory. It is needed to site educational problems in their appropriate context—psychological, historical, philosophical, societal. Together with the cognate content of selected academic subjects, these supply the ideas and attitudes one *teaches with,* not *to,* the pupils. That these studies cannot be applied in the ordinary sense of prescribing rules of procedures does not make them useless, but it is a use of which the user is very often unaware until he compares himself with others who do not have this context-building material, or until, in his own teaching, he reaches an impasse because there is a gap in context that he cannot close.

To complete the prescription for the fully professional teacher, we add the requirement that he or she be humanistic in the new sense of the term: that he be concerned about the individuality and personality of the pupil. It now seems a straightforward matter to say that the program for the preparation of teachers should be a judicious mix of these three components: rule-following skill, theory for application and interpretation, and sensitivity to human beings in general and pupils in particular.

But the matter is not that simple. Neither rule following nor humanistic "relating" necessarily requires formal study. The first can be learned through apprenticeship—right in the schoolroom, as many a teacher aide, no doubt, is doing; the second can be acquired informally in the community, in social work, and in groups of all kinds. Only for the *theoretical requirement* is formal study necessary. However, the theoretical foundations of teaching—both the behavioristic and humanistic—are being squeezed out of the teacher-training curriculum, and the arguments used are precisely that neither rule following nor charisma requires formal training, and that good teaching requires nothing else. If this argument is sound, do teachers need any formal "professional" study at all?

As long as the ideal of a truly humanistic personality, skilled in the art of teaching and fit to make autonomous decisions about teaching for every classroom, persists in the rhetoric of teacher education, there will be strong resistance to acknowledging the fact that the preservice training of teachers is overwhelmingly not professional. If, perchance, one could produce

2 million professionally trained teachers, we could not persuade the public to pay what it would take to recruit them in the first place.

Genuinely professional education for teaching calls for more extended specialized study than we now require, and a much longer commitment to a teaching career than most prospective teachers are willing to make. And these two factors are related. Less than a year's professional work is not much of an investment for a career. *

Teaching is a relatively inexpensive hedge (one is going through college anyway) against unemployment for men and a fairly reliable source of a second income for married women—especially after they have completed coping with their growing children. Such a modest investment does not invite or encourage a long-term professional commitment.

The oversupply of teachers that developed in the early seventies will not change the situation substantially. There is no reason to believe that as jobs become scarcer the preparation for teaching will become more demanding. On the contrary, as tax money for schools diminishes, there will be a greater incentive to hire paraprofessionals and part-time personnel, although this will not work for such specialties as teachers of the handicapped and school psychologists.

Nor is it to be taken for granted that the oversupply of teachers will necessarily reduce the number of teacher trainees for general classroom work. As a matter of fact, the current programs for teacher training are so nonspecialized that they are no impediment to employment in any number—I once catalogued fifty-seven—of occupations other than classroom teaching. Even practice teaching can be put to use in social work and camp counseling.

It may be that no country—even the richest—can afford the resources needed for providing a genuinely professional teacher

---

* I refer to the curriculum prescribed in many states for the secondary school certificate—about eighteen to twenty semester hours, of which eight to ten hours are in student teaching. Elementary school and specialty teachers have to do more. I am not including majors in an academic subject as professional unless pursued explicitly for teaching. Most bachelor degrees require a major.

for every classroom. It may be that if we could train technicians to perform most classroom functions by following rules, we might be able to afford a much smaller cadre at the professional level, a situation that obtains in medical practice.

One possibility is to give over didactics to programmed learning with or without the help of teaching machines, computer-aided instruction, and television. By didactics we mean any instruction in which the contents can be made explicit and in which the criteria for successful learning are objective. For example, the multiplication tables, facts of all sorts, reading, writing, spelling, solving algebraic equations, are all included under didactics. Most of the current rage for behavioral objectives makes sense in the mastery of skills and the acquisition of subject-matter contents. Didactics lend themselves to programming, and if there is any chance of increasing the school's productivity, it will be by the use of technology in didactics. Teachers trained to the rule-following level could manage this aspect of instruction, and they could be trained to this level with probably no more than two years of postsecondary work and paid accordingly. They might constitute 85 to 90 per cent of the school staff. The other 10 to 15 per cent of the teaching staff might include four-year graduates of schools designed to train professionals in teaching, much as four-year engineering schools train beginning engineers. From this group would come not only the overseers of the paraprofessionals and the designers of didactical teaching, but also whatever more subtle and personalized teaching a public school system can hope to offer.

The latter type of teaching one might subdivide into (a) heuristics, or teaching the pupil to discover for himself what didactics presents to him ready-made; and (b) philetics, in which the teacher concentrates on the emotional adjustment of the pupil. Both heuristics (sometimes called Socratic teaching) and philetics necessitate encounters between the teacher and pupil as persons; encounters of this sort cannot be programmed, mechanized, or mass-produced.

Even the professionally trained teacher will not be equally good at didactics, heuristics, and philetics, although one could expect every professional to have a working knowledge of all three. Some of the "encounter teachers" might be trained in the fashion of social workers and psychological group counselors; others might qualify by experience with children and youth in various forms of community work. The futile attempt to combine skill in didactics, heuristics, and philetics in the same person has been not the least of the causes of the failure of teacher-training programs. Didactics asks the teacher to function as an efficient machine; philetics asks him to be a warm, sensitive, concerned person; heuristics demands intellectual security and flexibility. Most teachers worry about didactics, and quite predictably they act as fairly inefficient machines. The chances for a well-programmed machine providing highly individualized didactics are better than for a live teacher doing so. But machines cannot deal with persons as persons, because they are not persons, but neither can live teachers deal with persons as persons unless they themselves are rather special kinds of persons. The number of human beings who can meet all qualifications—theoretical and personal—is bound to be far smaller than one would desire. Hence, most teachers we now train are destined to be unsuccessful teachers—on such an unrealistic standard.

These considerations impel me to blame the illusion that our classrooms are staffed by professional teachers as one of the most insidious causes of our slowness in making progress in the geuine reform of schools. It is as if we wondered why medicine did not progress if medical practice were carried on exclusively by nurses, technicians, and hospital aides. Yet, we have something like this on the teaching staffs of our schools, except that our teachers are nowhere so well trained in techniques as nurses are. Between pseudoprofessionals and genuine rule-following technicians, a good case could be made for the latter.

All that saves the teacher from mechanical following of rules is the perspective provided by whatever general education he picked up during the undergraduate years. Having been screened by the demands of the baccalaureate degree and selective admissions, teachers are academically competent. But this is not a pure plus. Lacking the experience and technique for teaching, they are frustrated in one direction; denied the power to make their own decisions as to what to teach and how to do it, they are frustrated in another direction. The result is a proletariatization of the teaching force into a white-collar labor union, bargaining and fighting for wages and good working conditions. The vague resentment against these ploys as "unprofessional" is misguided, not because this conduct is becoming to a professional—for a professional is never a hired hand or brain—but rather because it fails to realize how far from the professional the ordinary classroom teacher is.

Can the professional ideal for the classroom teacher be maintained? Not, I believe, for more than about 15 per cent of the total instructional staff. These, as indicated above, could be trained to a level comparable to a beginning engineer, lawyer, or architect and paid the going rate for such beginners, and they could expect the growth in responsibility and salary found in the other professions. Could it be done in the usual four undergraduate years? Yes, I believe it could. Unfortunately, none of the philanthropic foundations or the U.S. Office of Education and not many of the teacher-education institutions have their noses turned in that direction. All of these are more interested in sniffing the breezes for ways in which to deprofessionalize teaching and turn it into apprenticeship—while not relinquishing the professional pretensions.

As for the detailed organization of the curriculum for such a school, much could be said. The new standards for the accreditation of institutions preparing teachers adopted by NCATE (National Council for Accreditation of Teacher Education), properly understood and faithfully implemented, constitute one such design.

The design includes the following components and their functions:

A. *Study of the disciplines.* Although the NCATE standards do not specify the contents of this component in detail, it conforms pretty much to what most colleges demand for the bachelor's degree as general education. I would prefer to have general education completed in the secondary school—as it can be—and to use the college years to provide the prospective teacher with more preprofessional work in the academic disciplines. This *preprofessional* work in the disciplines would serve several purposes:

1. It would constitute a base for studying the contexts of educational problems. One needs to have studied psychology,

sociology, economics, history, and philosophy to make courses in the philosophy, history, sociology, and psychology *of* education worth the time invested in them. As matters now stand, the psychology course is expected to do the work of one in educational psychology, or the educational psychology course is expected to take the place of a study of psychology. This simply won't do.

2. It would supply content of what is to be taught. Thus one studies mathematics in order to teach mathematics, geography to teach geography. The disciplines one studies because one has to teach (although there may be other benefits) become part of one's professional training, just as being charming, although of benefit to all women, is part of the professional training of airline stewardesses.

3. It would give the teacher a broader conceptual context of what is to be taught. To teach mathematics, one studies mathematics, but it would be useful to study symbolic logic as well; not because one will teach symbolic logic to the mathematics class, but because the conceptual framework for mathematics includes symbolic logic. Similarly, one might study English history as a framework for the teaching of English literature. This is content to *teach with,* not necessary content to *teach to.*

B. *Technical proficiency.* The practical application of theory comprises three types of instruction:

1. Laboratory. Virtually all theoretical content in the professional program is amenable to some kind of laboratory exercise that illustrates or tests the theory. Theories of test construction, selection of materials, class management, the techniques of teaching—all can be illustrated and concretized by laboratory exercises designed for that purpose.

2. Clinical teaching. The clinic exhibits real cases being treated by the experienced practitioner, the sort of situation that is common in medical education.

3. Internship. While working on a real job, the candidate would still be under the general supervision of an experienced and credentialed practitioner. Such internship might be done in selected public schools, much as internship in medicine is done in selected hospitals.

These components of the technical side of teacher preparation customarily have been lumped together under practice teaching or student teaching (often lasting no longer than eight weeks). Some programs have tried to eliminate everything except internship—learning on the job; some have tried to make laboratory exercise do the work of all three components; a few have tried the clinical approach as the sole ingredient. These approaches have not worked, and one must conclude that all three components are needed. In a school such as I have in mind, they would be provided for deliberately. Only the internship might not be completed in the regular four-year course, although a start toward it might be made before graduation.

This is not the place to elaborate on the contents of each of the components in detail.* The organization of these contents might vary over a wide range, but, given a reasonable interpretation of these components, a school superintendent in Arizona and one in Massachusetts could expect a graduate from any such school to know certain things, to be able to do certain things, and to be able to accommodate himself or herself to a wide variety of school situations. Furthermore, there is reason to believe that these superintendents would be willing—I think, eager—to pay a premium for such teachers, and the professional organizations would, I hope, support differential pay for them.

Three pressures are converging to accelerate deprofessionalization of teacher education. The first comes from the liberal arts faculty member who honestly believes that a good major in a discipline is all that a teacher needs to teach. He believes, though he should know better, that all scholars are teachers, an assumption that the protesting college students, independently duplicating the experience of the ages, have shred to ribbons. If the assumption will not stand up at the college level, how can it survive—even in dilution—at the secondary and elementary levels?

The second push comes from a curious conglomerate of mili-

* I have argued this thesis in many articles in many educational journals over the last decade. "The Role of the Liberal Arts in Professional Study," *Journal of General Education,* April, 1966, pp. 50–68; "Criteria for the Professional Preparation of Teachers," *Journal of Teacher Education,* December, 1965, pp. 408–16; and "The Role of the Foundational Studies in the Preparation of Teachers," in S. M. Elam, ed., *Improving Teacher Education in the United States* (Bloomington, Ind.: Phi Delta Kappa, 1967), pp. 1–35, are a few examples.

tant blacks, existentialistic academics, and other reformers in and out of the school establishment. They all urge alternative schooling for any group that wishes it. Voucher systems, storefront high schools, community ventures, and the like are proposed in the name of freedom to innovate and improve. Whatever merit these schemes may have, they all seek the freedom to recruit teachers who need not be certified by the bureaucracy. Community workers, liberated housewives, Peace Corpsmen, and political activists, it is argued, are better suited for the free schools than are the standard brand. Obviously this does nothing for teaching as a profession.

In this connection, it is both amusing and instructive to compare the response of educators with that of other professionals to what might be called the "impostor" phenomenon. Every so often a bogus doctor or lawyer is unmasked. The impostor has done very well in practice despite little or no formal training and without benefit of a license. Law schools and medical schools do not regard these occurrences as reasons for closing up shop or turning themselves into schools for apprentices. Schools of education, however, do just the opposite; they see in the success of the impostor an innovative design for the preparation of teachers.

The same sort of inversion obtains with regard to pre-service and in-service education. In most of the standard professions in-service work is provided by highly specialized institutes that bring the practitioner up to date with the advances in research and procedures. Sharing a set of theoretical concepts, practitioners find it possible, in such institutes, to catch up after only a few days' attendance and study. In schoolteaching, the in-service institute, extension course, workshop, and the lately imported teachers' centers (from Great Britain) are used to take the place of a skimpy pre-service preparation. And there is a kind of practical logic in favor of this view: since there is no body of theory to guide the practice—or at least none that more than a few educationists are willing to accept—the prospective teacher is left to pick up the tricks of survival in practice teaching. It makes a kind of sense, therefore, to continue to let teachers find their salvation and that of the schools for themselves.

Finally, the education industries producing hardware and

software for the schools exert an important thrust toward deprofessionalization. Understandably, these firms are aiming at a
machine or a product that can be used with the minimum of
high-priced labor; otherwise, the benefits of mass production are
canceled out. Teacher-proof materials and methods are the appropriate goals for an education industry, and the whole perform-
ance-contract approach is peculiarly appropriate to industry. For
didactics, this is a logical development, and much of what goes
on in school—at any level—is still didactics: learning skills,
gathering information, solving standard problems. However, if
the savings potential in mass didactics is used to convert all education to didactics, this will be an unpardonable regression; one,
however, that school boards are not above perpetrating if the
taxpayer refuses to come up with sufficient funds for anything
more. But if these savings can be used for a strong, although
small, professional cadre of teachers, then there is hope for
better things.

From this group of professionally trained teachers would
come the decisions about practice, with all the variations that a
professional can safely permit himself to try. From him would
come the choice of the programs in didactics and the designs for
using them. From his ranks would come—after graduate study
and experience—the researchers, the supervisors, and even the
administrators for the entire system, just as higher echelons of
personnel in industry come from the ranks of engineers, of lawyers, and of accountants. The clients of these professionals
would be the individual pupils. What could be done en masse
according to rules would be done by machines or paraprofessionals. But diagnosis of educational needs and prescriptions for
meeting them are individual. They bring together the richness
of practice and the clarity of theory. Even with 15 per cent of
the teaching staff of a school prepared at this professional level,
it would be unrealistic to promise each child an "office" hour
each week with his teacher. But it would be reasonable to expect
that some teacher would know the educational profile of a given
child, so that he would be more than a statistic.

It is precisely this layer of professional competence that is
lacking in the American public school system, and that is why
the high-level theoreticians and administrators cannot get their

ideas implemented. Between the theoreticians and operatives there must be an interposition of practitioners enlightened by theory and freed by theory from mere rule following. The almost farcical attempts to evade the task of providing this professional layer are the prime cause of most of the ills from which the schools of America suffer.

CHAPTER IV

No Quality Without Standards

Profound changes in the meaning of "quality education" occurred at the start and in the middle of the sixties. The elementary and secondary schools were just about to gain the momentum for achieving quality in one direction when the direction changed. The first kind of quality, it will be recalled, had to do with making the school curriculum reflect "good" science, "good" mathematics, "good" history, "good" language and literary study. The second direction was that of redeeming the poor, the black, and, more recently, the young (of all ages) from discrimination and oppression—chiefly by the middle class. This latter direction, the new humanism, one finds expounded and urged at all levels of schooling.

Here, for example, is an announcement that appeared some time ago in the *Saturday Review* about a series of seminars on the alternatives to current educational systems:

Holt was to discuss obstacles to educational freedom; Edgar Z. Friedenberg was to tell how schools set youth apart from society into an arbitrary and unsocial role. Kohl was to take up "ways of subverting the school system from within" and Dennison was to conduct a workshop which will bring academic abstractions into "the realm of felt experience."

Of those listed as guest teachers, Ivan Illich, a frank advocate of the "deschooling" of society, is the most consistent. Illich wants to abolish schooling—at least for the developing societies. It is with respect to this new humanism that "quality education" is hard to define.

In ordinary language, quality means conformity with a standard. We grade apples and eggs; or we judge the extent to which something approximates an ideal, *e.g.*, the quality of an automobile, of a drama, or of a social system. What standards do we use when we demand quality education?

Sometimes the standard is a degree of achievement in such skills as reading, handwriting, or spelling. Or it may be the amount of knowledge retained after instruction in geography, history, literature, or some other academic discipline. We have tests for such achievement, and, on the whole, they measure pretty well what they purport to measure. The National Assessment Program uses this type of standard.

Some of the complaints about low-quality schooling in the ghetto refer to low achievement in standard curricular areas of conventional schoolwork as measured by standard achievement tests. Whatever the cause of the low quality may be, the meaning of inadequacy is clear enough. The meaning of low quality becomes less clear, however, when *one* of the causes of failure to learn to read is itself taken as the standard of school quality. For example, suppose it is charged that School A is a bad school because the children are apathetic and are not interested in learning to read. This criticism should not be confused with the standard of reading achievement, or even with the quality of the school itself, for not all apathy results in equally poor achievement, and not all apathy is caused by the school. It is good for children to be happy and active whether they learn to read or not. This is an intrinsic value. Whether a school is to be judged solely by the amount of joy and excitement it generates in its pupils is another matter.

Granted that learning to read is better accomplished in joy than in sorrow or apathy, achievement is achievement however the learning is accomplished. Are we bitter about the schools because children can't read well, or are we bitter because the children are unhappy or apathetic in school? Are the nations with the highest literacy rates the nations that have the most exciting, permissive, creative classrooms?

The confusion is mischievous, because the means for reducing some of the causes of poor scholastic achievement are not the same as the means for promoting achievement, although motivation is so important in learning that there is a wide overlap between readiness to learn and the ability to profit from instruction. But if the economic, social, and psychological impediments to school learning are massive—as they are in the urban ghetto— the injunction that the school's job is to make the pupils *ready* to learn, as well as to instruct, is glib to the point of irresponsibility.

Consider, for example, the following summary from one of the numerous reports on urban education:

Beyond the system's problems in coping with the increased numbers, lack of facilities, and lack of personnel, it has demonstrated a blindness in perception of the student of today's inner city. By and large, the system expected that student to be a failure, and unaware of its failure, has succeeded in creating the student in its own image. The teachers of the urban system are generally less educated, less able, and less experienced than those of the suburbs. They are too often of different backgrounds from their students. They gain little status for teaching the disadvantaged. For these reasons, and others, urban teachers are generally unsuccessful in relating to and perceiving their students.[*]

After considering the number of factors named (and unnamed) that have been identified as the source of the system's problems, one is still left with the impression that the urban teacher's blindness is the key variable. What causes the blindness? Poor education, less ability, and less experience than suburban teachers have, we are told. But the education, ability, and experience of the "better" suburban teachers foster precisely the middle-class biases that prevent them also from overcoming their blindness to the ghetto child's mode of seeing the world. And why does teaching the disadvantaged not gain status? Does status depend on professional competence or on the social status of the client? And, if the latter, is it perhaps because we lack a professional standard for "good" teaching?

And so the meaning of quality education moves from the straightforward standard of achievement to something much

[*] Wilson C. Riles, Chairman, *The Urban Education Task Force Report* (New York: Praeger Publishers, 1970), p. 186.

more complex and important, namely, to the kind of society of which the school is a part and to the articulation of the various institutions of that society so that a certain quality of life—whatever it may be—can be achieved for its citizens—from grade A apples, if you will, to a grade A society.

Another standard for measuring quality is the judgment of the connoisseur, the expert, the *cognoscente*. The standards for judgments about wine, rare books, chemistry, Egyptian archaeology, the history of Tudor England, and the Mets are the judgments of men and women who are acknowledged experts. Quality education, on this standard, is that type of schooling that helps the learner think, perceive, and judge as do the experts. Thus, a high-quality education is no great mystery, and an educated mind is not difficult to define and identify. The opposite of the educated man is the uneducated man, and the uneducated man is, on this criterion, 999 times out of 1,000 the unschooled man.

This standard of quality is the one that the schools embraced in the early sixties when there was much talk about "good" science, "good" mathematics, "good" biology, and—a bit later— "good" sociology, psychology, economics, humanities, and so on down the subject list. It is the standard that operates among the guild members of academe and its indentured apprentices. The criteria are clear, if not always enthusiastically accepted. And this standard prevails in the departments of humanities and the arts, as well as in the sciences.

According to this view, the liberally educated man differs from the expert only in the degree, not in the type, of expertise. He knows the same sort of chemistry as the professor of chemistry, but not in such detail; and the same could be said of economics, history, and American literature. The liberally educated man, so to speak, is an amateur in the intellectual sports. Most schemes for general education stipulated this amateurism in certain areas of the intellectual disciplines, *e.g.*, in the familiar distribution requirements found in many colleges. The rejection of this standard on the college campus by the *avant-garde* students and faculty at one end of the school spectrum, and by the advocates of the free university at the other end, is the most interesting educational phenomenon of the seventies. The frantic efforts of college authorities to liberalize academic requirements may defuse dissent but are often beside the point. Nobody will shed many tears over the abandonment of academic rules and requirements that are justified solely by their disciplinary value. Most of these requirements are intended to prevent the student from scattering his energies or to check on his diligence. Such precautionary measures may be appropriate in elementary and secondary education, but one wonders whether they are either appropriate or morally justifiable in higher education. If the student demand for autonomy is for freedom from such supervision, one can only applaud the rebellion; if the demand is for freedom to be scatterbrained and lazy without penalty, then it should be resisted. However, the student revolt may have an even deeper significance if it signifies a rejection of the guild system and its intellectual authority.

If the standard of the expert in the intellectual disciplines is denied, what other standards are available to define quality education? We might revert to the standard of the elites in the society, either the governing or the nongoverning elites, the classes in which leadership of various kinds resides. A good school was one that the aristocracy attended. It is the essence of a genuine aristocracy that is sets its own standard, since, by definition, it is the class of the best. By blood, divine dispensation, or the feats of the ancestors, this class regards itself as *the* standard. The secondary schools attended by the children of the aristocracy are the "good" schools and, according to C. Wright Mills, constitute the single most important factor in maintaining the value systems of the power elites. Since whatever this class does is, by definition, the best, the schooling it chooses is also the best—whatever its character and content. When these schools taught Latin, Greek, and the classics, that was the best curriculum. When they taught chivalry and military exercises, that was the best. If they had chosen to teach their young mineralogy and sword swallowing, that would have defined the best education, and the lower classes would have agreed. Although Harvard may have lost some of its aristocratic assurance in recent years, the quickest way to introduce a new practice or to abandon an old one in the American university is to have Harvard do it. Most academics cannot believe that Harvard could be wrong, and, to underscore a cliché, if Harvard didn't exist, we would have to invent it; there must be one institution in the system that does not take its norms from some other one.

If a society has various class types, these, too, can serve as models and standards of quality in schooling. The upper-middle-class entrepreneur, middle-range tycoon, and prosperous professional are success models, and whatever schooling they favor also becomes a standard regardless of content or functional capacity. The middle class, butt of so much recent criticism, apes the classes above it, although it pulls back from total imitation as the upper middle class gets too close to the aristocracy. It is hard to keep the social classes distinct, because in a technomeritocracy, the dichotomy between elites and masses tends to give way to a continuous ladder of achievement on which everybody has a position. As this comes to pass, quality in education is defined functionally—in terms, that is, of one's status on the ladder of achievement, rather than in terms of social-class membership.

The college-preparatory curriculum for the last quarter of a century has been the standard educational formula for the upper middle class and for much of the middle class as well. The lower classes turned to vocational training in the later years of high school. For the upper rungs of the meritocracy, then, a college-preparatory course in high school, a couple of years of general education in college, preprofessional work in the last two years of college, and then some sort of professional graduate work was the standard route. At each step, a uniform set of subjects was taught by the guildsmen, and the institution certified the graduates at commencement.

This standard is now being challenged by the counterculture, or Charles Reich's "Consciousness III," or the existential humanists. As yet, it has no clear social class by which it can be identified, but one must suppose that the members of the new "class" can recognize each other as readily as did knights of chivalry.

The gatherings at Woodstock and subsequent rock festivals did not attract a random sample of the population. Yet any attempt to lump all the *aficionados* of the new humanism into one commune is bound to fail. The flower children do not mix well with some of the Castroites and Maoists who may be found in the camp. All favor some form of ecstasy, but some prefer it with

drugs and some with violence. Not all are nomads and vaga-
bonds, and, although there is a uniform commitment to be oneself, the selves turn out to be far from uniform. All are against
cruelty, pain, and domination by others, but some of them do
not mind, on occasion, lacerating the hearts of their parents, the
scalps of the cops, and the feelings of those not yet on the road
to liberation.

How important is the emerging new culture, or youth culture, or counterculture as a source of norms for life in general
and for education in particular? The superior articulateness of
the new culture makes it seem as if there is a tidal wave toward
Consciousness III. According to the polls, the people's opinions
on the war and the environment are inching into line with the
liberal views on these matters, but very, very slowly. The hard-
hats, who cheered the Nixon war policy in 1970, were less favorable toward it in 1971, when the adventure in Indochina began
to hurt their pocketbooks.

The wave of public indignation against the conviction of
Lieutenant Calley on the charge of murdering civilians at My
Lai indicated how mixed human reactions can be. These judgments varied from "Calley was morally and legally in the wrong
but ought not to be punished, unless everyone else in the wrong
is also punished," to "Calley was legally and morally in the right
and ought to be given a medal for doing his duty." Whether this
mixture is evidence for a national movement toward Consciousness III is doubtful.

Reich's Consciousness I, with its emphasis on hard work,
character, and achievement, and its negative correlates of pig-
headed, dogmatic stubbornness and prejudice, is far from
oblivion. Nor can Consciousness II, the identification with the
impersonal efficiency of the vast technocratic society, be written
off as an episode in history that has had its day. If Reich is at
times implausible, he is most so in the belief that there is a genuine option between a modern society soaked through and
through by technology and a modern society that is not, the rejection of technology by upper-middle-class college students
notwithstanding. Indeed, as Peter and Brigitte Berger, a pair of
sociologists, writing in the New York *Times*, February 15, 1971,
noted half in jest, we may be at the beginning not so much of
the greening or blacking of America as the bluing of it. They

said that if sufficient numbers of upper-middle-class students "cop out" of the leadership roles in the technological society and choose not to play the achievement game in it, the more vigorous members of the blue-collar classes will take their places. Evidence of such a movement in higher education was noticeable in 1971, as open admissions were inaugurated in the public colleges of New York City. The hope that the technological society will wither or melt away under the love and creativeness of Consciousness III is vain, because, aside from holocaustal destruction of the world's population, there is no way to sustain even our present numbers without exploiting technology even further than we already have.

Few would quarrel with Reich's preference for a society in which people rather than machines, peace and co-operation rather than competition and war, truth rather than hypocrisy, friendship rather than exploitation, were the rule. The Judeo-Christian belief in the sanctity of the human individual, the ancient Greek dream of the ordered serenity of the good life, high hopes for conquest of evil through science, are not altogether different from the hopes of Consciousness III. What is new, perhaps, is a widespread intimation that we are approaching a divide in our history. The possibility of doing away with the evils created by technology through technology is so vivid today that many cannot tolerate any further delay in fulfilling the potentiality. But pessimism about actualizing the possibility is a brooding presence. History may be working up to another of its boiling points.

But what does all this mean as a standard of quality in education? What are the criteria of the new humanism by which we are to judge a school? From the literature of the existential humanists, it would seem as if a school is good if, and only if, the pupil is free—free to inquire, discover, grow, feel, and express his feelings. To extend this freedom to their students, "good" schools must themselves be free from the mores of the bad establishments and from the restrictions of academic requirements.

As one of the proponents of the new humanism puts it:

. . . love and freedom are integral parts of education, as they are of life. Allowing children to be happy emotionally and psychologically and to develop their full potential as human beings are more important to us then forcing them to learn to read or write and do arithmetic and homework. Happy children will become happy adults and happy adults do not make war, commit anti-social acts, or destroy living things.[*]

However, when the criterion is applied, what is one to say of situations such as Barbara Leondar found as a result of visiting and studying nearly 100 so-called free schools?

Freedom in the alternative school often means not merely avoidance of coercion, but absence of all restraints except those required for health and safety and for preservation of the rights of others. The free school student can, for the most part, do exactly as he chooses (and that includes choosing to do nothing) provided he does not endanger himself or unduly exasperate his fellows.

Furthermore, one activity is as good as any other, as the brochure of one California school makes clear:

Students are involved in such areas as mountaineering, creative sewing and design, organic gardening, computer building, word sensitivity, minority studies, existential philosophy, yoga, meditation, sex education, pottery, weaving, diving, geometry, and gourmet cooking.

Barbara Leondar argues that surely in these individualistic free schools the arts should flourish as nowhere else, but she found that

some students flit restlessly from one to another transitory attraction sampling a smorgasbord of interests and activities. Others sink phlegmatically into apathy and ennui. Few muster the doggedness and purpose to pursue a problem, aesthetic or intellectual, as far as it may lead.

There is, moreover, a sacrifice of privacy and silence for the sake of social growth. The faculty, by having to be almost continuously available to students, is

[*] Barbara Leondar, "The Arts in Alternative Schools," *Journal of Aesthetic Education* 5, no. 1 (January 1971): 75–93.

likely to disintegrate into an incoherent mix of harassment, crisis, and distraction. . . . The result, of course, is to deny students those models of sustained and disciplined purpose which might invite emulation.

Are these schools good or bad? Surely it is impossible to say without a great deal more information than these brief excerpts provide. Freedom as such is not a useful criterion for judging schools until we specify results of free activity, and when the result is stated generally as in the first of the passages quoted, we get the pathetically naïve dictum that happy people do not make war, commit antisocial acts, or destroy living things. Not only is the dictum false, but the notion that if schools keep the young happy, all will be well is vacuous until "their full potential as human beings" is added, but this takes us into something much more particular than a state of euphoria. It means reading, writing, science, and art and disciplining oneself to become good at them or at some other no less definite skills and knowledge.

Nor is ecstasy a much more useful criterion. After quoting Einstein to the effect that modern methods of instruction strangle the "holy curiosity of inquiry," George B. Leonard triumphantly—and quite correctly—announces that

life and joy cannot be subdued. The blade of grass shatters the concrete. The spring flowers bloom in Hiroshima. An Einstein emerges from the European academies. Those who would reduce, control, quell must lose in the end.*

But can one have it both ways? If the schools cannot quell ecstasy and creativity, then what is the point of indicting them for allegedly trying to do so? In *Twentieth Century Theme,* D. W. Gotshalk, a philosopher, diagnoses the turbulent state of civilization as owing to "ungoverned creativity."

These snippets are not cited to demonstrate a thesis in a scholarly fashion, but rather as samples of the agonizing one encounters these days in the popular literature about schools. Nor have I anything but sympathy for the unhappiness with the tur-

---

* *Education and Ecstasy* (New York: Dell Publishing Co., Delacorte Press, 1968).

bulent state of our civilization that these excerpts express. What gives me pause is their naïve notion of the role of social institutions in general and of the school in particular. Aside from the philosphical untenability of a concept of process without some sort of content and structure, which these views seem to presuppose, there is the quaint belief that any genuinely viable social institution will or can consciously and deliberately destroy the value system that it serves.

Even the social institution we call knowledge—the nearest thing we have that might qualify as an institutionalized critic of the culture—does not function by abandoning its own mission: to discover and disseminate knowledge. The schools can become the critics of the culture by inducting the young into the science, literature, and philosophy of the culture, not by fomenting free-floating anxiety, rebellion, curiosity, or even ecstasy. The criterion of school quality is not the amount or the intensity of excitement or freedom or inquiry by itself; the success of the school is measured by the degree to which these attitudes and enthusiasms are disciplined—yes, disciplined—by the intellectual and aesthetic inquiries embodied in the disciplines.

There may be, of course, other institutions that should promote enthusiasm, curiosity, and ecstasy for their own sakes. One thinks of the arts in this connection. Some of the encounter and sensitivity-training groups have this mission, and for them the amount of liberation and joy could be a valid criterion. But the function of these encounter groups, associated with the work of Rollo May and the humanistic psychologists, is not identical with that of schools, especially schools for children and youth. Whatever else schools may engage in, they must undertake instruction. Given a sufficient number of encounter groups, given success of the Women's Liberation movement, given enough disgust with war, we just might get a society that would sustain and be sustained by schools quite different in attitude and tone from those of today. If, for example, the teachers of 1985 will be liberated women and domesticated men; if the little boys and girls in their classrooms will no longer face a future ridden with anxiety about their sex roles, then, of course, the school will lose much of the atmosphere that it now exudes. If society in 1985 will have rationalized and controlled its technology, the schools will not unwittingly reinforce gross consumption of the gross national product; if in 1985 there will be no failure for children to fear, schools will not instill fear of failure. The attempt of the new humanists to convert the social order through direct change of the pupil's attitudes is misguided, because the school does not originate attitudes; it merely reinforces those to which the dominant group is already committed.

But what sort of social fantasy would impel one to conduct schools as if the real world is *already* like the world the Goodmans, Kozols, and Holts think (as would many of us) it ought to be? I see around me dozens of young college students who have succumbed to this illusion; they act and talk as if the world beyond the campus is not a world of scarcity, fear, competition, and absurdity. Should the schools deliberately reinforce this illusion? Is such hallucinating what is meant by social criticism?

To understand—by means of knowledge—the social reality is the mission of the school as school. To change that reality rationally is a commitment to which the school can contribute by the induction of the young into the cultural heritage, which is the record of social criticism. The school *in loco humanitatis* can do this without being politicized and without being turned into encounter-group therapy sessions.

Can the quality of the life celebrated by the counterculture be telling us something more about the quality of education than does the rhetoric of creativity, freedom, nonconformity? Of the prescriptions the counterculture makes for the school, respect for pupils as persons is the most prominent. Taken literally, the prescription is silly, because the kind of pseudoprofessional preparation most teachers receive and the sorts of tasks they must perform preclude the sorts of individualized encounters the prescription envisions. However, if the counterculture's prescription is taken as an indictment of the way the black ghetto child is regarded by white teachers, it is not silly at all.

Ralph Ellison's *Invisible Man* (1952) was but one of the books that vividly demonstrated the gap between the consciousness of the ghetto child and that of his white teacher. In the sixties many whites lived in black communities to get the feel of discrimination and oppression. Much was made of the white teacher's inability to identify with the value system of the ghetto child—his attitudes toward aggression, sex, and the family. Conversely, much was said about the ghetto child's inability to identify with the middle-class child's acceptance of competition, cleanliness, orderliness, and, above all, the importance of schooling.

However, the counterculture indictment went further. Not only the ghetto child was being misunderstood and oppressed. All youth was being exploited, stultified, and suppressed both in college and in high school, and from there it was but a step to say that all children, middle-class and ghetto alike, were being oppressed, stifled, and manipulated by the society.

I shall merely cite a few examples of the charges of impersonality and downright hostility to pupils that have been directed toward urban teachers:

School personnel . . . dislike and distrust youngsters. . . . more often than not they [youngsters] . . . find the school a jungle . . . and cannot defend themselves against the covert, lingering hostility of teachers [Friedenberg].

Teachers have been characterized as

people without any real concern for these children. . . . [They are] bewildered and desperate . . . and no longer have faith they can be teachers any more in their classrooms [Passow].

Another commentator said that the majority of children

deny their intelligence to their jailers, the teachers . . . who use fear and anxiety as instruments of control . . . and tend to mistake good behavior for good character. What they prize above all is docility [Holt].*

The citations could be expanded by the yard, but the solutions would still remain elusive. The element common to the solutions that are suggested seems to be freedom. Presumably the

* Edgar Z. Friedenberg, *Vanishing Adolescent* (New York: Dell Publishing Co., 1962), p. 26; A. Harry Passow, ed., *Education in Depressed Areas* (New York: Teachers College Press, 1962), pp. 19, 265; John Holt, *How Children Fail* (New York: Pitman Publishing Corp., 1964), p. xiii.

way to treat pupils as persons is to remove all restraints from them: school discipline, the emphasis on order, on cleanliness, on obedience to rules. In short, urban ghetto children are not deprived but depressed, repressed, and oppressed; remove the shackles, and the natural creativeness, intelligence, and desire to learn will blossom freely and fully.

There is some reason to believe that this would work for a part of the problem. Obviously, if restraints are removed, the children will be freer than they were before; whether they will then turn eagerly to studying the standard curriculum is not so certain. But that is the heart of the matter. If the goal of the new humanists is to set children free so that they can attain Reich's Consciousness III, then not sending them to school at all would be a plausible alternative, and it is one that would make many school children happy—even if nothing else were done. Or, if you like, we might invent institutions in which the young congregate and do their things without "uptight" adult intervention —communes, Woodstocks, day-care centers, social centers, or whatever—and we could, if we chose to do so, call them schools.

Some, like Kenneth B. Clark, would want the psychological atmosphere of the schools changed so that ghetto children could learn the skills and knowledge customarily taught to middle-class white children. Others, however, seem to be saying that even the curriculum of the white middle-class school is an imposition on nonwhite, non-middle-class children. Cultural pluralism is invoked as the ultimate validation for allowing each cultural group to learn what is "beautiful" for them and emphasizes the right not to study anything else. But logic will not let the argument stop there, for, if a child is to be really free, he should not be subject to the demands or values of his own ethnic group, either. Hence we are led to a school with an infinite number of alternative curricula (not only for actual pupils but also for all possible pupils) or as many alternative schools as enterprising educational entrepreneurs can establish with the help of state vouchers and grants from the foundations.

A school would therefore be judged by the number of alternatives it afforded the pupils, but what meaning is to be attached to quality education with regard to each alternative? If we remain true to the principle of freedom, can good quality mean anything other than "having been chosen freely"? If so, the content of the various alternatives cannot be judged at all; we thus arrive at the notion of quality without a standard, because the criterion has now become a subjective state that nobody can appraise with any claim to objectivity—not even its possessor.

However, it may be objected that this is a doctrinaire conclusion; that the new humanists are merely urging that harsh discipline and rote learning be abolished; that informal modes of teaching are more efficient than the conventional ones. Harshness in dealing with school children has been decried from time immemorial; exhortation in behalf of informal teaching also has a long history. This is why there is an art of teaching that some of us believe is worth cultivating. But thus far all schemes for informal teaching have been judged by their ability to achieve formal results. The question is whether informality as such, whether happiness of children as such, are sufficient criteria for judging the quality of schooling. It is the assertion of the latter thesis that is important and interesting.

The thesis can be sustained much more easily with the young child than with the adolescent. This follows from the principle that the younger the child, the less easily he deals with abstract ideas and the more he is tied to the concrete and the particular. High-order abstractions—such as "facts" and rules—are irrelevant to young minds, simply because they can't learn them as abstractions. So, if pressed, they learn them by rote. By rote even an infant can learn to say, "E equals mc squared."

However, when high school and college students invoke the principle of relevance as a justification for protest, the situation is considerably different. Adolescents can deal with abstractions —about as well as they ever shall—and they are in school because knowledge as organized abstract ideas is not available as incidental products of ordinary life activities—except possibly for the genius. When life predicaments can be resolved with common-sense generalizations, one learns by living; when common sense is insufficient, one has to learn by comprehending knowledge discovered and formulated by others. How far does common sense and personal experience go, these days, in thinking about pollution, inflation, the problems of health and peace? Rap sessions do not solve technical problems.

The rejection of the acquisition of knowledge not directly bearing on immediate problems by the protesting college student could be regarded as a form of parasitic ingratitude. It is easy to reject as irrelevant the formal study of chemistry and mathematics when one is quite sure that there are individuals and institutions who will study it and develop it. It is easy to reject technology if one is quite sure that the telephone system will continue to operate and that the supermarket will remain open until 9 P.M. A group of young people enraged about pollution drive to a rally in behalf of clean air in a car that belches pollutants from its exhaust; they gather at rock festivals where the plumbing is primitive, but where the music is propagated to the multitude by highly sophisticated electronic devices; expensively prepared health foods are consumed in unhygienic surroundings. Consistency may well be the hobgoblin of little minds, but consistent existential inconsistency in time destroys the credibility of even big minds.

This kind of mindless self-forgetfulness is hardly appropriate to genuine existential humanism; authenticity demands that one not forget one's debt to the tradition that is being rejected. The free university can propose to do away with all formal coursework, with examinations, and with required readings, because it presupposes a university that nurtures and disseminates the intellectual disciplines formally to somebody. A class on racial discrimination is nothing more than a protest meeting or a strategy meeting for action, if the resources of psychology, sociology, and economics do not exist to make the discussion more enlightened at the end than it was in the beginning. But how did these resources come into being?

Interdisciplinary inquiries come *after* the disciplines have been developed; and they were not developed so long as men wallowed in their own concrete predicaments. Scientifically, it is not profitable to understand water by confining oneself to the properties of drinking water and bathing water and navigational water. It was only when water was considered in abstraction from its numerous existential contexts—mythical, religious, physiological, agricultural—that a scientific understanding of its nature became possible. It was only when justice and courage and temperance became abstracted from the concrete contexts that engender them that philosophical inquiry into them became possible.

The clamor for relevance, especially in higher education, makes sense if one has already left Plato's cave and has become enlightened by knowledge. Then it does behoove us all to return to our human predicaments, individual and social, and to show that enlightenment did us some existential good. The demand makes no sense if it means that one will not leave the cave at all.

For a young man or woman to demand freedom from academic rules and requirements makes sense if he can accomplish their intent and results without them. If he is mature enough to use the library and the faculty resources on his own, then by all means he should be encouraged, urged, indeed, almost forced to do so. The onus of proving this maturity lies on the student, but a dislike of academic work and a preoccupation with social causes do not constitute sufficient proof. We may indeed be approaching the moment of truth in higher education, when only those who can use the resources of the university without the customary proddings and police actions will be given access to it.

In other words, when students demand more freedom in planning their studies because they no longer need the discipline of rules, requirements, and regulations, the administration and faculty should grant the request with enthusiasm. The amount of energy spent by institutions of higher learning in futile regulatory efforts is scandalous. The money would be better spent in enabling high schools to bring the student to the maturity level needed for higher education. If, however, college students demand freedom from rules in order to prolong their immaturity, then the sensible, although radical, response would be to send them home or to some other institution for further aging.

Quality education without standards is a meaningless and mischievous notion. Somewhere the standards of truth, goodness, and beauty must be made explicit, and somewhere it must be shown that tuition in these matters can make a difference in life. Such norms are available in the living tradition of each of the great domains of knowledge and the arts, and the school can be judged in terms of quality if these standards are accepted and used. Humanism can be a criterion if the norms of the studies we call the humanities are invoked. Philosophy, history, literature, art, have their critical traditions as the sciences do. To join the company of the learned and the wise in these domains—even as enlightened amateurs and cherishers—is the humanistic goal in its traditional and classical sense. But these humanistic traditions all require disciplined reflection on experience, as well as the mere *having* of it. They entail fine discriminations—finer than common sense yields or encourages; they call for a commitment to the superanimal possibilities of humanity rather than to its subanimal potentialities. It is the acceptance of this view that underlies the belief that the pursuit of knowledge is the central function of the university. Some have wondered whether this ideal has been abandoned. Is the professoriate no longer dominated by it?

The answer may be yes, but it may also be the answer of some of the students as well as of some faculty members who have succumbed to the demands of the market place. These students have rejected both the market place and the formal systematic search for truth. But is there any other kind of activity that is suitable for the university?

It is a question not only for the university but for the whole system of formal education. Once the university changes its role, the secondary and elementary schools may have to change theirs also. The seventies may be the decade when such a change may come about or gather sufficient momentum for us to discern what it may bring.

The issue is the degree to which the school, but especially the university, will devote itself to knowledge in the two forms it has achieved. One is for the purpose of its own development and dissemination—the disciplines as represented by the faculty of the colleges of arts and sciences: mathematics, physics, history, philosophy. Although these disciplines developed out of man's attempt to reflect upon the ways he invented to deal with his environment, once they achieved the status of conceptual structures with a logic of their own, their development became independent of their origin. Thus, for example, once mathematics became a deductive system, the fact that it grew out of the practical needs of mensuration could be bypassed. The guilds of professors and graduate students who work within these disciplines to develop and disseminate them constitute the heart of the university. Any attempt to reform the university that would seriously threaten the guild and its criteria for membership and reward is probably, and probably rightly, doomed to futility.

The university also houses knowledge organized in a somewhat different way. The schools of law, medicine, architecture, engineering, education, and agriculture—the professional schools—organized knowledge *from* the disciplines into knowledge *about* the problems of practice to which their graduates had to address themselves. In time, however, the new organization also became formalized so that one could speak of anatomy, physiology, pathology, endocrinology, medical radiology, and the like as "disciplines," and they could be taught with the same didactic rigor as the parent disciplines themselves. These acquired the status of professional disciplines.

It is the study of formalized knowledge in pure or professional disciplines that is now under attack and forcing the university to cast uneasy glances over its shoulder and at its curricula. The attack has many forms, but the most familiar are that instruction should be organized in terms of neither of these disciplines but rather in terms of (1) social problems, *e.g.,* pollution or war or racial discrimination; or (2) personal problems. This is the usual import of the demand for relevance.

Traditionally, however, general education has consisted of the formal study of the disciplines in the arts and sciences, and professional work has consisted of the professional disciplines, so the attack asks for a radical reorganization not only of the curriculum but of the intellectual training and habits of the majority of the professoriate.

The challenge to the traditional style of the university is made more serious by the charge of overqualification. It is said that most jobs do not need as much formal study as is now prescribed; there is pressure to reduce the amount of disciplinary work in schools of medicine and law, to take only two examples. The case of formal study in preparation for teaching was discussed in the previous chapter. The reduction of formal disciplinary study for general education is also in the wind.

It is time, therefore, to rethink the claims made for disciplinary study for both general and professional education, and this has to be done in terms of the individual and society as a whole. In a technologically developed society, the theory represented by the disciplines is indispensable, but for how many? For example, basic research in nuclear physics must continue, but how far down the engineering ladder must one prescribe formal study of nuclear physics? Could we get along with a relatively small, elite cadre of theory people in all the professions, and, likewise, could we get by with a relatively small part of our population receiving a highly abstract sort of general education? Could the bulk of our people be trained to the apprentice, rule-following level as far as their vocation is concerned? Could their general education be reduced to basic skills of literacy and the information receivable from the mass media?

These themes will come up again in this book, and perhaps there may be a way of bringing about the interpenetration of knowledge and the human predicaments that will be more effective than those that are being challenged today, but in the meantime we ought to be wary of those who peddle the nostrum of quality without standards. At best, this is sincere nonsense; at worst, it is quackery.

An accumulation of facts and a detailed knowledge of theory in any domain of knowledge is possible and useful only to the specialist, and the subtle insistence of "good" professors that all their students study as if they were to become their apprentices, *i.e.*, as if they were to become specialists, is what has been nibbling steadily at the roots of general education in our colleges and universities. Probably the really "good" professors, as members of the guild, can do little to change this attitude, and one hesitates to urge that they should. But neither should we force the student to play the professor's game, if he wants a general education and has not yet opted for some profession or specialized field of graduate study.

Without abandoning the disciplinary structure of knowledge and instruction or disbanding the disciplinary guilds, we may still be able to effect general education. First, the really "good" professors of a discipline are in the best position to decide which minimal set of components of a discipline—theoretical, factual, procedural—are *essential* to thinking correctly and critically

within a given domain. Second, "good" professors can participate with students and colleagues in attacks on such problems as
pollution of the environment, war and peace, racism, sexism, and
the other manifold ills of the social order. And by participate I
do not mean reading a paper and listening to other papers on the
problem. By participation I mean exerting the strenuous effort
needed to understand the categories and language and procedures of the other fellow's discipline as it tries, so to speak, to put
the common problem under its own stencil. I use the word
"strenuously" advisedly, because neither professors nor students
really know as yet what cognitive and emotive processes are involved and how they are involved in interdisciplinary thinking,
feeling, and deciding. The art of collective deliberation—with a
variety of disciplinary perspectives—has to be cultivated, and
there is no reason why the school should not practice this cultivation from its earliest grades, but especially as the stencils of
the various fields of knowledge are being learned in high school
and in college. This art is not part of any disciplinary course, and
it is not always advisable to make it so.

If relevance is interpreted to mean a demand for testing the
structure and content of the intellectual disciplines on socially
important problems, then the demand is wholly reasonable and
urgent; if the demand for relevance is taken to mean discussion
of social problems without studying the disciplines, or the substi-
tution of discussion for such study, then one can rightfully become alarmed at both the demand and the press of the younger
members of the faculty to meet it.

CHAPTER V

The Cost of Quality and Equality

If the current attacks on the public schools are symptomatic of a general social malaise, the financial predicament of these schools is even more so. All the agencies that supply social services—welfare, the police, public transportation, pollution control, as well as the schools—clamor for more and more funds, while their deficits grow larger and larger. What is even more discouraging is that we seem to be unable to reduce substantially the gap between needs and resources, so that the various agencies have to compete with one another for the available tax dollars. These phenomena taken together give rise to the fear that the mechanisms we have devised to deliver social services have about reached the limit of their capacity. Nor is the pessimism confined to public agencies; in recent years our vaunted telephone service has impaired its image of reliability, while the disordered railroads have surrendered control of passenger traffic to a government agency. Ralph Nader has made a shambles of the claims to efficiency and credibility of our largest industrial combines. Are we, then, facing a general institutional breakdown, a kind of social bankruptcy?

I lack the expertise and the gift of prophecy to say at what point the overload of the system will cause it to disintegrate—perhaps a coincidence of a big blizzard and strikes by the transport and communications workers—as did the notorious "one-hoss shay," but if it does, it may furnish us with the opportunity to reassemble the social order in a way that cannot be done so long as we can keep on patching and shoring up the old system. What we have now is an unstable mixture of private entrepreneurship and government activity, with every element in our society trying to exploit the public treasury for its own advantage. By and large the rich and powerful have done better at this game than the have-nots, but the pressure from the latter is growing—they are taking the rhetoric of the liberals literally. But the social reality is on their side, too, for the haves cannot continue to prosper in a highly interdependent technological society if there are too many under-consuming have-nots.

Should a great social earthquake occur, there may be a period of relative chaos followed by a long stretch of the doldrums, but I am optimistic enough to believe that a new institutional pattern will emerge, and that it will be able to deal with our social problems somewhat better than the one that it displaces. Whether the new arrangement resembles some form of the corporate state or a democratic form of socialism, I don't know, but the odds seem to favor more public control of social services than less.

It is not clear at which stage of the general disintegration the public school system has arrived; it has not yet broken down, but the numerous votes against school levies are not good omens. Furthermore, in recent years the public has learned to tolerate school shutdowns, although school boards strive frantically to avoid them. Teachers' strikes have been responsible for some of the unscheduled vacations, but the sheer lack of funds when the school authorities reached the bottom of all the wells they could think of is the more usual cause. Up to now there has always been one more well the waters of which revived the school, but it is now conceivable that the schools of Chicago or Los Angeles will remain closed for a whole school year at a time.*

* The fear of schools shutting down is a phenomenon that is associated with urbanization. In our agrarian days, schools were shut down quite frequently —often when the scholars shut out the schoolmaster—but such cessations occasioned little social or individual disruption. It is a quite different story when closed schools release hordes of children into the streets with nothing to do and with plenty of opportunity for mischief. Cf. David W. Swift, "Changing Patterns of Pupil Control," *The Educational Forum*, January, 1972, pp. 199–208.

To be sure, even in chaos the people will not be without their schools. A good many of them will spring up as each group of like-minded families establishes one to its liking. This is precisely what some groups are doing now or would like to do now if they could afford it. That the fragmentation of the schools will continue once the social system transforms itself is unlikely, for if it is a system, schooling will be one of the key institutions within that system; the need for integration that engenders and sustains a society, especially a modern technological society, will not let the schools elude the net of interdependence.

Perhaps this is why the schools cannot respond creatively to the challenge of the day by themselves. A school reform without the parallel restructuring of the economy, the health services, and the relief of the poor and the aged makes little sense. If social dislocations continue to deform children faster than societal mechanisms can straighten them out, then it is silly to proclaim that a more efficient method of teaching reading or a change in the composition of the school boards will redeem the children and the social order to boot.

The support of the public schools involves a mixture of social, moral, and financial considerations. Underlying many of the issues is the tension between two equally strong sentiments: one is to allow each citizen to provide the kind of schooling he deems best for his children; the other is that all children have an equal right to schooling that will maximize their potentialities for whatever they conceive to be the good life. We have, on the whole, satisfied the first sentiment much better than the second. Money may or may not be the key to quality in education, but lack of it is one key to inequality. School support is also tied up with school control, and this, in turn, is related to what people believe schools ought or ought not to do and teach. Some people want the schools to overthrow the industrial-military-business complex; others wish to impose the kind of efficiency measures used by that complex on the schools.

Just how important is schooling? The accepted view is that its social benefit is beyond question and the individual benefit even more so.

In the now-famous *Serrano* v. *Priest* decision, the California Supreme Court declared, "We are convinced that the distinctive and priceless function of education in our society warrants, indeed compels, our treating it as a 'fundamental interest.' "

To those who counsel deschooling and repudiate compulsory-school-attendance laws, this court decision offers little comfort:

> Today, education is perhaps the most important function of state and local governments. Compulsory school attendance laws and the great expenditures for education both demonstrate our recognition of the importance of education to our democratic society. It is required in the performance of our most basic responsibilities, even service in the armed forces. It is the very foundation of good citizenship. Today it is a principal instrument in awakening the child to cultural values, in preparing him for later professional training, and in helping him to adjust normally to his environment. In these days, it is doubtful that any child may reasonably be expected to succeed in life if he is denied the opportunity of an education. Such an opportunity, where the state has undertaken to provide it, is a right which must be made available to all on equal terms.

One measure of the importance of schooling is the extent to which the schools are utilized. In 1969–70, 77.1 per cent of the eighteen-year-olds were being graduated from high school, and of these 59.8 per cent were going on to college.* This is certainly an impressive degree of utilization.

Another measure is the amount of money spent for schooling. Table I tells at least part of the story.

Clearly the dollar in 1970 was not worth as much as in 1960, so the increase in total expenditures from $24.6 billion to $70.3 billion is not so impressive as one might think; during the decade, moreover, total enrollments went from 45 million to 58 million, an increase of nearly 40 per cent. The expenditures per pupil in average daily attendance were $375 in 1959–60 for public elementary and secondary school pupils, $783 in 1969–70, and are expected to rise to $986 in 1979–80.

Large as the totals spent for education are, the amounts spent for all schooling, public and private, at all levels, represented about 7.5 per cent of the gross national product in 1969. About 5 per cent of the GNP went for elementary and secondary

---

* Statistics of Trends in Education, 1959–60 to 1979–80, National Center for Educational Statistics, 1971.

TABLE I

(U.S. Office of Education Financial Trends in Education, 1959–60 to 1979–80, March, 1971)

Total Expenditures by Regular Education Institutions	Unadjusted Dollars		Constant 1969–70 Dollars
	1959–60	1969–70	1979–80 (Estimate)
(Billions of Dollars)			
All levels	24.6	70.3	97.4
Public	19.6	57.1	78.4
Nonpublic	5.0	13.2	19.0
Elementary and secondary schools	17.9	45.4	55.2
Public	15.8	40.8	49.7
Nonpublic	2.1	4.6	5.5
Institutions of higher education	6.7	24.9	42.2
Public	3.8	16.3	28.7
Nonpublic	2.9	8.6	13.5

school education. Governmental expenditures for all functions in 1967–68 were 16.2 per cent of per-capita income, and for education 6.51 per cent of per-capita income, or $205.93 per capita. Perhaps the situation is better described by the fact that even at an annual per-pupil cost of $783, this expenditure amounts to about $.70 an hour for a seven-hour, 180-day school year, and one can hardly hire a baby-sitter for that much. So far as I know, no new automobile can be purchased in the United States for $783, nor can one be operated for much less than that in a year. On this scale, public schooling is still a bargain, even if it provides nothing more than custodial care. Lest we are tempted to denigrate the custodial function of the school, let us remember that we rely very heavily on schools to keep children, especially urban children, off the streets during the day and thus out of daylight delinquency.

I do not want to stress, as one well might, the relative priorities of cosmetics, motorcars, dining out, vacation travel, and schooling in our spending habits, because taxes are not paid or resisted solely on consumer preference. Most social services— government, fire protection, garbage collection, and road maintenance—are public necessities, not private luxuries, whereas consumers' value priorities are exhibited in the luxuries they seek, *after* the necessities have been secured.

Nonetheless, among the social services some are more postponable than others—garbage collection and snow removal cannot be postponed for long. Education can be. After all, the children are not in school all summer, and although individual households are tested severely, the nation survives. All men by nature, Aristotle announced, desire to know, but ignorance of the things taught in school is not unbearably frustrating. At best, the benefits of education are deferred gratifications even for oneself or one's own children; to invest cheerfully in these deferred benefits for the children of others or for the nation as a whole is to ask for more farsightedness than our schools have been able to produce in most of our citizens.

A more ambiguous factor in evaluating the importance of schooling is the counterculture's doubts about it. One line of its attack is based on the allegedly low correlation between schooling and economic success, although a recent study showed that, of families with incomes of $25,000 or more, 69 per cent of the family heads had at least some college training; by contrast, of those families with incomes of less than $3,000, some 65 per cent of the breadwinners had less than twelve grades of schooling. Another impugns the value of success as measured by middle-class standards (do you need schooling for Consciousness III?). A third doubts the value of compulsory schooling. Ivan Illich, for example, might grant the value of schooling for those who can profit from the economic opportunities of developed countries, but not for the peasantry of underdeveloped countries. Unless we return to a preindustrial form of society—which I consider unlikely—schooling will continue to be valued by most of our people for one or all of three reasons: for occupational competence, for discharging the duties of citizenship, and for trying to wrest a tolerable quality of life from the constraints of a technological society. Schooling will continue to be in high demand.

High demand, however, does not necessarily mean that the people will be willing to expend large amounts of tax money for education. Schooling could be supplied by private sources entirely and be bought and paid for by those who wanted it. Adam

Smith thought it ought to be a transaction between a teacher and his customers so that healthy competition and incentives would prevail:

The endowments of schools and colleges have necessarily diminished, more or less, the necessity of application in the teachers. Their subsistence, so far as it arises from their salaries, is evidently derived from a fund altogether independent of their success and reputation in their particular profession.*

Milton Friedman, in our day, is more or less of the same opinion. Schooling goes public, so to speak, when it is thought to yield a public benefit that a considerable number of individual citizens might neglect. This is a necessary precaution, for little in history supports the belief that individuals will tax themselves *voluntarily* for anything other than to avert disaster. Voluntary support for armies, the relief of the poor, the aged, the orphaned, and the education of the young has been a slender reed on which few governments have been willing to lean.

But education also goes public when large numbers of individuals who cannot afford as much schooling as they would like insist on having it. Thus the citizenry wanting less schooling than the state thinks it ought to have and those who want more than they can afford to buy in the private sector make public support of education necessary.

In our own country, at least, the schooling of the poor could not be left to the poor or to the philanthropy of the rich. Permissive legislation had to be supplemented with mandatory statutes; tuition schools had to give way to fully tax-supported schools, and voluntary attendance to compulsory attendance. As long as schooling is regarded as a communal benefit, it probably cannot be otherwise—a minimum must be mandatory, and for the poor the minimum tends to become the norm. If vouchers were given to the poor for schooling, would they spend it for schooling—if schooling were not compulsory? And if they could get better schooling by supplementing the vouchers with their own money, could they afford to do so? It would be surprising indeed if the

* An Inquiry into the Nature and Causes of the Wealth of Nations (London: 1776, 1784; New York: Random House, 1937), p. 717.

poor ever ended up with much more than the minimum required by law—that is what being poor in our type of society means.

That schools compete for public funds with welfare recipients is not without its irony, because our practice of levying taxes for schools had its origin in the poor laws of England early in the seventeenth century. In the sixteenth century, England was faced with problems of unemployment, the support of the indigent, and their control in matters of crime and morality. The poor laws, as codified in 1601, provided for both the use of taxes to relieve the poor and the authority to supervise their lives. The parish appointed overseers of the poor, who were empowered to levy taxes, to collect the levy, to build workhouses, to put the poor to work, and to place their children in workhouses or to bind them out as apprentices.

Under these laws (reformed again in 1834) many children were sent to America, and in 1642 the Massachusetts lawmakers, noting that

this court [legislature] taking into consideration the great neglect of many parents and masters [of apprentices] in training up their children in learning and labor, and other employments which may be profitable to the commonwealth, . . .*

went on to charge the selectmen to see to it that these children could "understand the principles of religion and the capital laws of this country." Furthermore, parents and masters who did not abide by the statute were to be fined. Virginia passed similar ordinances for the care of orphans and children of the poor. So acute poverty was originally responsible for public schools, which are now being asked to redeem the victims of poverty.

Granted that schooling as measured by utilization and expenditure is important to the American public, how is expenditure related to (1) the quality of schooling, and (2) the dictum: Equal access to equal quality?

Some advocates of school reform believe that quality of education is a function of expenditures. They therefore concentrate on correcting the injustice that is produced by unequal expendi-

* Ellwood P. Cubberley, *Readings in the History of Education* (Boston: Houghton Mifflin Co., 1920), p. 298.

tures. Other reformers, however, deny that more money will improve the schools so long as the middle-class establishment school boards, teachers, and administrators are spending the money. Hence their efforts are directed toward changing the attitudes of the faculty personnel or, better still, changing the personnel altogether.

For a long time—and perhaps in the minds of most people even now—the relation between expenditures and quality was taken for granted. The discrepancy between schools in Southern states and those of the North was generally explained by the difference in expenditures; so was the difference in the quality of the schools provided for blacks and whites.

The difference in quality between rural and urban schools was explained in the same fashion, although the density of population in the city made certain savings possible. Sparsity of students in the rural districts deprived their schools of the diversity of curricula and special programs available in large schools. The movement for consolidation of small, rural school districts and for the bussing of pupils into centralized regional centers was argued on these grounds. Hence some of the current attempt to break up large schools into a multitude of little red schoolhouses, each doing its own thing, is puzzling indeed.

Much as the disparities between rich and poor districts, between black and white schools, were deplored; much as we were startled by the large, stagnant pools of functional illiteracy uncovered by the draft in both of the World Wars, it was not until the mid-sixties that we were really jolted by the difference between the quality of the schools in the inner city and almost everywhere else. By quality I mean in this instance not only the amount spent on the schools, but also the relatively low rate of achievement of their pupils in the basic scholastic skills.

Why this revelation should be so shocking has puzzled me for some time. After all, we had lived with copious pockets of illiteracy for a long time. As recently as 1960, for example, Alabama had an illiteracy rate of 4.2 per cent; Georgia, 4.5 per cent; and Louisiana, 6.3 per cent.* Professor Leo Fay, a reading specialist at Indiana University, cleared up one part of the puzzle. He

* U.S. Department of Commerce, Bureau of Census, *Current Population Reports*, series P–23, no. 8.

noted, if I recall his remarks correctly, that illiteracy and a low order of intellectual skills generally are less dysfunctional in rural areas than in the city—presumably because there is a good deal of gainful work in the country that would not penalize illiteracy unduly. Consequently, it is only when illiterates migrate in large numbers to the city, where there are relatively few occupational opportunities for the poorly schooled, that inability to read, write, and compute become highly visible disadvantages. I did not ask him whether Southern cities had more employment opportunities for rural immigrants than did Northern cities, but as Southern cities become more and more industrialized, one would guess that the difference would not be as important now as it once might have been. All big cities seem to be having the same sorts of troubles.

With the blossoming of the civil rights movement and civil rights legislation, black citizens everywhere, but especially in the inner city, could hardly avoid seeing how disadvantaged they were, not only with regard to schooling but also with regard to the social and economic conditions that make it possible for children to profit from schooling. The militant leaders of the ghetto were sociologically more astute than some of their educational comrades who joined them in the reform movement. The leaders quite correctly said: "We need more of everything: relief, housing, jobs, and schooling." Their educational allies, for the most part white and affluent, said: "All we need is to take the control of the schools away from the middle-class bureaucracy and hire humanistic teachers."

If we go with the leaders, the public expenditures for the reform of schools in the inner city will have to go well beyond that needed to provide equal facilities and instruction. Getting the community ready to profit from instruction will take even more public funds, and yet there is no easy alternative to this wholesale rehabilitation of the inner city. Even bussing the children into the "best" schools—for which, in certain instances, a case can be made—will do little for the situation as a whole, although a few individuals may well have their whole lives changed by the experience.

But let us return to those who hold that quality in school depends on money. The arguments for this view are based on the belief that quality has at least the following three dimensions: teachers, facilities, and programs. In each of these dimensions it is held that the higher the expenditure, the higher the quality.

The teacher-salary level is the most important fiscally since it constitutes so much of the total budget. Does quality schooling mean highly paid teachers? If we could agree on the meaning of quality, we might give a straightforward answer to this question. Since we cannot do so, we revert to the operational standard of quality, namely, the socioeconomic status of the school's clients, that is to say, "good" schools are schools patronized by well-to-do people, and "good" teachers are teachers who are hired to teach in such schools. On this criterion the wealthy suburbs get the "best" teachers. A community made up of upper-middle-class residents, with children conditioned to the values of that class, offering a high salary schedule and, if possible, a delightful climate, will have a good teaching staff.

What the distinctive characteristics of teachers so recruited are is not easy to say, but two may be encountered more often than others. One is that they are more likely to have been graduated from "good" colleges than their more unselected fellow teachers; the other is that many of them have moved in from other communities. They thus have a little more of the pioneering spirit, and, other things being equal, this is a plus in almost any calling.

The effect of higher salaries on teacher mobility is damped, however, by collective bargaining. It works this way: many teachers, especially females, for one reason or another, prefer to work in their home communities. City teachers are peculiarly loathe to leave the city. These homebody teachers often sacrifice a good deal—including money—to work at home. However, with collective bargaining, it is possible to have one's cake and eat it, too; one can force up the salary scale at home.

The proposition that a teacher's salary should be proportionate to quality of service is further fudged by the fact that remuneration of service personnel reflects the cost of living more than it does the quality of their services. Haircuts and food stuffs are no better today than when their price was a fifth of what they are now. The increased price merely means that barbers and grocers have to pay more to live; their clients have to make up the difference; quality has little to do with it.

Somehow this fact of economic life has eluded the most vociferous advocates of accountability in the public schools. Apparently they believe that with each increase in the pay scale of teachers, they have a right to expect an increase in efficiency or quality or whatever it is they would like the schools to accomplish.

Their reasoning, one must suppose, runs something like this: teachers, like everyone else, work to get a salary. These salaries, which make up the bulk of the school budget, should produce a certain amount and grade of educational "product." Increased salaries should produce more "product" or a better "product" in one of two ways: either by lowering the cost of production through more efficient methods, or by increasing the effort per unit of time. Since it is difficult to increase productivity without a dramatic use of technology, the accountability men urge greater use of technology, but they also feel that money should act as an incentive to greater effort.

Consider, if you please, the following excerpt from the *Education-Training Market Report* of November 8, 1971:

Incentive Pay Project: Office of Education is negotiating with four school systems to conduct incentive pay projects. Two cities, Cincinnati, Ohio, and Jacksonville, Florida, will conduct experiments under which teachers will be paid bonuses based upon pupil achievement. Two others, San Antonio, Texas, and Oakland, California, will pay bonuses to both teachers and parents. All schools have agreed to participate and final details are now being worked out.

Some $750,000 of Title III Elementary and Secondary Education Act funds have been allocated to projects. *Spokesman at OE has described program as "kind of performance contract for teachers and parents."*

As part of project, OE has entered into $251,000 contract with Planar Corp., Washington, D.C., to establish data bank, and $200,000 contract with Education Turnkey Corp., Washington, D.C., for management support. Another $320,000 will be used for bonuses and other school district costs.

Test and control schools will be designated in each of four districts with 600 test and 600 control children. All 4,800 children will be given standardized tests during program, but which tests and how tests are to be administered have not yet been determined.

Performance will be measured against normal expected progress. Teachers who do one-tenth better during test period will receive *25 percent of maximum bonus of $1,200.* Teachers who improve performance by 20 percent will receive half the bonus; teachers who reach 30 percent improvement will get 75 percent and those who improve pupil performance by more than 30 percent will receive full bonus.

Parents will be paid on same basis up *to maximum of $100 for each child's* progress in schools where both teachers and parents are eligible for bonus. Bonus will be paid only for 2,400 children in test schools.

This experiment should be followed with great interest, because it might show (1) whether the participating teachers had been loafing on the job; or (2) whether they were incapable of improvement despite the money incentives; and (3) whether there is any relation between rate of improvement and current salaries of participating teachers. As for parents, if their $100 bonuses help more than a $300 bonus to teachers, we might pay the teachers' salaries to parents. Why the pupils are not given bonuses is hard to say, except that schemes that have done so have been criticized—presumably on moral and educational grounds. But these objections, one would think, would weigh also against money incentives for teachers and parents. How, by the way, can the U.S. Office of Education be made accountable for spending $750,000 of the taxpayer's money for this kind of project?

The plain fact is that if we knew how to rate teachers in a way that would be credible, we would have had merit pay schedules long ago. In Utah a school merit committee spent several years and nearly $250,000 without getting satisfactory answers to the following questions: (1) Can we define and measure good teaching? (2) If we can, how can these measures be related to a salary program? * Long before the unions estab-

* Gale Rose, "The Utah Story on Merit Salary Schedules," cited in Charles S. Benson, *The Economics of Public Education* (Boston: Houghton Mifflin Co., 1961), pp. 433–36.

lished collective bargaining, administrators could not find criteria that would give them the courage to assign salaries on merit. Moreover, the task differentiation within teaching is too small to warrant fine gradations in salaries. Accordingly, years of service plus credits beyond the initial baccalaureate degree serve as the major differentiators. In all likelihood, these are somehow related to quality, but nobody really knows how, especially since the criteria of quality are themselves so vague.

The hope that teachers could be judged and rated by the achievement of their pupils as measured by tests must also be regarded as optimistic.

At best, tests which are sufficiently well studied to deserve attention provide only a hasty survey of a pupil's knowledge, square only inexactly with the purposes of a particular teacher, and are several years behind advanced thinking about education. Teachers do differ stably in the amount of various knowledge which their pupils gain from their instruction . . . but ordinarily these stable differences are not sufficiently large to be of practical value for salary differentials. Teachers usually are so closely grouped with regard to the gains which their pupils make that the low standing teachers would evidence considerable dissatisfaction if they received lesser salaries than did the high standing teachers for this reason.[*]

In general, although teachers' remuneration has risen steadily over the last fifteen years, about doubled, to an average of $8,840 a year, they do not receive salaries as high as holders of baccalaureate degrees in other fields, such as engineering or accounting. This is understandable in the light of the scanty professional education teachers receive and the relative ease of entry into what is politely called the profession.

In 1957 the Bureau of the Census reported that about 32 per cent of the male and nearly 4 per cent of the female professional, technical, and kindred workers received an income of $7,000 or over, but in 1959–60, the National Education Association indicated that only 10.8 per cent of classroom teachers received salaries in excess of $6,500. Even taking into account the

[*] David V. Tiedeman, ed., *Teacher Competence and Its Relation to Salary* (Cambridge, Mass.: New England School Development Council, 1956), p. 58.

relatively large proportion of female teachers, it is difficult to think of teachers as unusually affluent either in absolute or relative terms. At any rate, while quality education is no doubt related to quality of teaching, teachers' salaries are a very dubious index of teacher quality.

School facilities, furniture, equipment, textbooks, supplies, and the like constitute another cluster of expenditures by which quality is judged. Although they are not the most important ingredient in the mix, it is amazing what clean, spacious rooms, decent furniture, decorated walls, good landscaping, and adequate play areas can do for the morale of teacher, pupils, and parents. No less important is what lack of them can do to that morale. Costs for these items have mounted. New buildings demand large capital outlays, which, in turn, necessitate special levies or bond issues. With the enrollment in the lower schools stabilizing, new building construction may decelerate, and we may be able to do more to bring older buildings up to par, but it is doubtful that reluctant taxpayers will be persuaded to finance building outlays of any kind without the prod of heavy enrollment pressure.

The third factor, innovative programs, like the first, suffers from the criterion infirmity. The rapidity with which innovations are introduced and dropped, only to be picked up a decade or two later, inspires little confidence in mere up-to-dateness.

For these reasons, public schools look to the federal government and philanthropic foundations to put up funds for special programs and services. Thus, in addition to such special grants as those for vocational and agricultural education, the U.S. Office of Education in recent years has helped with programs for educationally deprived children, library resources, supplementary education centers, education for the handicapped, bilingual education, and dropout prevention in elementary and secondary schools.

Some communities have been the beneficiaries of grants from private foundations to undertake educational experiments, usually noticed in the press as an "imaginative breakthrough." Relatively few of these ventures survived the life of the sustaining grant. There are a good many reasons for this failure, including the fact that innovations, when adopted on a large scale, entail huge expenditures and massive dislocations in the existing facilities. More fundamental, however, is the lack of any body of accepted theory or expertise in terms of which one can tell in advance something about the viability of a project or experiment. This also may help to explain why the not inconsiderable outlays for research and development by the U.S. Office of Education (over $96 million in 1971) have borne so little demonstrable fruit. The most demonstrable and valuable of these gains is the training of a large number of competent educational researchers, but in the absence of a cadre of educationists who share common credentials and a criterion of quality, researchers do whatever interests them or whatever project can be funded. All of these considerations, of course, cast some doubt on the equivalence of school quality and school expenditures, at least so far as elementary and secondary education are concerned.

In a way, it is misleading to mix up the meaning of "good" schools and "good" colleges and universities, because it is far easier to agree on the kind of quality that costs a lot of money in higher education than in elementary and secondary schools. At the university level, laboratories, equipment, highly specialized professors working at the forefront of a field, extensive library resources, are very expensive. Even so, to legislators and laymen, these "quality" items are far less essential than to the members of the academic guild who do research and graduate teaching. It is of little use to defend heavy appropriations for such items on the ground that they will attract superprofessors, who in turn will attract supergraduate students, who in time will become superprofessors. As one legislator, seeing the budget request for the library, remarked, "Hell, they've got more books now than anybody will ever read."

Having vented all of these doubts about equating quality and expenditure, there is a point beyond which one cannot deny that the quality of schools and their costs march together, and at that point, equality of educational opportunity must be discussed in terms of money. A few observations on what equality of opportunity, if taken seriously and strictly, might mean for school support are in order.

If by equality of opportunity one means an equal chance to land in the social or vocational slot for which one's merit qualifies him, then only a special kind of society can provide such equality. Such a society would have at least as many slots as there are people who want to qualify for them. If there are more who can qualify for any position than can be employed, then some qualified persons will be treated unequally. Thus, if 1,000 American citizens could qualify for a seat in the U.S. Senate, choosing only 100 would leave 90 per cent of the aspirants disappointed and feeling, quite correctly, that the opportunities for senatorial standing were not equal. This is almost always the case in our society, so we tend to fill the vacancies with people who are both qualified and available, but without weighing them against all other qualified persons. This creates another sort of inequality of opportunity: that of visibility. Suppose, for example, there are openings in a firm for ten executive positions. Unless the firm undertakes a world-wide search for all possible candidates and weighs their qualifications on a very fine scale, visibility and familiarity may decide among those who are equally competent. Thus a man or woman known to the hiring officer will be chosen over those he does not know but whose qualifications may be quite adequate.

It is this kind of advantage the socially disadvantaged lack. Even when equally qualified and when the hiring agent is determined not to employ unqualified personnel, considerations other than the qualifications for the post come into play. Social position, friends, family, college acquaintances, racial prejudice—all de-equalize opportunity. Admission to college, winning of fellowships, initial appointments, promotions—all involve more than qualifications. The person who is disadvantaged may properly complain that merely providing opportunities for schooling that, objectively considered, are equal does not in fact equalize the power to exploit opportunity; that special consideration should be given to the special inequalities from which he suffers.

Providing for equal educational opportunity may mean something more than spending the same amount of money per pupil, but chances are good that it means at least doing that. Thus, spending the same amount of money for schools in black and white neighborhoods may not of itself equalize educational opportunity. Therefore, bussing children to provide the integration component may, under certain circumstances, be justified. On the other hand, when expenditures are not equal for schools in black and white neighborhoods, it makes little sense to bus children from the more expensive schools into the less affluent ones.

Perhaps one more note on quality and equality may not be amiss. Quality education in the mind of the public is identified with the kind of schools children of the elite attend. If this smacks too much of snobbery, then let us say that good education is defined by the schools to which successful parents send their children—in our time, the parents and children of the upper middle class. The educational expenditures of this class go beyond the money spent for schools; an intellectually stimulating environment, books, travel, and instructive leisure-time activities are also included. In these circumstances, the school budget can be used to sustain and exploit the rich environment that well-to-do homes can supply. If less-advantaged children are to have equal educational opportunity, an equivalent school budget is not enough; enough must be spent to provide an equivalence of environment as well. Or, if equivalence of environment is too rigorous a requirement, then it may not be unreasonable to insist on home and communal environments that do not negate the effects of the school expenditures.

In the famous *Brown* case in 1954, the Supreme Court held that segregated schools could not be equal even if expenditures were equal, and in the *Serrano* v. *Priest* case in 1971, the California Supreme Court ruled that schooling opportunity could not be equal if financial resources were unequal. Taken together, the two decisions leave us with the conclusion that equality of expenditure is a necessary, although not sufficient, condition for equality of educational opportunity.

The California decision seemed to say that, insofar as quality of schooling depends on monetary availability, differences in schools should not be permitted to be a function of the number of tax dollars a school district can raise for their support. The court held that the plaintiffs had grounds for claiming that they were discriminated against, because the community was poor and had a low tax revenue. Children attending school in a district that had a slim tax base should not receive schooling inferior to that of children living in a district that is affluent in this respect.

The California case reopens a bag of difficulties that has been with us for a very long time, for it is no news that school districts finance their schools largely (about 50 per cent, it has been estimated) from the local property tax. Furthermore, it is common knowledge that states, and districts within states, vary greatly in the amount of property available for taxation and the rate at which it is taxed. It has been estimated that in 1929–30 differences among the states in personal income accounted for 62 per cent of the variation in expenditures per pupil, and in 1959–60 it accounted for 70 per cent of this variation.*

Further, it is well known that ability to pay for schooling and willingness to levy taxes for this purpose do not go together. Thus, one wealthy community in California in 1969 had a tax rate of $2.38 and spent $1,232 per pupil, whereas in a neighboring district the tax rate for that year was $5.48, but the community had only $578 to spend per pupil. Again and again it has been shown that regions with relatively low resources make stronger efforts to support their schools than do some of their more prosperous counterparts.

There are, however, some other wrinkles that mar the use of the local property tax for schools. One is the pressure to keep the tax rate down in order to attract industry. This reduces the amount of money available for social services—at least until the move succeeds in luring large amounts of taxable property. School boards are reluctant to raise the tax rate in large amounts, and since quality is so hard to define and demonstrate, they tend to increase expenditures on the basis of increased enrollment only. Due to slow reassessment, yield of taxes on real property lags behind price increases, especially during inflation.

Charles Benson points out that in agrarian societies a levy on land had a fairly close relation to the ability to pay taxes, but when most of the citizenry are employees, no such relation between land and income exists. Moreover, inasmuch as personal property is relatively easy to conceal, it is increasingly being excluded from the tax base, so that the portion of the property tax levied on households has come to represent a tax on the consumption of housing and is therefore regressive. To skew matters further, a farmer or landlord can shift the tax on real property to the consumer or renter. The owner of a private dwelling or the renter of an apartment cannot.

* Benson, p. 62.

Add to this the fact that the state and federal governments are constantly withdrawing real estate from the local tax rolls for parks, buildings, highways, and the like, and the complaints of the taxpayer, especially the householder, are not hard to understand. For householders who are pensioners with fixed incomes that do not keep pace with inflation, every increase in taxes is a step nearer to real poverty, which, we are told, was the lot of over 20 per cent of our senior citizens in 1971—and yet these very senior citizens will have to be provided with more and more social services as time goes on.

Inflation also means marketing more expensive school bonds, while at the same time shrinking the purchasing power of borrowed funds. Inflation cuts down the value of fixed grants-in-aid, so that, all in all, poorer districts are lucky if they can meet their current needs, let alone engage in research or provide special services.*

Finally, the assessment of taxes on the basis of market value of the property alone disturbs the balance between costs and benefits. A house assessed at $100,000 does not require services from the local government five times those of one assessed at $20,000.

There are, I am sure, other and more subtle economic issues involved in depending on property taxes for so much of the support of the schools, but so far as equality of opportunity is concerned, it is clear that the practice in and of itself is a major obstacle to achieving even a semblance of such equality.

The local community resources for the support of schools depend on factors over which it often has little if any control. Level of employment, wage rates, the size of its industrial tax base, for example, may reflect national or market conditions. Once a community suffers an economic decline, things go from bad to worse. At the same time, it has to raise the tax rate to provide an ever-decreasing amount and quality of social services. This, in turn, drives out of the community those who are best able to pay taxes, so that "some communities have been practically reduced to taxing the unemployed for their own relief." †

* *Ibid.*, p. 511.

† Mabel Newcomer, *Central and Local Finance in Germany and England* (New York: Columbia University Press, 1937), p. 203. *Cf.* Benson, pp. 174–75.

So much for the evils of relying on the local tax resources for schooling. What are its advantages? Mainly, they encourage fiscal responsibility and local control. It is argued that if the state or federal government gives money, it will exercise control over the expenditures; if it does not monitor expenditures, the money will be squandered.

Of course, in practice there is rarely full control by the state for every dime that it might allot to a community, but neither is there complete laxity. Nor is there any assurance that local funds will be spent more wisely and carefully than federal or state grants. So long as there is a mixture of funds, taxpayers may be expected to play the watchdogs over expenditures, or, as Benson puts it:

All that is required is for a sufficient percentage of funds to be local so that the taxpayer (1) feels the financial burden of his demanding more—or more expensive—services and (2) feels the financial relief of some improvement in local efficiency. There is no magic percentage of state aid at which such sensitivity becomes dead.*

There remains to consider the alleged virtues of local control over the schools, which might be impaired if the state or the federal government paid too large a share of the costs. It is argued that each locality has peculiar educational needs, and who better than the local citizens know how to meet such needs? It might be countered that there is a minimum of schooling that the state or the nation requires for the public good, regardless of the idiosyncrasies of the individual district. Most state constitutions specify schooling as a state responsibility.

Knowing what is best for its children depends on the community, and precisely the poorest communities are least likely to know what is best for their children, even though they ardently desire the best for them.

It is sometimes urged that as centralization increased, bureaucrats in Washington or Albany or Boston could achieve thought control over the schools, and a deadly uniformity would descend over them. There is reason for entertaining these fears, but here again freedom and diversity are not in themselves unqualified goods in this matter. Their value depends on the peo-

* Benson, p. 231.

ple who will exercise freedom and utilize diversity. A bigoted community can use local control for one purpose; a liberal community for another. The optimum use of local control comes when it is exercised within the parameters of norms that are independent of the voters' wishes. For example, the local community can make a better curriculum choice appropriate for its own situation if it acknowledges the norms that define good physics, good literature, good mathematics, and good history—norms that are not legislated at the polls.

No group, if like-minded about what is good, true, and important, wishes to dilute the mix, and so it wants control of its own school and its own school budget. But the argument takes different forms depending on whether the group is rich or poor. The rich group wants autonomy and control of its own budget, because it can give more to its own children if it doesn't have to share the wealth with poorer neighbors. The poor group, however, does not want autonomy unless it can get resources to augment its own; it does not want to be deprived of benefits for which it cannot pay out of its own resources, but it also wants the autonomy that the richer communities enjoy. Now, who is to judge whether poor groups can use their autonomy as wisely as rich groups?

One other argument for local control is often advanced, namely, that decentralization allows greater freedom in experimentation and therefore greater progress.* Probably this is so. Richer districts will experiment more freely than poorer ones, not only because it costs money to experiment, but also because wealthier communities are made up of more highly educated citizens, who are in a better position to think about such things and to become dissatisfied with what is—or is not—being done about them.

Nonetheless, as much educational reform has been triggered

---

* In this connection, the experience of New York City with splitting up its school system into thirty-one or so districts, each with its own board, is not encouraging. According to Albert Shanker, President of the United Federation of Teachers, the districts have "refrained from adopting educational innovative programs" (New York *Times,* November 28, 1971). Furthermore, Shanker asserts that the voter turnout for school board elections was a mere 15 per cent.

by the need to provide common education for the masses as by the desire to improve elite education for the classes. Conversely, the sort of innovations that exclusive schools do try may or may not get down to the poorer districts, especially if they are expensive and if the districts are stuck with local control and limited to local support. Group instruction, grading and grouping devices, motivational schemes, are the result of having to teach large numbers at low cost. Meeting individual differences, providing a rich variety of experience, and using first-rate materials traditionally have been the province of elite education. The attempts to provide these benefits for all children by simply asserting that public schools ought to do so is as mischievous as it is silly, unless the resources and conditions of elite education can be approximated for all children. Perhaps they can be, and I suspect that by the wise use of educational technology they might. But technology calls for large initial capital investment, and without help the poorer districts cannot make that investment

And so we come to the necessity of funneling funds to local districts from state and federal sources as well as making taxes other than property levies available to the local agencies.

Grants-in-aid have a long history in this country, and formulas by the dozen have been devised to meet the demand for equal benefits, equal opportunity, and equal sacrifices.

As early as 1901 Ellwood P. Cubberley was seeking a formula for equalizing inequalities induced by local taxation differentials. Another design was promulgated widely by George D. Strayer and Robert M. Haig. Later still, Paul Mort, Harlan Updegraff, William P. McLure, Francis G. Cornell, and many others grappled with formulas for equalization. But it is difficult to come up with a formula that will insure both equality of opportunity and equality of effort and sacrifice.

In most plans of this sort, the rich districts get more benefits than the poor ones, for to the rich all grants-in-aid are the topping on a rich pie, whereas to the poor all such grants merely bring them up to the subsistence level of bread and minimum butter.

By 1960 payments from the state represented about 40 per cent of the total revenue for public elementary and secondary schools, with another 4 per cent coming from the federal government. But states, like municipalities, are complaining that they are reaching their limits of capacity to pay for local services. In Illinois, for example, a state income tax was passed recently on the grounds that it would relieve the burdens of local communities by making help available for schools, relief, roads, and other social services. But two years after the passage of the tax, the state was in just as much of a financial bind as it was before—the cost of the services had outrun the increased revenues, so that city after city, especially Chicago, was seeking help to meet threats of school closings several times a year.

What are the alternatives to the local-property-tax method? A Washington lawyer, John Silard, in a New York *Times* article (September 2, 1971), sees four:

Redistribution of the local property tax on an equal, statewide basis, with an option that local communities may still tax themselves for education extras.

Requirement of strict equality of expenditure, based on a "one-child, one-dollar" concept.

Focus upon equal education rather than equal dollars, under which a community would be allotted enough money to provide a certain standard of education.

Measurement of how much money should be spent by determining each child's needs, keeping in mind that it would cost more to educate a "culturally deprived" child than a middle-class one.

But consider these alternatives. So long as local communities can tax themselves for educational extras, the inequality of schools will be maintained; equality will be for a minimum standard.

If one insists on a strict numerical equality of expenditure, then differences in costs of construction, teachers' salaries, and transportation would give some districts an advantage and put others at a disadvantage.

To focus on equal education rather than on equal dollars would be fine, but again richer communities could supplement this minimum by extras that would impair the equality.

The last alternative, of course, is the ideal one: to each according to his needs; but the first half of the classic socialist formula also applies, namely, from each according to his abilities;

and the application of this cannot be foreseen in a society that tries to maintain a mixed economy with overlapping public and private sectors.

So long as we have a mixed economy, we shall probably have mixed systems of delivering education, medical care, and social security. As our society becomes more and more technologically mature, and as interdependence tightens its net over all of our activities, it will become more and more difficult to find purely private sectors of activity and support; anyone doubting this need only examine what has happened since the thirties. Certainly medical care, welfare, and schooling will go public, just as railroad transportation has and airplane traffic probably will. But, as was noted at the beginning of this chapter, there will be more patching before that day comes, and until then, equality of opportunity will have to be qualified in many ways to keep the rhetoric and the reality in some kind of match—with the courts every so often reminding us that the match is far from perfect.

What are these patchings? The improvement of assessing real property is one, but what are the chances that the numerous political considerations that enshroud our assessment procedures can be overcome? Rather small, one would think. Another route is to use local sales and income taxes, a route that some municipalities are taking, although somehow they do not seem to reduce the gap between proliferating needs and resources very impressively. More state aid is an answer, but the state governments are screaming about as loudly as the mayors· of the large cities that the federal government must bail them out in the very near future, because, among much else, the federal government has pre-empted so much of the tax potentialities. So where does the patching end? In Washington. QED.

Out of 51.3 million pupils enrolled at all elementary and secondary school levels in the fall of 1969, 5.7 million, or about 11 per cent, were in nonpublic schools. The percentage in nonpublic institutions of higher learning is, of course, far higher, nearly 26 per cent. So we have a large number of households in which expenditures for schooling has to be added to what is being paid by that household for schools in the way of taxes. As was shown in Table 1, this amount in 1969–70 was about $13.2 billion, of which $8.6 billion went for higher education. These households in many instances resent this "double cost" and perennially argue that state aid be given to private schools; in other words they would like to retain the privilege of selecting the schools to which they send their children—a form of voluntary self-segregation—but they would like to do so partially or wholly at public expense. This is not a new idea.

In the first half of the nineteenth century, public schools often charged tuition, whereas some private schools received public funds. The great common school movement powered by James Carter, Horace Mann, and Henry Barnard not only made the case for the public benefits of schooling but also argued that to achieve these benefits the schools should be supported by public funds and operated by public authorities. It was difficult to regulate private schools, and the poor, they thought, were not really competent to choose schools, a position that most of the medical profession holds with regard to the consumer's wisdom in choosing drugs and physicians.

Today the need for both regulation and operation of schools by the state has been called into question. Support yes, regulation maybe, but not operation. The attempt to introduce a variation of the *laissez faire* doctrine into schooling has led to the revival of Milton Friedman's notion of a voucher system,* which promised to yield the blessings of local control and public benefits, not to speak of driving inefficient schools out of business.

We are experiencing strong pressures for state aid to private schools and colleges, and, while at the elementary and secondary levels the issue is largely constitutional, it is not so in higher education. Religiously founded colleges have received the benefits of scholarships and governmental research contracts. More direct governmental aid to private colleges is being demanded.

In the seventies the constitutional question may recede behind the fiscal and moral ones as far as the elementary and secondary schools are concerned. The patrons of private schools say that if their schools are forced to close for lack of funds, the burden would have to be shifted to the public schools—and this might be the straw that would break the taxpayer's back.

---

* "The Role of Government in Education," in Robert A. Solo, ed., *Economics and the Public Interest* (New Brunswick, N.J.: Rutgers University Press, 1955).

The moral argument is that private schools offer alternatives and challenges to a "monolithic" public school system. Voucher schemes use this argument extensively and intensively, although some of these schemes envision giving parents choice among public schools as well. Presumably, if this argument is cogent, many parents are dissatisfied with some or all of the public schools. Whether or not the closing of large numbers of private schools will break the taxpayer's back, I do not profess to know —there are those who doubt the inevitability of either the closings or their dire consequences. But even if these consequences were to ensue, they do not cancel the constitutional question in the case of religious schools. This does not mean, however, that the constitutional question will not be evaded if the money question becomes sufficiently crucial. The contention that aid should be given to private schools because the taxpayers are disenchanted with the public schools should also be taken with a grain of salt.

The financial plight of the schools, one must reiterate, is more the result of the taxpayer's dislike to pay taxes rather than of his dissatisfaction with the schools. The rapid increase in school building after World War II, the need to provide schools for new housing developments, teachers' strikes, and collective bargaining contracts made school costs highly visible. The opportunity to vote down school bond issues was too good and opportunity to miss for many taxpayers. Here at last was a foe that the taxpayer could transfix with the stroke of a pencil; here was one wad of money that would not be spent. He would probably do the same to many other public spending proposals given the same opportunity.

Those who were disenchanted with the public schools, and had a right to be, were the inhabitants of the inner city and of Appalachia, but they rarely led the fight against bond issues—the bond issues, in any event, were rarely for their benefit anyhow. But the writers who rushed into print and royalties with harrowing tales that public schools incarcerated poor children against their wills and systematically lowered their IQs seized upon the tax revolts as an opportunity to launch a general attack on the public schools. Among the ploys of the attack was a call to return the schools to free enterprise. Later came more sophisticated versions of the voucher plans. By now it is difficult to tell which of the motivations are financial, which moral, and which merely Machiavellian.

The main issues involved in the controversy as to whether or how far the private sector should be allowed to take over schooling, especially at the elementary and secondary levels, seem to be of two sorts:

First is the argument against taxation without benefit. Nonparents argue that they do not benefit from the taxes they are forced to pay for the support of the public schools. It is estimated that 5.6 million children attend private schools, about 11 per cent of the total elementary and secondary school population. Almost 90 per cent of these are in Catholic schools. Parents who send their children to private schools say they are the victims of double costs: taxes and tuition.

Second is the argument from the *laissez faire* economic ideology to the effect that free-market competition among schools will improve their quality and lower their costs. The fittest will survive or those that survive will be the fittest. This argument covers two subordinate theses: one, that such a system will give the consumer freedom of choice—and that is good; and another, that the competition will encourage experimentation and innovation as a way of winning the competition—and that is even better.

About the only defense one can make for school taxation without proportionate benefit is that everyone benefits indirectly, namely, that schools yield a social as well as an individual benefit, much as public roads and police forces do. Furthermore, it might be argued that a social service has to go public when there is a reasonable doubt that individuals will not voluntarily pay for the collective benefit or even for their own individual benefit. That is why the schools went public in our own country. It was to prevent a large proportion of the population, mainly the poor, from neglecting the schooling of their children. There is little reason to believe that the situation has changed sufficiently to return schooling to private discretion. If schooling is a public benefit, the plea of nonequal benefit to the taxpayers loses its force.

Parents with children in private schools could argue that they were not injuring the benefit of education to the state, and that therefore they should be excused from the payment of school taxes or be given tuition grants to compensate for them. Supposing that attendance at a private school does serve the public good adequately, it still may be the case that if private enterprise in schooling is encouraged, public schools will be destroyed, and that may or may not preserve the public benefit for which they were established. That such encouragement is a threat to public schools is admitted by voucher advocate Christopher Jencks:

Either tuition grants or management contracts to private organizations would, of course, destroy the public schools system as we know it. . . . And if, as some fear, the public schools would not survive in open competition with private ones, then perhaps they *should* not survive.[*]

If it is so clear that the agency established to protect the public benefit will be destroyed by opening schooling to free competition, then the private benefits that such competition might provide for certain individuals would not override the danger to the public good, and to excuse such individuals from school taxes would not be warranted. This is especially relevant when it is far from certain that schools that survive in the competition will necessarily be the best schools, or that one could expect the rule of the free market to operate in this field any better than it operates in other sectors of the economy.

As for freedom of choice, it already exists for those who can afford it, so presumably the force of this argument depends on the right of those who cannot afford private schooling to avail themselves of it. This has led to great elaboration and subtilization of the simple voucher system envisioned by Milton Friedman so as to make all "good" schools equally accessible to all who wish to attend them. However, if it takes a great bureaucracy to manage the public schools, what sort of bureaucracy will be needed if the qualifications and modifications of the various voucher plans are to be implemented? Furthermore, once all the regulatory measures are provided for, there will be about as much of the free-market competition left in the system as there

---

[*] "Is the Public School Obsolete?" *Public Interest,* Winter, 1965, p. 27.

is now among the public utilities. In other words, to provide for freedom of choice, free competition, and equal opportunity is quite a trick.

However, I am not at this point interested so much in the legal and moral implications of turning the schools over to the private sector with or without regulation. The important point is whether or not such a move would provide more money for the support of the schools. It would do so if private management were less expensive than public, or if fewer people attended schools or attended them for shorter periods of time. But private schools, once they lose the benefit of using church personnel as teachers, find that their costs soar as do those of the public schools. Private schools might, of course, if unregulated, get away with using noncertificated teachers, but this would arouse the wrath of the teachers' unions as soon as private school enrollments became large enough to challenge public school enrollments. With regulation some kind of certification would be reinstated, and the pressure for increased salaries would operate as it is now doing. As for quality, one can easily get the mistaken impression that private schools are better than public ones if one compares the few private schools that have good reputations with what the media and the romantics are saying about the public schools. As a matter of fact, some of our poorest schools and colleges are private, and some of the most flagrant abuses of customers are perpetrated by some proprietary schools. The latter-day apostles of *laissez faire* claim what even the fathers of the doctrine never quite dared to hope for, namely, that private enterprise guaranteed moral virtue; all they claimed was that the strong, the ruthless, and the able would probably outlast the weak, the sentimental, and the less enterprising of the competitors. That the strong and swift, having once taken the lead in the race, would not hesitate to make rules so that those trailing could never catch up troubled the conscience of our Founding Fathers, and so they did not rely wholly on Adam Smith's *Wealth of Nations* to serve as the Constitution of the United States. This may explain why they promptly appended a Bill of Rights to it.

If school attendance remains compulsory, it is difficult to see how private management of schools would either augment the resources available for education or diminish the costs of it. If freedom of choice is encouraged, the decentralization process will accelerate the fragmentation of the "system" into smaller and smaller units, and this does not augur well for economy. If competition drives the total cost of schooling down, then less, rather than more, will be spent for it. If nonusers are not taxed, the total sum available for schools will thereby be diminished. One "answer" might be to develop reasonable alternative patterns within the public school system.

This leaves us with several noneconomic benefits that are promised if the "monolithic" public school system is challenged by private schools—especially if these private schools had access to public money. One is diversity, and another is experimentation.

Historically, private schools have not been noted for either their diversity or innovation. Catholic schools certainly did not claim these virtues and until very recently did not regard them as virtues. The prestigious, independent Grottlesex secondary schools have not enjoyed the reputation of being either politically or educationally radical. A prudent forecast would indicate that if all our schools went private tomorrow, the distribution of conservative and radical practices would remain just about what it is now.

Just as the vaunted daring and nonconformity of the private schools as a class is mythical, so is the doctrine that the public schools form a monolithic system. In the fall of 1969 there were more than 18,000 operating school districts in this country, and much of the brouhaha about the public schools is caused by the extraordinary range of diversity in resources, attitudes, curricula, organization, and practices. We do not have national textbooks, and in many states there are no prescribed state texts. There is no national curriculum, no national system of teacher certification—indeed, as I have pointed out repeatedly, there is not even the semblance of consensus on what quality in schooling or teaching should mean.

So while equalizing opportunity does mean differentiating schooling to meet a diversity of needs within the school population, at the same time it can and does mean some equalizing of resources and the diminution of many types of diversity that now exist.

I do not know what measures we shall use or invent to meet the financial crisis of our social services, but one would hope that turning the schools over to the mercies of what LaNoue has called the voucher constituency will not take place. The nature of this constituency supplies the reasons:

> There is a latent coalition prepared to support vouchers, and it won't be led by the gentlemen scholars from Cambridge and Berkeley. The coalition is the one Kevin Phillips proposed in *The Emerging Republican Majority* (Garden City, N.Y.: Doubleday, 1970). It is composed mainly of Southern Protestant nativists and Northern Catholic ethnics —plus, I would add, a touch of the far right and the far left. Aid to private schools was one of the ways Phillips suggested that coalitions might be brought together. The danger is, then, that while the intellectual debate focuses on ideal vouchers, the true voucher coalition will rise up to take command of the idea.*

If we recognize the inequities of the present method of financing public schools through heavy reliance on the property tax, and if we refuse to forget the regressive nature of many sales and excise taxes, about the only alternative left is the income tax—local and state, as well as federal. Some form of sharing in that greatest of tax resources will have to be devised for schools as well as for welfare, transportation, and environmental repair.

In the meantime, schools would be well advised to examine their willingness to accept accountability for noninstructional services, which either are incidental to instruction or are most conveniently dispensed at the place of instruction. From 1910 to 1958 sums spent for auxiliary services in transportation, food, and various health programs rose from $5 million to $1.5 billion.†

In 1967–68 the total expenditure of public funds for transportation of pupils (excluding capital expenditures) was $981,006,-000, at an average cost of $57.27 per pupil. For that year the total of expenditures for "other services" in the public elementary and secondary schools came to almost $2 billion.‡

* George R. LaNoue, "The Politics of Education," *Teachers College Record,* December, 1971, p. 318.

† Werner Z. Hirsch, *Analysis of Rising Costs of Public Education,* Paper no. 4 (Washington, D.C.: Government Printing Office, 1959).

‡ U.S. Department of Health, Education, and Welfare, ed., *Digest of Educational Statistics of 1970,* p. 55.

These are important social services, but they represent charges against the school budget, and, more to the educational point, they are charges against the time school personnel have to devote to pupils. If citizens want these services, then they should be charged to the social agencies responsible for health, housing, transportation, welfare. It does make a difference out of which budget these monies come, because these expenditures are lumped with those for instruction when the school levy is up for a public vote.

The same advice might also be given to institutions of higher learning. They would be perceived by legislators and donors as lighter burdens if they divested themselves of the multitude of noninstructional services to which they have mortgaged themselves. Housing is one; providing public athletic spectacles is another; feeding students and staff is still another. Students do not appreciate these parietal ministrations in their behalf and, left to their own devices, could probably secure them as cheaply as the university can provide them.

The nonacademic staff required to provide and monitor these services is huge and powerful, and in no small part these services create the need for universities to maintain security forces of their own in addition to the police forces of the community. Once parents are convinced that their eighteen-year-old children will do just about what they please in the way of personal virtue and vice—regardless of adult supervision—higher education can rid itself not only of the budget burden but also of the *in loco parentis* role that this budget reflects.

Functions that are only incidental to instruction have a way of achieving the same importance as the instructional ones. Once a specialized group of workers depends for a living on carrying on these functions, their claims to a livelihood and economic security cannot be given lower priority than that accorded to other employees. But there is the added factor that as student bodies become larger, even instructional functions are split up into subspecialties and handed over to specialists, with their special titles, staffs, and offices. Counseling, admissions, discipline, planning, and what not become semiautonomous units, among which lines of communication have to be instituted and maintained. Of course, in no time at all, the director of communications becomes a necessity, and he needs an office, staff, and budget of his own. The attempt in the name of efficiency to increase specialization can only go so far before it takes more time and effort and money to be efficient than to do the job. And there is a similar limitation on the extent to which education can match the diversity of its offerings and services with the diversity of needs of individual students.

Thus it has come to pass that the hundreds of courses listed in the university catalogue have not made it more certain that the individual student will tailor his studies to his individualized needs. There is now the problem of deciding among the plenitude of alternatives, and so cadres of counselors—academic, career, and psychological—have to be hired to guide the student— or to tell him to go and guide himself. Students complain that the complicated procedures for finding the right advising agency and the right person within the agency takes more time than the counseling session does. As a result most of our students consult roommates, friends, and classmates and make their choices on criteria that are almost never mentioned when the budget for counseling services is drawn up. This says nothing against the value of counseling, but it says much about the assumption that institutions must be as complicated in structure as are the lives of their clients.

There is another way of meeting individual needs in education, and the financial stringencies now upon us may favor our considering it. Schooling has always depended for its fundamental justification on the theory that what is learned in school will be generalized to function in a wide array of life circumstances. If this theory is denied, then the wisdom or efficiency of studying *for* living rather than learning *from* living becomes dubious. For highly specific skills and knowledge, on-the-job training is probably more efficient than more general study. It may just be that schools have gone so far in the direction of specificity that the value of schooling is no longer as credible as we would like. If the schools are to be entitled to their share of public funds, they may have to rely more on the ability of individuals to adapt a highly generalized curriculum to their own needs, and may have to expend less effort trying to dispense with the need for the individual to do so.

CHAPTER VI

Accountability — Why Not?

Nothing is so tempting, so frustrating, and so characteristically human as the search for villains and heroes.

The tempter is our incurably moral nature. Harness an undesirable state of affairs to the thought that it could have been otherwise, and we are off on the search for someone who, at the critical moment, made the wrong choice. If *only* Eve had not eaten of the apple and offered it to Adam; if *only* Caesar had not crossed the Rubicon; if *only* President Johnson had not accelerated the Vietnam war; if *only* Lieutenant Calley had refrained from indiscriminate shooting at My Lai . . .

Blame it on our ancestral anthropomorphism or on human nature: our model for apportioning praise and blame is still an individual confronting a situation that offered him several alternatives, the consequences of which he could foresee, understand, and control—and among which he could choose freely. Only in situations such as these is it proper to raise the moral question: Did he do the right thing? Did he do his duty? Was he obliged to do what he did?

Consider the following judgments. The telephone company should have prevented a breakdown in communications. The electric utilities are responsible for pollution of air and water. The post office services are disgraceful. The Democratic party is to be blamed for inflation. The Republican party is responsible for the recession. The schools have failed. These are, we might say, corporate villains.

The services rendered by these collective enterprises did not come up to the expectations of those who passed moral judgments on them, and surely had somebody made a different decision, things might have turned out better. But try identifying those decisions and tracing them to their source, and you experience the twentieth-century syndrome, the frustrating search for a moral agent who did what he should not have done or omitted to do what he should have done. Every event has its causes, and these causes are events that, in turn, have their causes, so the more thorough the search for the villain, the surer one is to end up with putting the blame on Eve, for had she not eaten the apple, et cetera ad infinitum. As Kant put it, in one of his antinomies of reason, the notions of an infinity of causes and a First Cause are equally rational and refutable.

The reflex response to frustration by a social institution is to condemn and punish it as one would an individual guilty of a fault. We're not going to let "them" get away with it; we'll hold them accountable, make them reveal what they have done and see whether or not it is what they were supposed to do. The schools have failed; let's make them accountable. Let them prove that they have produced the results for which they took our tax money. If they have failed, let us give them no more money or not so much as they asked for; or let us direct—if we can—that it be given to other schools that promise to do better. Perhaps we can even send somebody to jail.

Who can quarrel with accountability? It seems part of the cosmic balance that right should be rewarded and wrong punished. An individual or an institution "getting away with it" violates our sense of justice and fairness. Not to be outraged may be a mark of moral insensitivity.

Nevertheless, holding an institution, a government, a nation, accountable is not the same as holding an individual responsible. The conditions for a moral choice cannot be satisfied by a collection of people, because, strictly speaking, there is no collective mind, conscience, or will.* Each individual in the collective can

* Those who speak of the mind of God or the will of God do not, I take it, equate it with the sum of the minds or wills of any group of people.

be held morally responsible for his decisions and acts, if the conditions for moral choice are fulfilled. However, since these conditions imply forethought, fidelity to some principle of the right and the good, knowledge of possibilities and consequences, it is only metaphorically true that the collective can be held morally responsible for its actions.

Each individual German in World War II, given the conditions of the moral situation, was ineluctably responsible for the "final solution" of the "Jewish problem," for, if he was willing to take the consequences, he could have protested and resisted the brutal edicts of his government. More compellingly, so was each member of the "government," given the conditions of the moral situation and the superior quality of its information. But what can you do to individuals who, admitting their moral responsibility, nevertheless had so little power individually that it is difficult to find punishments that are proportional to their share of the total evil?

Punishment for the acts of a government or institution must be inflicted either individually, on those who were both morally in the wrong and had sufficient power to execute or refrain from executing the decision, or collectively, by imposing reparations, fines, and opprobrium on the total population. Membership in the collective makes it just for everyone, regardless of his own role, to suffer some of the consequences of the collective decision and to reap some of its benefits; without such an arrangement, societies would be impossible.

So, although the distinction is not so sharp as one would like, we may speak of holding an institution accountable and yet not *morally* responsible. It is accountable insofar as it causes events (morally or otherwise). For an institution to deny that it causes events is to plead complete impotence, thereby justifying its immediate abolition. If an institution does cause events, then it makes sense for individuals or groups to judge their effects and to take steps to prevent an institution from causing a particular event or to persuade it or even force it to bring about this event rather than another. One can, therefore, hold an institution accountable without the imputation of vice or virtue that is appropriate only to moral agents. For example, it is a truism that schools as institutions are to be held accountable for conforming to the laws laid down for their governance. This may be an important kind of accountability for the school board, but not for the individual teacher, because little of his conduct is governed by law. Similarly, fiscal accountability, both in expenditures and in honest bookkeeping, is expected of school authorities, but it is not central to the accountability of teachers.

Although legal and fiscal accountability need involve no moral issues, their real import is to serve as indices of moral accountability. The school board and its hired personnel are thought to be obligated to parents, pupils, and the electorate. This obligation is thought to include furnishing evidence that the obligations have or have not been met. Failure to meet these obligations or an unwillingness to give an account of them are therefore regarded as moral lapses.

We shall not change our speech habits readily; nevertheless, in discussing the accountability of schools, it helps to remind ourselves from time to time that we are talking about (a) what the school as an *institution* can reasonably be expected to do, and (b) what power it has to do it, rather than talking about good guys and bad guys. This is an important difference.

With these distinctions in mind, let us examine some of the talk about school accountability. One can imagine a legislator or a citizen saying, "I can't find out why the school didn't produce equality in reading achievement among all the pupils. They didn't deliver the goods, so let someone else try." Entering into a performance contract with some education industry presumably would provide for accountability. This indeed is what Gary, Indiana; Portland, Oregon; Texarkana, Texas; Jacksonville, Florida, and scores of other communities have done.

Communities may be wise or foolish to enter into such contracts, but what accountability means when they do is quite clear—in any event, legal counsel for both parties should make sure that it is. However, when accountability is defined as a contract to produce a specified result, the contractor may or may not be held accountable for the method he uses. For example, in Texarkana, allegations were made that the contractor had been teaching for the test. Was that cricket? He may use odd methods of motivating the children and the teachers. The contractor might well retort, "You wanted these results; we promised to get them; you got them; what's the beef?"

There is something admirably tough-minded and sporting about this no-excuses approach. But suppose the results contracted for are accompanied by other less desirable results. Is it sporting to victimize those who sustain the undesirable results? Should the school board shrug a collective shoulder and say, "Sorry, you win some, you lose some"? Even with clear-cut contracts bristling with sharp-edged objectives and with tests that can be used to find out whether or not the contract has been fulfilled, the moral question is not wholly irrelevant. The pupils are not parties to the contract, but they are the objects of it, and if they cannot negotiate for themselves, somebody—the parents or the school boards or the state—is morally and legally bound to do so. So unless one writes everything educationally relevant and important into the contract, accountability may not achieve what its advocates with their tough talk think it will. For complete accountability, the school board making the contract must be held accountable for the kind of contract it makes.

It may be argued that everybody in the game—teachers and administrators, as well as school boards—is accountable for total results, good and bad. The argument does cut all ways, and precisely because it does, if taken strictly and seriously, its cutting edge is dulled. In practice, accountability is applied selectively. As a punitive measure it selects as criteria those results that the punisher values and those he would like to devalue. He who has to render the account, on the other hand, selects those results as criteria over which he has full control. Unless the judger and the judged agree on what is to be accounted for, the accountability doctrine loses much of its superficial rightness.

As an example, consider a superintendent who has been converted to the new humanism. He persuades the school board to let him move his schools in the direction of open classrooms, group-therapy sessions, and involvement of pupils and teachers in community affairs—on the side of good causes. A group of parents demands that he be held accountable for their children taking drugs, indulging in premarital sex, and speaking disrespectfully about the flag and country. Given sufficient determination and money, this debate could be dragged through the courts for years without the lines of argument ever meeting.

It is worth noting, in passing, how handy performance contracting can be for school boards and school administrators.

School boards, feeling the pressure from their constituents, transmit it to the superintendent and his administrative staff. They, in turn, try to transmit it to the teachers, and presumably the teachers exert the pressure on the pupils. However, the analogy of pressure being pumped along from one station to another is inaccurate. At each stage, the pressure has to be transformed into a set of different operations. The administrator is told by the board to see to it that the children learn to read, and no nonsense. The administrator has to do more than tell the teachers to teach ghetto children to read. He has to hire teachers, find the means for instructional materials and the space for instruction, and organize the right sort of remedial programs. This the board does not have to do. The teacher, in turn, cannot, in response to the pressure from the superintendent, simply turn on the reading spigot. She may or may not know how to teach ghetto children to read, and some ghetto children may not have the environmental incentives to read, and there may or may not be the right materials and the space and the equipment. School superintendents don't teach children to read.

Or the teachers' union may decide to call the teachers out in order to teach the school superintendent and the board a lesson —that without teachers school will not keep. This generates a counterpressure, which is transmitted to the board and to the parents. Again the demand is that something be done, which can be done only by personnel at each level in the bureaucracy doing their "own thing."

How tempting, therefore, is the offer of a Pied Piper who promises for an appropriate fee to take all the pressures upon himself. A huge weight is lifted from everybody's shoulders— with the exception of the pupils. As for the contractor he gambles; he wins big or loses big. But he never loses more than money. If he fails big, the superintendent may lose his job and the board may be turned out at the next election. In the backwash of such failure, parents and pupils always lose.

So performance contracting has attractions in addition to the desire for efficiency. It also offers a moral holiday—a freedom from responsibility. Things may not turn out right, but then they may, and even if they do not, one can, for a time at least, put the blame on somebody else and get a good night's sleep every night. By 1970, according to a survey reported in the *American School Board Journal* recently, two out of three boardmen favored performance contracting.

Should the public schools be held accountable for producing a given level of achievement in reading, writing, and arithmetic? Have they been successful? This is not the place to discuss the facts—or, better, the statistics. According to the *Digest of Educational Statistics of 1970,* issued by the U.S. Department of Health, Education, and Welfare, in 1960 only 2.4 per cent of the population (fourteen years and over) were illiterate as compared to 11.3 per cent (fifteen years and over) in 1900. This means that the schools have not failed utterly, but, of course, that is not the issue that propelled accountability into the educational literature in recent years.

The point is that (a) illiteracy is greater among socioeconomically depressed parts of the population, and (b) the measures used in the statistics do not disclose the full extent of dysfunctional literacy or functional illiteracy. But what constitutes adequate functionality? Reading the newspaper, comic books, high school textbooks, technical reports? Few of us are functionally literate in all materials. I do not wish to dismiss the issue or to obscure it, but neither is it fair or sensible to give the impression that reading is a simple skill mechanically taught, learned, and used. Indeed, if performance contracting does nothing else, it may disclose the multiplicity of social and cognitive factors involved in reading. Not the least of these factors is a culture in which the importance of reading is valued and devalued at the same time.

A more global type of accountability in schooling than a contract to teach children to read or to do computation in arithmetic is assumed by a school when it promises to prepare pupils for the next higher step on the educational ladder. Grade school undertakes to ready the pupil for high school, and good high schools prepare the graduates for entrance into good colleges, and good colleges feed the good graduate schools. If there is anything remotely systematic about the public school system, this ladder is it.

On this criterion American schools have succeeded quite well. True, there is some doubt as to whether all those who want to climb the ladder have the academic and intellectual qualifications to do so; but this means that the criterion for accountability, rather than performance of the school, may be subject to criticism.

One might urge that the schools be held accountable for preserving academic standards at a certain level, as, for example, the schools are expected to do with the eleven-plus examination in Britain. The British system holds the schools accountable for upward mobility in school for some and for flatly preventing such mobility for others—on no other basis than scholastic achievement in a prescribed curriculum designed for an intellectual elite. The same criterion has been used in the French *lycée*. In recent years elitism and the traumatic effects of the fierce competition on pupils have come under attack. The educational demands of a society on the road to industrial maturity, which will be discussed in a later chapter, are not congruent with a sharp dichotomy between mass and class schooling. In all European countries since World War II, more of the population are receiving more schooling, and just as they are recapitulating American industrial development, so are their school systems repeating some of the American experiments with comprehensive high schools, guidance programs, vocational counseling, and more flexible curricula. As might be expected, the American mistakes are also being repeated.*

In the United States, however, qualifying pupils for further schooling is as variable a criterion as functional literacy. Promotional policies within the elementary and secondary schools cover a wide range of tolerance. Some schools promote everybody; some do not, but the reasons for nonpromotion can very from poor attendance to laziness to low scores on a standardized achievement-test battery. As for college admissions and promotions, there is even greater flexibility. One can take courses for

* At one exclusive secondary school in London, the man who does the vocational counseling is called the careers master. This title is significant in two ways: first, it is no longer taken for granted that graduates of this school will go to Cambridge or Oxford—they may go into more vocationally oriented universities; second, the English are far better than the Americans at exploiting the connotative power of words: witness the difference between "vocational counselor" and "careers master." In this connection, the faith of those who say that there will always be an England is justified by road signs announcing, "Roadway liable to subsidence."

pass-fail grades or for variable units of credit or for no credit at all. The student can earn credits by taking courses, studying abroad, doing apprentice work in the "real" world and in workshops of infinite variety. In short, the traditional American unit of credit—one class hour plus two or more hours of outside preparation—is about as stable as the purchasing power of the American dollar. I am not arguing the merits or demerits of this traditional academic accounting system, but if the unit has lost its stable value, then the degrees earned by collecting these units are equally elastic, and if this is the case—as it is—then how schools shall be held accountable for preparing the young for college is something those who demand such accountability ought to explain.

We can take another step in holding schools accountable. Suppose we say that the schools should be accountable for character. Let us say that the schools should certify that its graduates will cherish certain given values and will embody them in their own behavior. Writers on education have always said something of this sort, and many would say so today. The adults in the community would like the schools to keep children away from drugs, from casual sexual intercourse, from disobedience to their parents and the police, and from delinquency in general. On the positive side, it is urged that children be taught to love their country, right or wrong, respect constituted authority, and work for a high standard of living.

Now schools do undertake to produce results of this sort. The school board rhetoric commits the public schools to this type of outcome, but only certain private or independent schools are really under "contract" or "covenant" to do so. Religious schools enter into tacit covenants of this sort; so do the socially exclusive schools, such as Groton and St. Mark's; so do some of the military-style secondary schools.

Indeed, with some ingenuity and Porter Sargent's guidebooks, one can pick a private school that will promise to do for a boy and girl just about anything the parents want done: entry into Harvard, Yale, or Princeton; learning to ride a horse; speaking with a military bearing and deference to elders; social confidence, social restraint, remedial reading. Of course, the covenanting school does not admit clients indiscriminately; it takes only those with whom it can probably succeed, and it guarantees nothing. Further, it has resources to employ staff who can reasonably be expected to accomplish what the school promises to do.* Above all, these schools reserve the right to send the boy or girl home for whatever reason whenever they choose to do so. Usually, but not always, the schools insist on a nonschool environment that is in keeping with the results to be achieved.

When public school officials allow the public to assume that public schools, too, will be accountable for character and personality, they are acting irresponsibly. Virtually none of the conditions that make it possible for the "independent" private day or boarding schools to be held accountable exists in the public school.

There is an even more fundamental difficulty in holding schools responsible for character and personality development. I refer to the neohumanistic rhetoric about the search for identity and authenticity, the self, which the public schools are accused of suppressing and distorting. Some of these humanists take an almost Sartrean view that the true self is created from moment to moment by commitments to specific courses of action. Others, like the late Abraham H. Maslow, speak of a *real* self that is there to be discovered and developed. The school, on all of these views, takes the role of a guide or helper to enable the individual to find his true self. Just what this means in the way of a curriculum is hard to make out, except that the object of study is the self, and the method is some kind of therapy, introspective or extrovertive. Maslow quotes Carl Rogers as asking:

How does it happen that the deeper we go into ourselves as particular and unique, seeking for our own individual identity, the more we find the whole human species? †

* These resources are not necessarily used for high teacher salaries. Although the variations in private schools make generalization dangerous, salaries in some of the schools are lower than in urban public high schools. This is explained partly by the fact that often there are no certification requirements to be met, but more important is the lack of bargaining power —which public school teachers have—to establish salary schedules. Most important, perhaps, are the nonmonetary rewards that association with a socially elite institution bestows; when these count, they count a lot.

† Abraham H. Maslow, "Some Educational Implications of the Humanistic Psychologies," *Harvard Educational Review*, Fall, 1968, p. 690.

To some, the answer might be fairly simple, namely, that there is a human essence, contrary to what Sartre alleges. But neither Maslow nor the other humanistic educators seems to draw from this the consequence that once the human essence is discovered we might do more than practice introspective grooming behavior in the classroom. We might study the cultural materials that try to understand the human essence. So long as training for character or development of personality is an idiosyncratic search, however, the public schools can no more be held accountable for this sort of outcome than can Billy Graham for saving souls.

It is in connection with the matching of schools to the needs of the pupils or, more correctly, to the wishes of the parents, that the voucher system achieves whatever plausibility it has. If justice means that what is good for the rich is also good for the poor (by no means a self-evident proposition), then justice demands that the poor also have a choice of life outcomes and schools to achieve them. This is the professed creed of the private enterprise system—a variety of goods, plenty of competition, and a fair chance to bid for consumer favor.

Incidentally, if parents are to have a real choice, why shouldn't no school be one of the alternatives to which they are entitled? Perhaps they would like to use their vouchers for travel, for loafing under the trees, or for subscribing to the Book-of-the-Month Club.

The use of public monies by individuals to secure a service from a school of their choice is pretty much like the present system of Medicare and Medicaid, whereby Medicare pays money to or for patients who can choose their doctors and hospitals. We are told that this system is well into the disaster stage. Nursing homes of dubious quality, spectacular rises in medical costs, and abuses by physicians were not prevented by giving patients "free choice," and these abuses could have their counterparts in the voucher system for schooling. To be sure, precautions will be built in, we are told, so that the poor will have the same access to the "good" schools as the rich, that blacks will not be turned away from schools of their choice, and that the dull child will be as welcome as the bright one. Unfortunately, 'twas never thus. No system of controls has protected the poor, the gullible, and the ignorant from the depredations of the wily and vigorous entrepreneur. Already hundreds of enterprising men and women are ready to get into the private school business. In education, as in commerce, the free market makes sense only if it is really free, but how long has it been since we have had a really free market? How long does really free competition remain fair to those of unequal endowments? How long before those who pull ahead in the competition establish rules that insure their staying ahead?

Would the voucher system make schools more accountable than the public schools are now? Well, it would certainly motivate schools to keep their customers happy, and it would give parents a chance to try something else if they were not happy. In this sense, the voucher system would provide for accountability. However, it would shift the real responsibility from the school to the parents, for it would be up to parents to change schools if things were not going right, because alternatives would be available.

This view of accountability has not figured in the arguments of the proponents of the voucher system; on the contrary, one hears that vouchers will make the schools accountable, and the bad schools will be driven out of business by the good ones. But this supposes that the parents can tell good schools from bad ones on criteria other than the reports of their children and the general reputation of the schools with other parents.*

The medical profession sometimes forbids physicians to advertise in the ordinary sense, that is, to laud themselves as good physicians. This is so, I am told, because the profession does not believe the lay public can judge the merits of such claims. Only a physician can make such a judgment. Physicians do not judge each other's competence by popularity, although patients often choose physicians on no other criterion.

Are parents in a better state with regard to judging schools?

---

* As a sidenote to the sort of objectivity we find in evaluating educational proposals, the voucher system had as one of its most vigorous advocates Christopher Jencks, of the Harvard Graduate School of Education. The Office of Economic Opportunity, aware of the reservations that many "educationists" had about the voucher plan, resolved to finance a feasibility study. Guess to whom the grant for making the feasibility study was made by the OEO—it was to the Center for the Study of Public Policy, in Cambridge, of which Mr. Jencks was a codirector at the time.

If they could, would they be buying millions of books on how to cope with children? Would they be sending them off to school at all, if they could educate them so much better themselves? Or is it really the case, as some aver, that the schools are the cheapest day-care centers one can devise?

In one community, a study showed that a $20,000 residence in the neighborhood of a "good" school brought as much as $1,500 to $2,000 more on the market than a comparable one in a neighborhood where the school was thought to be only fair or inferior. Yet nobody interviewed could say why one school was good and another bad; the reputation was enough, and the reputation was built by parents blessed by the sort of children who did well in school. In time the neighborhood became a paradise for schoolteachers.

Was it a good school for ghetto children? Who knows? As the price of real estate in that neighborhood rose, the ratio of black children to white fell. If black parents were given vouchers, would they have chosen to send (bus) their children into this "good" school? Would the children have done well? A thousand ifs spring to the tongue as one tries to answer such questions. The sad fact of the matter is that about the only working criterion for judging schools today is social class. The schools patronized by the successful classes are judged to be the "good" schools regardless of what is taught there or how it is taught and regardless of how happy or miserable the pupils are. Snob value aside, how else is the citizen to think about the "goodness" of schools? If schooling does make a difference to success in life, then obviously the schools patronized by the successful strata of society are the good schools. If schools don't make any difference to success, then what difference does it make whether a child attends one school rather than another—convenience and cost being equal? That parents will choose schools that promise to train their children *out* of the success routes of the day and into some counterculture is precisely what parents will *not* do, the effusions of the self-appointed emancipators of modern man to the contrary notwithstanding.

Of course, you may say, "Why not ask the educationists to tell us which is the better school?" This is what we do in our judgments about lawyers, architects, and doctors. There's the rub! The educationists no more agree on criteria than do their critics. If the voucher boys have their way, the school scene may resemble the church scene in Los Angeles; pick up the paper on Saturday, and you will find a dazzling variety of alternative routes to salvation listed for the following day.

All of the foregoing siftings through the complexities of accountability lead to the conclusion that, where schools are concerned, the demand for accountability is valid only under certain limited conditions.

1. The special function of the school is clearly identifiable and agreed upon.

2. The outcomes for which the school is held accountable are well within its control.

3. There can be agreement on or acceptance by the public of some common body of teachable knowledge, skill, and value that all children within the educable range at the school can be expected to study.

4. The standards for quality are clear; either in the form of instructional tests for specific segments of instruction, or in the form of standards within recognized domains of knowledge, as determined by experts in those domains.

5. The members of a profession are recognized as experts— whether teachers or administrators—in various special aspects of the educative process.

6. There is some consensus on educational theory—at least with respect to terminology, topics for study, and methods of inquiry.

The condition having to do with an identifiable function is important, because otherwise schools would be held accountable for everything, which is absurd. This injunction would seem platitudinous were it not for the loudly asserted fallacy that since the child is a whole, his schooling cannot minister to only one aspect of his life. To be sure, the division of labor in society can be abandoned, but if it is, there is no point in asking the school, or for that matter the home or the state, to be accountable for anything.

The greater the elapsed time between the end of instruction and the time when the pupil uses or misuses his schooling in non-school life, the smaller the accountability of the school for either failure or success. Success or failure in life is the result of such a complex of factors that the mind boggles at analyzing even a simple sample of it. Take, for example, the success of a mechanic at his job. This does seem like a straightforward case: man learns skills; man is employed to use skills; man uses skills; man is a successful mechanic.

Ah, yes, but what about that good-natured bouncy wife of his and those three bouncy children who keep his motivation high? What about his love of automobiles nurtured since adolescence by a train of curious circumstances? What about a half-hundred other little coincidences that caused many roads to converge on what now seems to be a simple path? Change the bouncy wife to a termagent; add the frustration of an ambition to be an automotive engineer, a penchant for extramarital experimentation, and a fondness for gambling on the horses, and what happened in the school for mechanics would become trivial.

Or take, as another common example, the effect of attending college on life. Do the courses one studies make a difference? Yes, I believe they do, and if you don't believe it, ask a friend who has not gone beyond high school to read the special sections of the Sunday New York *Times* or other reading material with a similar cognitive demand. Two things will be obvious. Your friend, although he may be an intelligent, alert chap, will not be able to manage terms and concepts that he has not studied formally. He may take a guess at such concepts as homeostasis, gross national product, atonal music, symbiosis, but that's about all. The other thing that becomes clear is that many of the topics treated in the special sections are of no interest to him.

I would hold a college accountable if its graduates could not manage discourse on a wide variety of topics at this level of sophistication, for if general education accomplishes anything, it should broaden the intellectual interests of its beneficiaries and equip them with sufficient knowledge in many areas to read, discuss, and think with the categories of an educated man.

But I would not hold any college responsible if some of its most literate and thoughtful graduates turned out to be despots, breeders of wars, great humanitarians, or saints. Life is more than learning, and the most enlightened education can only predispose the individual to meet each predicament of existence with the forms of thought and feeling that have been distilled by the living traditions of the educated culture. Only the individual can decide the right thing to do in a particular situation; all his education can do is predispose him to want to do the right thing and enable him to reflect—if there is time—on the possibilities and consequences of defining the situation in this way or that. Men with the same sort of formal education become Democrats and Republicans, liberals and conservatives, Schweitzers and Nazis. What makes the difference? Who knows? Early childhood relationships with others; all sorts of psychological and social factors—these perhaps can be dug out by an interested biographer if one is important enough to warrant a biography. For the rest of us, these deeper existential eddies do their work and are either not noticed or forgotten—but of this one can be sure: they are almost never the overt concern or result of deliberate instruction in a school.

This is why, one might suppose, our attention has been called to the affective factors in both life and school. The awakening of this country to racism and its consequences was the shock that uncovered social and psychic inadequacies not only in the children of the black ghetto, but in the entire population. Clinically, the mass acts of the American people are symptoms of sickness, of a sick society, if you like. I say "clinically" and "mass acts," as if a society could be brought into a clinic and observed as one might observe a sick individual. Of course, this is only a way of speaking and a dangerously slippery one at that. Yet when all is said in the way of exculpation, each one of us as individuals either did or did not condone or act on moral issues. And however these results crossed and crisscrossed, our government has been supported in unsupportable wars, and our industrial machine has been sustained by our purchases in its wasteful, polluting ways.

Has the school produced this sickness, this slackness of moral tension, this heedless hedonism, this lack of foresight? Of course it may have, because schooling is part of the history of the individuals who became sick, but the same schools figured in the history of individuals who are not sick and those who, though sick, recognize their illness.

Can the school provide the prophylaxis against this sickness?

I do not know, and it is hard to know, because we are not even sure of what is a sick soul and a healthy one, and we are far from knowing precisely what produces either. Once the purely animal state in a state of nature—whatever that might mean—is ruptured, the human psyche oscillates between the superanimal and the subanimal, and either move, if it goes the slightest bit beyond the tolerance level of the community, will be called soul sickness. Is a sensitive child well or sick? Is a stolid child well or sick? Are homosexuals well or sick? Is the search for means to maximize sexual pleasure a sign of health or sickness? Is ambition a sign of health or sickness? Is success healthy or not? Until one has satisfactory answers to these questions, the school cannot define "maturity," "good emotional adjustment," "good relationships," or any one of the array of question-begging epithets used in discussions of this sort.

A child so battered emotionally that he cannot be instructed by ordinary methods has no place in the ordinary classroom with an ordinary teacher and ordinary classmates. His place is in a special classroom or clinic with personnel who at least make some claim to special knowledge and techniques. It does little good to blame the ordinary teacher for the child's maladjustment. A frustrated teacher is a bad teacher, just as a frustrated pupil is a bad pupil; put them together and you have an intolerable situation, and that is precisely what has been done in many ghetto schools. To speak of school accountability in such tragic situations is itself a sign of diseased logic.

The emotional sickness for which the school as a school is accountable is that caused by (1) the failure of the school (its personnel) to treat pupils as persons or, better, as clients to whom they have pledged their best efforts at instruction; (2) insisting the pupil do what by all available evidence he cannot do; and (3) allowing the pupil to perform at levels of quality well below what, on good evidence, is his capacity.

Is this too simple a view of the matter? Perhaps, but let us leave to the psychiatrists the more devious and convoluted causes of emotional maladjustment. For one thing, by the age of six, the time for the very early childhood trauma has gone by. For another, the types of maladjustment I have mentioned are all within conscious experience. Finally, group therapy, encounter sessions, and sensitivity training, whatever their merits, demand skills and training that classroom teachers do not ordinarily possess.

Teachers have been accused of not caring about the emotional difficulties of their pupils (a deficiency in philetics) and that this deficiency is the major obstacle to pupils' wanting to learn. Even if this were true, which I doubt, it does not follow that the care and concern a teacher ought to have for a pupil is that of a doctor (mental or physical) for a patient. Bad tonsils may also make a pupil hostile to learning, but the teacher is not therefore charged with removing the tonsils before trying to teach arithmetic; yet something quite analogous is expected in mental and psychic indispositions. The care and concern that can be demanded of a teacher is for the pupil as a learner, a potential learner; the frustrations he is accountable for are the frustrations caused by inappropriate tasks; and the major character malformation the pupil has the right to be protected from is that which results from being allowed to get away with much less than he can really do.

While talking about making the public schools accountable, it is well to remember that they are public. In this country, "public" means not only that the schools are open to all, but also that they are supported by taxes collected from everyone whose incomes and property are liable to taxation. Furthermore, up to a certain age, attendance is compulsory for every child, and the attendance must be in some school approved by that public agency the state. There is no justification for a common school unless there are common needs. This is not incompatible with cultural diversity and individual needs. It may be true that all Americans need a telephone, but not that all must have white, green, touch, or dial telephones. Common needs do not exclude individual diversity, any more than a common theme precludes a host of variations. The basic needs of the social order furnish the common theme; a rich and enlightened society affords endless opportunities for variation. But without a theme, what is the meaning of variation? For this reason, cultural pluralism without some cultural unity is chaos, just as cultural unity without diversity is dull. Destroy commonality and for what are public schools accountable?

A common language is a serious case in point. It may be advisable for some American children to speak or at least to comprehend more than one language. In an earlier mood America tried to do away with multilingualism for the same reason that it encouraged immigrants to forget or suppress the alien ways of the old country. This was a "new" land, a refuge from the persecution and poverty of the old countries—else why did the immigrants emigrate? Of course, only the more recent immigrants were expected to abandon their native language and culture entirely.

Inasmuch as the non-Indian settlers of the new land were all fleeing from somewhere and from something, it was not really fair to demand suppression of original culture from only the later arrivals, but this was not decided by logic but by conquest, so that although we emerged from the Revolution with an ideal of a distinctive American character as a nation, this did not result in abandoning English as the national language. On the contrary, a common language was to be the strongest solvent for ethnic diversities, as the floods of immigration swelled in the latter half of the nineteenth century.

Now it is one thing for certain ethnic groups to want bilingual instruction because the children and parents had no adequate opportunity to learn English. Perhaps they arrived only recently from other lands. But it is quite another to demand that the public schools be bilingual so as to preserve the Spanish or Indian or black culture. The singleness of language is itself no great matter aside from convenience, but in this country the common language was to be the gateway to common ideas and aspirations to a new community, not the preservation of all ethnic differences.

To the more radical historians of education, this messianic and evangelistic mission of the school was a mask concealing the exploitation of the public schools by the rising middle class for its own advancement and profit. Some of this debunking, no doubt, is justified; no epoch is invulnerable. But Horace Mann, the first secretary of the Massachusetts Board of Education, created in 1836, and one of the indefatigable workers for a free public school system, was not a hypocrite when he defended the public school in terms of this ideal. Indeed, free education was

supposed to incorporate men not only into the Commonwealth
of Massachusetts, but into the commonwealth of men. Along
with the economic aggressiveness of the middle-class entrepreneur went a political faith that Gunnar Myrdal was to call the
American Creed. Inchoate and inconsistent as the mixture of
Greek humanism, Christian dogma, and English common law
was, it adumbrated an almost subconscious belief in human dignity, law, and the democratic process, a kind of humane liberalism that in recent years has been derided as "tired" by those
impatient with it. To the consensus achieved for the high-order
evaluations embodied in the Creed, Myrdal credited the ability
of this country to unite rich and poor, native and immigrant,
members of all political parties. All justified their claims in its
name. It is this commonality of evaluation—not merely unilin-
gualism—that the new humanists are rejecting. Why has this
happened? Perhaps one reason is that the ideal envisioned a type
of community that is no longer typical in our society.

The democratic ideal as envisioned by Horace Mann and
much later by John Dewey was exemplified by the way in which
the New England village was governed. Free farmers, free
householders, free businessmen and tradesmen, not differing
greatly in wealth, power, and knowledge, could reason together
in the town meeting about local problems. This was New England participatory democracy, not Athenian mobocracy or representative republicanism. This was a genuine community, and the
language of the schools talked of democracy in these terms long
after a technologically complicated and interdependent society
had destroyed that kind of community. For this cultural lag it is
hard to forgive the public schools.

Nevertheless, the passing of the New England village community—the community of free and approximately equal individuals—did not mean that all unity and all commonality had
also disappeared. Is there no set of knowledges, skills, and attitudes that the nation presupposes if it is to survive as a democratic society in some sense of that word? Does not the technological system itself impose a certain uniformity of demands on
education? But more on this later; for the moment, what becomes of accountability and, indeed, of the notion of the public
school itself if we adopt a radical cultural pluralism? To how

many different cultural units is the school to be accountable? And what agency is to be accountable for the sort of schooling that is needed to keep a highly developed, technologically mature society from shattering into a thousand fragments like a body dismembered by centrifugal forces? Have the celebrants of alternatives, decentralization, and unlimited cultural autonomy thought of their own accountability? Extreme cultural relativism, the principle invoked to justify cultural pluralism and ultimately anarchic individualism, is an interesting philosophy, but a misleading description of social reality. It makes social life impossible because each man—not man as distinguished from God—becomes the measure of all things. And if schooling has any relevance to social reality, cultural pluralism cannot rule the curriculum, and alternative programs cannot be multiplied indefinitely. For the school to be accountable, its responsibilities must be limited and to some extent directed to common goals.

Once the accountability of the public school is cut down to matters of instruction, school climate, and organization, that is, to matters of curriculum and the organization of teaching and learning, the question of autonomy to make decisions in these areas becomes paramount. Responsibility extends as far as and no further than autonomy.* Shared responsibility and shared authority are equally incoherent notions. They are euphemisms for escapes from responsibility and accountability.

This sounds strange in view of the benefits claimed for sharing decision making with all those who have even the remotest interest in the outcomes of the decisions made. But morally, responsibility does not exist where there is neither the freedom to choose nor the power to make choice effective. The more authority and autonomy are shared, the less responsibility each part

---

* I realize that this has a dogmatic ring and needs further explanation, but I am trying to avoid long digressions into technical points of ethical theory. The slave is accountable to the master, although he has zero autonomy with regard to decisions, but he is responsible only if he has some alternative and a reasonable freedom to make a choice. Thus he may be responsible for his decision to obey the command of the master, although he had no voice in issuing the command. Although it makes sense to say that teachers are accountable for obeying their superiors, it makes little sense to say that they are responsible for the decisions of their superiors; their responsibility may consist of no more than the freedom to quit the job.

has for the total effect. Especially pernicious is the notion of delegated authority, which is a form of bureaucratic sadism. Delegated authority means to the delegatee, "Do it at the risk of being reversed if your superior chooses to reverse you." What has been delegated is not authority but risk. Understandably, delegatees make sure of approval before they exert the authority. But this is a strange kind of authority, is it not?

Participation by citizens, parents, labor leaders, in the affairs of the school, when it extends into the domain of instruction, results in confusion and dilution of responsibility. We have about reached the point where the school plausibly can disclaim responsibility for even those instructional outcomes that clearly ought to be its responsibility. This has come about in the name of the right of smaller and smaller political units to make decisions about instructional matters, and the rights of ideologists to control the school as a means for shaping society in the image of the ideology that haunts them.

For example, local communities in recent years have attacked the Board of Examiners of New York City because civil service examinations prevent them from employing such teachers and supervisors as they want. Especially vehement were minority groups, who argued that the examinations discriminated against them.

Another example is the current push against all required courses for college degrees. This is based on the view that each student is the best judge of his own educational needs. Here the unit of educational decision is the individual.

The recent breaking up of the New York City school system into thirty-one quasi-independent districts for the control of elementary schools was defended on the ground that in this way the schools would conform more closely to the wishes of the parents of the pupils of those schools.

Free schools that have sprouted up in many parts of the country carry the fragmentation even further than control by local districts. These schools cater to parents who want their philosophy of life reflected in a style of schooling. Because such schools cannot subsist on private tuition, moves are made to secure public support for them or to incorporate them as alternatives within the public schools.

Yet all of these developments become minor when compared to the abdication of authority for the curriculum and the conduct of instruction by school personnel. Indeed one can hardly blame the citizens for making educational decisions—even on details of school management—when the school authorities admit that they lack either the knowledge or the courage to make them. It would be far more wholesome to hold school administrators accountable for abdicating their responsibilities than to hold schools responsible for decisions the citizens have made.

We return to an old theme: a school that cannot appeal to the consensus of the learned has no choice but to be guided by *vox populi*. A school, unlike some other social institutions, is accountable to an impersonal client—to knowledge itself—and in a way this allegiance is basic to its obligations to other clienteles.

When it comes to apportioning responsibility in terms of power and influence, one can no longer stop with the *de facto* administrative apparatus of the schools or the teaching staff or the school board or the State Department of Education. Sizable portions are to be allotted to the philanthropic foundations, their allies in the U.S. Office of Education, and the communications media that select a particular educational proposal or individual for publicity. These New Establishment agencies certainly wield influence, but one hears little of their accountability for what the schools have done or failed to do. It is no wonder that even a commission generally sympathetic to private foundations could note that foundations have remained "a kind of closed society in an era when openness is a byword." *

Can the school be held accountable for results? Yes, but only for the results of instruction when that instruction reaches a testable state. Instruction in skills and knowledge can be tested reasonably well; the uses of schooling in nonschool situations as yet cannot be tested directly. I believe we can devise ways of estimating the over-all uses of schooling in life, but such devices do not now exist. The more the pressure for accountability mounts, the more the school will confine its work to results that can be

---

* *Foundations, Private Giving, and Public Policy: Report and Recommendations of the Commission on Foundations and Private Philanthropy.* (Chicago: University of Chicago Press, 1971). See also Joseph C. Goulden, *The Money-Givers* (New York: Random House, 1971).

tested. The more this is the case, the less responsibility will the school be able to assume for those long-range life outcomes to which schooling should contribute.

The school can be held strictly accountable for what the best expert opinion regards as the appropriate procedures, materials, and organization of the instructional process. In an imperfect world, it makes sense to say, as do the physicians, "The operation was successful, but the patient died," or "The case was handled perfectly by the lawyer and the judge, but the verdict was unjust." Professional expertise and ethics try to define the responsibility of the professional. At best, the definitions do not solve the hard cases, but the principle is clear. The professional is responsible for knowing the "best" practice and for having the "best" available knowledge at any given time. The profession determines what it is reasonable to expect the professional to know and to do. But note that this excuses the professional from responsibility for the ultimate goals of man and society. As a man and as a human being, he must make a moral decision as to whether he will use his professional skills in behalf of goals that he cannot approve. If a chemist cannot in good conscience work on developing defoliants, he can refuse to do so—if he is willing to take the financial consequences of his choice. Moral heroism has its costs. An individual may have adequate reason for not being a moral hero—one's duty to one's children, for example, may surmount other obligations—but one does not necessarily lose moral stature by following conscience in one direction rather than another; it is by *ignoring* or *defying* conscience that one forfeits a claim to moral integrity. It can be seriously compromised when one is unwilling to bear the consequences of heeding conscience. Thus, when in good conscience the school superintendent cuts the budget drastically, moral integrity demands that he seek out and live with the consequences that will affect the victims of the cut.

And all this brings me to the main reason why the schools cannot be held accountable for the really important outcomes of education. Schools not only lack the autonomy for making the decisions that determine the success or failure of the enterprise, but more important, there is no professional cadre to provide criteria for judging the educational process. Public school personnel simply do not acknowledge any coherent body of knowledge on the basis of which they might legitimately and convincingly claim the authority of the expert. For one thing, no coherent body of such knowledge exists; what knowledge there is fails to command sufficient acceptance to render the notion of a professional expertise plausible.

There is no set of ideas about anything in education that the professional teacher or teacher of teachers feels obliged to learn or to consider. Members of coteries cite each others' works, but not the works of other coteries. Research is rarely replicated. Each graduate student is encouraged to produce something new, with the result that we have mountains of research studies, but no basic literature. This is one reason for "newness" being so widely used as a criterion by funding agencies. A practice is good if nobody can recall its being done before, and a benign neglect of history assures us of never-ending originality.

It is only by poetic license that we can call teachers in the public schools professionals. As fairly well-selected four-year college students, they have the intellectual capacity to become professionals, but for reasons I have already discussed in Chapter III they are, for the most part, white-collared classroom operatives. Despite the rhetoric of professionalism, the teaching force has quite rightly found itself more advantageously allied with the unionized worker. Salary, working conditions, tenure—these are the problems with which perforce they have to be concerned, because they are treated as employees with limited responsibilities and virtually no autonomy. If I seem to approve of this proletariatization of teachers, it is not with pleasure. I, too, have shared and worked for the ideal of a professional teacher for every classroom, but since this ideal is probably not realizable for more than a small fraction of the teaching force, it is better for the vast majority of our teachers to bargain collectively for whatever advantages they can, rather than to sacrifice these benefits for a professional status they do not have and probably will not have in our time.

These facts make it difficult to hold the schools accountable even for correct procedures as determined by professional expertise. When the experts cannot agree on what constitutes an expert, when some experts counsel school officials to do nothing

without advice from their clients, we must conclude that either
the experts are wily manipulators of public opinion in behalf of
their masked intentions, or that they really do not know what to
do until their clients make up their minds for them.

Can one blame the public for turning to journalists and the
foundations for guidance on the public schools? As a matter of
fact, do not the professional organizations like the American Educational Research Association and the American Association of
Colleges for Teacher Education invite these laymen to their annual conventions to hear "wholesome criticism," and perhaps to
find answers that they themselves cannot produce? Can one
blame the black community or the Eastern intellectuals or the
redneck communities for demanding control of their own
schools? Society abhors a vacuum of authority; today all sorts of
bids for authority in education are being sucked in to fill that
vacuum. The polite words for this chaos are "alternatives" and
"cultural pluralism."

Perhaps every synthesis has its day, and, as it breaks up, a
struggle for new authority must follow. At such times it is better
for many alternatives to fight it out with each other rather than
to have the field usurped by one aggressive party. I think we are
in such a period now where both schools and society are concerned. What is the prognosis for the new unity or the new synthesis? That depends on the destiny of the modern technological
society. But until that new unity emerges, until there is a clear-
cut division of labor among the school and other social agencies,
until the activities of schooling are monitored and directed by a
strong professional class, the talk of accountability, understandable and proper though it may be, smacks more of recrimination,
impatience, and vengeance than it does of genuine concern for
the education of the young.

CHAPTER VII

Education for a Benign
Technological Society

Not long ago I read somewhere that Congressmen wanted access to computers in order to have the information needed for decision making. This surprised me a little, because I was under the impression that Congressmen got all the information they needed from lobbyists and an occasional visit with the folks back home. I should have known better. For some time now, politicians have been relying on specialists for much of their information; tactics and strategy emerge from consultation with public-opinion pollsters and professional image makers.

At the international level, as the spy movies tell us, gathering information and buying, selling, and assessing it are almost as important as the moves made by diplomats and heads of state. All of which is witness to the fact that all uses of power depend on knowledge power. This has always been true insofar as knowledge guided action, but in modern times action without highly sophisticated information is often impossible. The knowledge that is involved in the exercise of military, industrial, and political power is likely to be technical, esoteric, and highly specialized.

This fact has radically transformed the task of the schools. It has done so in several ways. For one thing, what C. P. Snow

called the literary culture is no longer sufficient for the educated
citizen; it has to be supplemented by the scientific culture. In the
second place, the motion of a society toward technological maturity renders questionable the almost unquestioned assumption
that there is to be one sort of schooling for the elite and quite
another kind for the masses.

As to the first point, the schools are faced with the problem
of how to teach the highly specialized and diverse disciplines so
as to make them useful to the citizen as distinguished from the
specialist. The scientific community, as represented by the American Association for the Advancement of Science, has taken the
view that for this purpose science should be taught as a process.
"Science—A Process Approach" is a kindergarten-through-sixth-
grade program, which leads the child to comprehend science by
looking at the world somewhat as the scientist does.

Beginning with very simple situations, the child observes, classifies,
uses numbers, measures, communicates, predicts, infers, and ultimately formulates hypotheses and does simple experiments. In the
process of these activities of the scientist, he incidentally acquires an
impressive body of information that now is functionally meaningful
for him. At present *Science—A Process Approach* is being used by
well over 50,000 teachers throughout the country, with approximately
2 million children. *

Presumably what has been done with the physical sciences
will also have to be done for the behavioral disciplines that are
now struggling to achieve scientific status. We are confronted
with the problem of packaging the results of the knowledge ex-
plosion for instruction so that the pupil can understand them
without being overwhelmed. This problem must be solved by
the scholars before the educationists can do much about it. In
this task the physical scientists have much the easier time, for
they share a broad area of agreement as to the nature of the
problems to be dealt with and the concepts and methods of dealing with them. By comparison, the areas of agreement among
social scientists—for example, in sociology, social psychology,

* William Bevan, "The General Scientific Association: A Bridge to Society
at Large," *Science* 172, no. 3981 (April 23, 1971): 351–52.

and economics—are scanty indeed. In the physical sciences, therefore, it is possible to teach a structure that organizes a great range of phenomena, whereas in the social disciplines, the lack of such a structure leaves us with much matter and little form. Despite these difficulties, it is expected that schooling will enable the citizen to assume the cognitive stance of the sociologist and economist, as well as of the physical scientist. Nothing less, it is fair to say, will enable him to understand, much less cope with, the social problems of the day. The need for all of the citizenry to display this degree of cognitive versatility was ignored in the dual system of schooling.

To be sure, the whole tradition of liberalism has rejected the dual class system in principle and, to some degree, in practice. The cornerstone of this philosophy was the concept of man as a rational being endowed by his Creator or Nature with certain inalienable rights. Education as the key to self-development was a necessary means to implementing these rights. Hence, as far back as Condorcet's report to the French Legislative Assembly in 1792, it was clearly enunciated that equality of educational opportunity meant a system of state schools open to all for basic primary education, supplemented by professional training for the development of individual potentialities.

However, this philosophy of education simply emphasized that the elite would draw their membership from the talented among the total population, and not from a restricted group of individuals. In due course, there would be what Vilfredo Pareto called a circulation of the elite. This, of itself, does not abolish the radical difference between the elite and the masses. The poor boy who "made it," who acquired membership among the elite, did not remain in the masses politically or intellectually, and, what is perhaps even more to the point, he usually acquired his elite education because he was chosen by the elite for co-optation, rather than the other way around. Equalizing educational opportunity, in principle at least, makes it unnecessary for the child of the lower classes to depend on co-optation by the elite before educating himself for membership among them.

But how often in history have we had societies in which membership in the governing or the nongoverning elite depended solely on ability? Originally the governing elite may have established themselves by managerial skill or military might, but thereafter dynasties were established to perpetuate the conquest beyond the life of the conqueror. From then on, membership in the elite depended more on family position than on native or nurtured ability, for ability was nurtured primarily only in members of the elite, although the church often encouraged lowborn but bright boys to develop their talents. This hereditary system of elite maintenance breaks down when the major roles in the society demand the same type of education, although in varying degrees.

As long as the vocational duties of the elite were not functionally dependent on their formal schooling—as they were not for the Chinese mandarins and the British civil servants and the sons of bankers on State and Wall streets—the distinction between elite and mass education could be maintained. For the elite, education was directed to the social life of the prince and the courtier or the highly placed civil servant. In societies that valued the literary culture, literary education was part of elite schooling; when knowledge of science became a mark of high culture, elite schooling included that also. In this country, a liberal education, including the humanities and the sciences, is still considered appropriate for the leaders of the society, apart from their occupational roles.

For the masses, on the contrary, minimal literacy, industriousness, piety, social docility, and some form of training in the more menial occupations were considered sufficient. In short, the leaders could do without specialized training in the vocations, and the masses could do without general education. But in a technologically mature society, the elite cannot do without specialized training for vocation, and, if the society is to be democratic, the masses cannot do without general education. And if this were not enough to shake the dual system of education, the need of a mass production economic system for a high rate of consumption, not to speak of civic virtue and personal sanity, would certainly do so. Large pockets of economic and cognitive poverty are incompatible with a growing, technologically based economic system.

I do not know just when these transformations began, but it seems clear that the process is now well on its way. As far as the elite are concerned, it is difficult for them to find success routes that do not require some sort of formal study of a more or less specialized sort. Politics may be the exception, but even here a career in law or a good business background helps. However, as was remarked at the opening of this chapter, even the art of politics now calls for ancillary expertise or at least some access to it. The Senator who heads an appropriations committee, or indeed any other important committee, perforce must become familiar with highly specialized knowledge. Today the State Street banker may still want his son to go through Harvard with at least a gentleman's *C* and appropriate conviviality, but he may insist on some study in the Harvard Business School before letting the young man assume his position at the bank. In sum, every elite—military, priestly, industrial, political, intellectual— requires specialized training, and, if success is not always determined by merit alone, it is no longer determined merely by birth or even by birth plus character and diligence. Our society is approaching the state of a technomeritocracy.

The ways in which the militant young and their middle-class and upper-middle-class parents view the technomeritocracy constitute the most radical of the generation gaps. Scientists are shocked that the young do not regard the marvels of technology as unmixed blessings and that they are reluctant to join the priesthood of science. Parents are dismayed that their young, after expensive educations, are not eager to qualify for one of the professions or for a place in the business world. The university, geared to serve a technomeritocracy, is disconcerted when the "relevance" of its mission is not only questioned but assailed by rocks and epithets as well.

Granted that the technomeritocracy is guilty of all the evils attributed to it—ruination of the environment, depersonalization, demoralization, all of the horrors of "megatechnics" as detailed by Lewis Mumford for nearly half a century, and especially in *The Myth of the Machine: The Pentagon of Power* (1970)— what are the chances, since we cannot reverse the Industrial Revolution and return to a preindustrial or even a prepostindustrial world, of resuming control of what Mumford calls the Megachine? Is it possible, in short, to reintroduce into the technomeritocracy those humane and humanizing values that the success of the megachine seems to have driven from our midst? Can we have a benign technomeritocracy?

I shall not venture an answer, except to speculate that, without developing our technological apparatus even further than we already have, we cannot possibly sustain our own, let alone the world's, population for very long. The destruction of this technology or the abandonment of it would be a drastic form of population control, and it seems very unlikely that it will be chosen. I do not wholly share the current pessimism about technology, because whatever else it does it creates the potentiality for new value every time it augments human power, and once that potentiality is created, it is up to human beings to use their imagination and will to exploit that potentiality in a genuinely human and humane way. As one of a myriad of possible examples of this, Athelstan Spilhaus, president of the American Association for the Advancement of Science, writing of the "next industrial revolution," remarked:

I believe we must base the next industrial revolution—a planned one —on the thesis that there is no such thing as waste, that waste is simply some useful substance that we do not yet have the wit to use. . . . If American industrial genius can mass-assemble and mass-distribute, why cannot the same genius mass-collect, mass-disassemble, and massively reuse the materials? *

What will happen to the masses in a technomeritocracy? It will no longer do to give them a minimum of literacy, some simple vocational training, and enough piety to keep them resigned to their station in life. Vocationally, they, too, must be specialized, but also highly adaptable. To function as medical, electronic, or food technicians, they need more than simple literacy and rudimentary computation. Indeed, technical training schools want about the same sort of linguistic and mathematical skills for admission as schools of engineering. Furthermore, we are told that vocational specialties will be so short-lived that the most useful vocational preparation will be a package of intellectual resources that will enable a man to change jobs with a minimum of trauma. On the assembly line of mass production, the intellectual demands are more modest, yet we take for granted

* Editorial, *Science* 167; no. 3926 (March 27, 1970).

that the worker can read and understand directions, specifications, and, where necessary, blueprints. We also take for granted a general understanding of machinery and a rudimentary appreciation of the scientific substructure of technology and machines. The importance of this implicit machine consciousness is sharply silhouetted when sophisticated machines are introduced in underdeveloped countries. The workers can learn to operate the machines, but all sorts of odd responses occur, because the general scientific mentality that is embodied in machine consciousness is not part of the culture.

What this means for the formal schooling needed for a vocation is not wholly clear. We have assumed that somehow the more formal schooling the better, and especially as the proportion of white-collar jobs to blue-collar jobs increases. By 1975 it is estimated that we shall need 20 per cent more of these white-collar workers than we had in 1970. Almost all the young now attend high school, and more than half of those who are graduated from high school attempt some form of postsecondary schooling. How necessary is this increase of formal schooling to success on the job? James W. Kuhn, writing in *Saturday Review* (December 19, 1970, page 55), commented that

as of 1968, twenty-seven million employed workers—about 37 percent of the civilian labor force—were contributing productively to the economy, even though they had received less than twelve years of schooling. Among these dropouts are two-and-a-quarter million professionals, technicians, managers, and business proprietors, as well as more than four million men in the skilled crafts. These workers acquired their skills and proved their worth to employers by learning on the job.

Yet the 1969 Manpower Report of the Secretary of Labor predicted that

even in semi-skilled trades a high school education or prior skill training or both is likely to be increasingly necessary as the supply of persons with such preparation becomes larger.

Employers will cream off the candidates with the greatest amount of formal schooling regardless of the nature of the job, but is the formal schooling necessary?

In recent years the suspicion has spread that formal schooling has been oversold. Books such as that by Ivar Berg, *Education and Jobs: The Great Training Robbery* (New York: Praeger Publishers, 1970), and such articles as "The Myth of the Well-Educated Manager," by Sterling Livingston (*Harvard Business Review*, January–February, 1971), stress the lack of correlation between success in formal schooling and success on the job. By increasing the academic requirements for the vocations, it is charged, important functions, such as nursing, are understaffed. Professional schools of medicine have been under pressure to reduce the time spent on academic studies so as to turn out physicians at a faster clip. Similar tendencies are operating in law schools.

Automation of industry, moreover, seems to have exerted a much smaller impact on education required for employment than had been predicted, and the whole issue is beclouded by the current charge that employers use schooling as a screening device to keep minority groups out of jobs. There is also the fact that during periods of prosperity, employers tend to increase educational requirements and, in times of depression, to cut them down. As an example of the latter tendency, one hears reports of industrial firms preferring applicants with the A.B. degree rather than an advanced degree, because they will accept lower beginning salaries. Apparently the difference in degree does not make an equivalent difference in the value of the applicant to the employer.

The contradictory views on the need for schooling to make one's way vocationally are not easily reconciled. Of course, the discrimination hypothesis may be sound, but long before the civil rights issue became acute, employers used educational qualifications as screening devices. For a long time it was thought that scholastic achievement was virtually equivalent to intelligence, and for training purposes an employer would rather have intelligent learners than stupid ones. Finally, low correlations between job success and school achievement neither establish nor preclude causal relationships. The more widespread the possession of a college degree becomes, the less it becomes useful for differentiating workers, and so much of schooling makes no pretense to be job-oriented that it would be remarkable if really high correlations were the rule rather than the exception.

It may be that, although in a technologically mature society theory is of supreme importance, the number of individuals who have to master any specific portion of that theory in great detail can be quite small. For example, the better the refrigerator, the more theory goes into its perfection, but, once perfected, the user need know nothing of the theory.

By breaking up the practice of medicine into numerous sub-operations, the cognitive demands of each may be reduced, and a paraprofessional may be trained in less time and with less understanding of the total operation than would be required for the man who would be responsible for the general practice of medicine. The same might be said for any of the high-level professions. This fragmentation of tasks is a natural development in a technological society. So long as a sufficient number (although it may be quite small in proportion to the total work force) have a grasp of the theory that rationalizes the practice of a profession and provides the authoritative ideas for progress in it, the number of practitioners without the theory can be quite large. Thus, the average medical practitioner no longer has to be an expert in radiology, pathology, anesthesia; there are specialists in these fields to whom he may turn for guidance. And these specialists, in turn, have to know less and less about the construction and operation of the devices they use; technicians with the appropriate know-how can be hired to design, manufacture, and service the machines.

Nevertheless, we are far from having a fully matured, automated industrial machine, and it remains to be seen just what proportion of workers will be needed for jobs that require a minimum of cognitive competence. Computers eliminate assembly line workers, but they engender needs for computer technicians, programmers, operators—symbolic ancillaries of the machine-controlled machines.

Well, then, what sort of schooling does the maturing technological society seem to prescribe? The received doctrine is that the diversity of occupational slots in and of itself dictates highly specific job training to be undertaken as soon as possible—and certainly not later than the seventh grade. Moreover, part of the received doctrine is that occupations divide into two sorts: one for the literate elite, and one for the masses; one class works with one end of the spinal column, and one with the other. I submit,

however, that a high order of specificity in occupations does not
necessarily imply an equally high order of specificity in schooling.

A technologically mature society institutes an extraordinary
number of gradations in a single occupational spectrum. When
the economy is working in high gear, it approaches the ideal of
enabling almost any pattern of talent and training to be matched
with an appropriate job. The import of this situation, although
not obvious, seems to be that everyone needs a sufficient ground-
ing in the basic skills and disciplines to get specialized training
for some vocational role in the technomeritocracy, and, if necessary, to shift from one role to another as the job market changes.

That a long period of general education is indicated in a
technologically mature society may be argued, of course, on
other grounds as well. Work at a gainful occupation may not be
the greatest source of social or individual significance, despite
the wide range of vocational potentialities within the system;
assembly line workers are showing increasing resistance to
highly routinized operations. This means that for many people
who will be doing this sort of work, other avenues for significance and satisfaction will have to be explored, and general education may be one of the means for doing so.

For these reasons I agonize much less than the majority of
my colleagues about early and specific vocational training for
everybody, but especially for the masses. However, there are
other considerations that lead me to believe in a prolongation,
rather than a diminution, of general education in the secondary
school.

First, as the writings on the low correlation between school
and jobs show, success on the job involves many factors that are
beyond the power of formal schooling to supply. The implica-
tion of this finding, if it is true, is not that the schools should
supply these qualities, but rather that people should go to school
for other reasons. Second, for a vast array of jobs, specific vocational training can be secured in a relatively short time, as adequately on the job, perhaps, as in school. This means that general education, to facilitate receptivity to specific training and to
a variety of such training, is the more important resource to be
supplied by the elementary and secondary school. Third, al-

though work will continue to be important in the society of the future, its importance will be greater to the system than to the individual—except for a small minority of high-level professionals and creative workers. Finally, I am apprehensive about the ready acquiescence of minority groups, the poor, and other disadvantaged segments of the population to the notion that training for jobs—any jobs—as soon as possible, is the panacea for their difficulties. Far from being a panacea, this notion leads to the drastic reduction in the amount of general education available to the children of the disadvantaged, and this condemns them to perpetuating their disadvantages indefinitely. The dual system of schooling is good neither for them nor for society.

On the consumer side, the technologically mature economic system demands that the workingman become conditioned to an ever-rising material standard of living; he must forever be trading up his house, his car, his boat, his vacation. Otherwise the benefits of mass production cannot be exploited. This means not only a high rate of consumption of material goods, but also of newspapers, magazines, books, television sets, attendance at movies, and sports spectacles. To be sure, we have not yet satisfied everyone's basic needs for food, clothing, and shelter, but if we did, it would not be enough to keep the vast economic machine humming as it must to sustain itself. More services in health and education, more expenditures for leisure-time activities—these are the demands that incubate one new industry after another. Chain nursing homes, mobile homes, snowmobiles, air travel, air conditioning, cosmetics, are but a few examples of growth fields that depend on the masses being able to live well above the subsistence level.

One consequence of mass production of supersubsistence goods is that the difference between the elite and the masses in their leisure is diminished. First of all, the masses do have some leisure. Further, no sooner does the jet set discover a vacation paradise than the tourist industries contrive a low-cost-version package for everybody else. Mass and class imbibe the same drinks, see the same movies and television programs, and wear the same sorts of clothes. The differences in cost and refinement are still there, but they are not differences in kind.

The mass market, therefore, is the dominant market; its size and health is the key to the gross national product and the gross national taste. Exotic variations in clothes, amusements, and culture in general are extrusions from that market, not essentially different from what is traded in that market. For this market to grow, the desires of the masses have to be expanded, and this means that their education has to be traded up, as well as their houses and automobiles. And any effort to escape from the mass market in any domain—ideas, clothes, amusements, art, morals —is attended by great effort and not a little pain.

To reiterate a point made previously, a thriving, mass technological society cannot afford significant amounts of either material or cognitive poverty. We realized this in the mid-sixties. The large pockets of poverty that seemed to be a permanent part of our society, and the race discrimination that exacerbated the problems of poverty, as well as in no small part causing them, shocked us. It was a jolt to both our humanitarian and economic sensibilities. And when such a double shock occurs, we have one of those golden moments in history when humanitarian, economic, and political advantages converge. It is only now, in the seventies, that rampant exponential consumption is being questioned, largely on ecological grounds; nonetheless, economists shudder at what would happen if Americans stopped living well beyond their means. The depression-inflation of the early seventies illustrates this thesis; the key to prosperity is the purchasing power of the masses, and when savings pile up in the banks, the production indices droop. All the proposed remedies seek to release funds for greater production that will promote more employment and, in turn, more consumption. The occurrence of the depression raises the question as to how the technologically mature society will be governed—whether the existing mix of public and private sectors can manage such a society. I must leave the answer to those competent to discuss it, but, whatever it may be, the demands made by the system on the schools will be those of a technomeritocracy.

Perhaps the most important impact of the shift from a dual class-mass society to a single-ladder technomeritocracy on education is in the realm of citizenship. In a totalitarian society, it may still be possible to condition the masses to follow their leaders. In a society presumably committed to democracy, the citizen has the duty (not merely the privilege) to make decisions in accordance with his concern for the public good. Some may wish to quarrel with making political activity a duty even in a democratic society. One could argue, for example, that not even the most zealous citizen can participate in every political decision. Or one might say, "I delegate the privilege of decision making to the voters who choose to vote on Election Day, and since I do this freely, I have not really abdicated my duty to democracy." One can, in this way, excuse oneself from a good many onerous civic chores, but sooner or later a decision will be made the consequences of which are repugnant to the nonparticipant. At that moment he has to ask himself whether, in letting slide his rights to decide, he contributed to the wrong decision and thus acted immorally.

However, as with any other moral situation, the moral agent is involved with consequences and knowledge as well as with intentions and conscience. All social issues that amount to anything do have a moral dimension, and the first moral obligation is to become knowledgeable about the issues so that the decision will be moral in the light of the best available knowledge of causes and consequences. In simple situations—*e.g.*, whether to put the new sewer on the north or south side of the roadway— the needed knowledge may be readily available, and the pros and cons can be brought out clearly in a series of council meetings or town meetings.

Unfortunately there are no simple societal problems left. Shall I favor a system of social medical insurance, or shall it be left to enlightened private enterprise? Giving industry a quick write-off on capital investments sounds like unfair privilege for the wily tycoons, but what if the write-offs help to produce full employment? Shall there be tax-exempt municipal bonds? If there are, millionaires can avoid paying income taxes; if there aren't, then municipalities may have to pay higher interest rates for their borrowings, and this will increase local taxes, and so on, world without end.

But where do I get the information and judgment to make these decisions? I can get them already packaged by reading a favorite columnist, or I can consult my party leader, or I can ask a drinking companion. A philosopher of my acquaintance relied a great deal on his barber's dicta as guides to political judgments. If, however, I have any notions of making up my own mind and being my own man, I had better prepare to spend some time reading fusty, dusty discussions on economic questions. And if I am to make up my own mind on foreign policy, abortion, drug legislation, space exploration, pollution, and aid to parochial schools, I face many more yards of reading and many more hours of discussion. If I am told that this do-it-yourself kind of citizenship is not really necessary, that it is sufficient to choose among the experts and be guided by them, then on what criteria do I choose among experts of whose fields I am relatively and sometimes absolutely ignorant?

I submit that good citizenship in a modern democracy is not radically different for the elite than it is for the masses. Most of our elite are nongoverning, and they, too, have to arrive at political decisions on the basis of knowledge that they either cultivate for themselves or take on the authority of others. The elite do not have civic problems that the rest of us are spared, and I cannot see that the moral obligation to become informed and to participate in political activity is any greater for them than for the rest of us.

Good citizenship, however, entails more than knowledge about issues and alternative solutions. It requires what used to be called wisdom. Wisdom is knowledge about relative values, and there are no specialists in wisdom. It is not surprising, therefore, that in the modern university one cannot find either students or professors of wisdom, for the professors, at least, are all specialists. Even the specialists in moral philosophy would disclaim the title of "wise men." A student seeking to study wisdom would not find it in the catalogue, and if he persisted in trying to register in courses for wisdom, he would end up registered for treatment in the psychiatric clinic. Some such frustrated students precipitated riots. Clearly the students were wrong in the matter of riots, but were they really wrong in thinking that they ought to be hearing something about wisdom from their professors? A vague memory of the ideal of liberal education stirs the conscience of even the most specialized professor, so that he does not have the heart to say that the search for wisdom is irrelevant; he can only demur that it is irrelevant to his own specialty. When the student replies that his specialty is irrelevant to wisdom, what is the professor to say?

Wisdom, the key to both personal and civic virtue, is the perennial problem of pedagogy. The Greeks were puzzled by the fact that the sons of Pericles had not learned wisdom, and whether virtue could be taught troubled Socrates throughout the early dialogues. Protagoras, the great Sophist, thought there were no specific teachers of virtue, because everybody, the community as a whole, was forever teaching virtue. But the kind of virtue he had in mind was that of conforming to the mores, and in a modern society civic education has to go beyond that.

In addition to knowledge about social problems, the good citizen needs (1) value schemata, or hierarchies, that enable him to reflect in a systematic way on alternatives for action; and (2) the art of moral reflection itself, especially as it is carried on by groups.

The source of civilized value schemata is the humanities and the fine arts. In the early years, what is right and good are identified with the expectations of one's parents and peers. Later the larger expectations of the community define the right, the decent, and the good. But in the developed forms of literature, history, and philosophy, one finds the search for principles that transcend these *de facto* expectations. It is in the name of these principles that moral codes have been challenged and sometimes changed. Perhaps, as some have argued, *e.g.*, Lawrence Kohlberg, children have to go through stages from amorality to moral autonomy in a definite sequence. If so, then some sort of analogous sequence of moral training and education could be derived for the kindergarten, primary, and later grades in school. Learning to obey rules in the early years may be a prerequisite for making autonomous moral decisions in later years.

However, at the secondary level, one might reasonably expect that the pupil in the first six years of schooling had absorbed, through varied but constant exposure, the moral norms of the cultural heritage through story, precept, and example. High school, it seems to me, is the time to cultivate more systematically the value norms of this heritage, especially as they are exemplified in the great works of the humanities. For these works are the abiding records of man's experiments with moral reflection and revolution.

This training by itself, however, although helpful and perhaps even necessary, is not sufficient for civic competence in a modern society. The knowledge of the various disciplines, both scientific and humane, has to be reorganized so that it becomes relevant to social problems. This reorganizing is learned by practice in studying social problems so as to determine what knowledge is relevant to them, what alternatives exist for their solution, and what the consequences would mean for the value hierarchy that the individual is creating: the schema that, in the long run, will define his Self. The arts of collective deliberation involve more than knowledge and good logic. They call for sensitivity to the values of others, to conflicts among value schemata, to syntheses that are more than compromises among the conflicting parties. This has been the great contribution of group dynamics to the deliberative process so essential to democratic thought and action. Unfortunately the affective factors in group deliberation have sometimes displaced the cognitive ones altogether.

I think it is obvious that what I have sketched as civic education is no more than general education; that wisdom is an achievement rather than a separate field of study. Wisdom comes as one tries to use the concepts of the disciplines and the insights of the arts to make the problems of life intelligible. The secondary school is the ideal time to pursue this sort of wisdom, because the adolescent likes nothing better then to talk about "life." At this time the full force of interdisciplinary thinking is brought home to the student. It is interdisciplinary not only because different scientific disciplines contribute their categories to mapping social problems, but also because the value schemata of the humanities are fragmented by the interests of various groups in the society. Only the individual mind can integrate these diverse interests into a value judgment and later into a commitment, just as only the individual can integrate the diverse categories of the various disciplines into a context in which the social problems stand revealed not only in their complexity but also in their fundamental unity.

This, it seems to me, is the prescription for civic education in the benign democratic technological society. If it resembles the liberal education reserved hitherto for the elite, then so be it. But will it be a benign technomeritocracy? It will be if the civic pattern of the technomeritocracy is an enlightened democracy, not a mobocracy and not a colony of efficient ants.

I realize that this kind of talk may elicit hoots of derision from those who do not believe that a technomeritocracy can be either benign or democratic. For them, the notion of general education for both the elite and the masses or, better still, for a single body politic, varying in many ways but always in degree rather than in kind, is either utopian or hypocritical. It is thought to be utopian because no society can be wholly benign and because machines, in being nonhuman, must inevitably be inhuman. It is thought to be hypocritical because the promise of education as a means to the good society is an "opiate" that diverts the wretched from making the revolution that alone will bring in the new and better society.

This brings us to the third dimension of schooling for a benign technological society—that of personal freedom and integrity. I shall not repeat all the talk about alienation that by now is no less tedious for being true. But I would point out that all social constraints alienate the individual at the moment that he does not feel like being constrained, and it is a melancholy fact that all revolutions substitute one set of constraints for another. Schooling should be concerned primarily with the kind of constraint that is imposed on the individual by his own incompetence, by the kind of emotional disturbance occasioned by inability to meet the demands of the social order—when he acknowledges these demands as valid and worthy. If John is emotionally disturbed, how much of his malaise is caused by his inability to function well as a citizen, a worker, a husband, or a parent? Some constraints are more rational than others, and some are more avoidable than others. Really humanistic education helps one to think clearly about proper and improper constraints, and merely rallying the young to the barricades as a way of lowering frustrations is not an adequate substitute for such thinking. The new humanism counsels revolt against the technological society; the really modern humanism asks the school for the intellectual resources wherewith to wrest individuality and integrity from the constraints of technology, and this is possible because technology creates possibility as well as constraint.

One of the more benign possibilities of a technologically well-developed society is the homogenization of the quality of individual life as well as of vocational and civic activity. In the quality of personal life, as in the latter domains, the differences among groups tend to become differences in degree rather than in kind.

There was a time when the noble classes did not regard the masses as capable of experiencing beauty, love, or romance. The masses needed no fine art, presumably because they had no fine feelings. The folk song, the folk dance, the folk play, and folk humor did well enough for the masses. Serfs and peasants led a simple life, and it was thought that their joys and sorrows were also simple. The general use of common folk as subjects for the fine arts is a relatively recent development.

The sharp discontinuity between the affective life of the elite and the masses was made plausible by the belief that the slave and the peasant lacked the imagination and sensitivity to reflect upon their experience. And one must suppose that if human beings exhaust their energies on sheer physical survival, there will be little left for imagination and sensibility. But first the middle-class citizen and now the workingman have been freed sufficiently from drudgery by technology to allow their latent powers of reflection and imagination to come into play about their identity, about freedom to leave their habitat, to experiment with sex, and to shake the foundations of the establishments they were reared to respect. The workingman can be as "human" as the elite, or more so, if he so chooses. For example, we do not think it impudent for the mass production worker to complain that he is not happy on his job; he too has the right to be bored.

But aside from occupational stresses and the psychological problems of adjusting to children, there are the tensions created by racial animosities, the changing role of the family, ethnic loyalties, and the cognate difficulties these bring. Beyond such specific inevitabilities, there are the more general clouds—of war, of pollution, of nuclear threats—that hide the workingman's sun as much as they darken the world of the occupants of the rungs of the ladder above him.

This is not to say that all distinctions of class have vanished or will soon vanish. There is still much talk of middle-class values, the ways of life of the upper middle class, and the doings of the rich and fashionable. Birth still counts. With the help of the columnists, the worlds of society and celebrity are still carefully distinguished. The Roosevelts, the Rockefellers, the Kennedys, the Nixons, the Johnsons—to speak only of some occupants of the political elite—are very distinguishable.

The point is that the homogenization produced by the technological society has rendered some of these social distinctions functionally irrelevant, however interesting they may be to social historians and the readers of gossip columns. Alienation, lack of communication, loneliness, anonymity, latent cruelty—these plague us all, whether we are high on the social scale or near the bottom. The differences are in the money, time, and education available to the individual to cope with the same set of problems. One of the positive results of the awakening to the plight of the poor and the black was the awareness of the similarity between the emotional problems of the "lower" classes and their social "superiors," for we may well have lapsed into the habit of thinking that they had somehow regressed to a state of quasi-animal simplicity and did not really feel the psychic blows that so easily wounded the sensibilities of those around them. The literature on black culture should have corrected this kind of ignorance; the need for pride in self endures even after centuries of slavery and pseudo emancipation; the need to belong to a group can never be wholly eradicated; the temptation to identify with the aggressor and to hate oneself is always lurking behind the next encounter. Ralph Ellison's *Invisible Man* made it impossible not to realize how thoroughly our categories of perception and interpretation are oriented toward whiteness as good and true and beautiful, with blackness as their opposites. Not all intelligent whites may subscribe to the dictum that black is beautiful, but they can no longer believe that black is ugly or that white is the only possible measure of the pleasing.

The old humanism argued that human happiness is a state of being that covers a whole lifetime, and that the human race has a heritage of thought and feeling regarding the conditions for happiness. More important, it has a tradition of reflecting upon those conditions. To induct the young into these traditions is to accept them into the larger human family and not merely into local groups, whether racial or national; to exclude them from induction is to exclude them from the family. Given the induction into the basic human themes, endless variations are possible; otherwise life degenerates into a conglomerate of variations in search of a theme.

And so it turns out that for happiness, as well as for vocational competence and civic adequacy, a fairly straightforward scheme of general education seems indicated. The great intellectual disciplines are the stencils that, when placed on raw experience, disclose their intelligible patterns. To think *with* these stencils is to think and feel as do the learned and the wise who have painfully wrought, criticized, and rewrought the heritage over centuries. How we learn to use these stencils and to integrate them is a matter of teaching strategy and tactics, and, although important, they are not fundamental.

The really new humanism will insist that these resources of mind and feeling should be used not only to understand and exploit the new technology for material power, but also for new life forms. There is no lack of freedom in the technological society, but it is not the old freedom of merely individual effort. The new freedom almost always involves collecting strength from other individuals so that freedom becomes effective through power.

There is no lack of opportunity for individuality in the technological society, but the new individuality is achieved through self-cultivation so that one can think for oneself and form tastes that can be truly justified by experience and reflection. The new society makes such self-cultivation amply available to those who have the self-discipline to avail themselves of it.

The social order need not be oppressive if we have enough intelligence and energy and education to keep the bureaucracy within bounds and our priorities straight. Courage, temperance, justice, spirituality—all of these are killed not by technology but by insufficient self-cultivation, insufficient imagination, and insufficient sensitivity. For individuality to survive requires great effort, and merely changing the system will not relieve us of the necessity of such effort. No system can force that effort, although some systems discourage it more than others. A benign technological society is possible if our education is directed vigorously and relentlessly toward giving individuals the intellectual resources to keep it benign. Among these resources the most neglected are the fine arts.

In the search for freedom and individuality, we gingerly mention art now and then, for the artist claims to exemplify this search in his own life. At least this has been the image of the artist nurtured in the romanticism of the nineteenth century. *La Bohème,* with its undernourished romantics living in garrets and fighting a crass materialistic culture, is still a widely accepted image of the artist. This life style has been co-opted by the counterculture, so that it is now impossible to distinguish the artist by his unconventional dress and behavior. Sexual freedom, drugs, contempt for the *bourgeoisie,* odd eating habits, are no longer the stigmata of the struggling and rejected painter, writer, or musician.

Why a materialistic civilization has not rendered its artists extinct is a puzzle. Even today the artist who can make a decent living by his art alone is a rare phenomenon. In the struggle for survival the aesthetic qualities would seem to have low value. Yet the artist has survived because there have always been crumbs from somebody's table to keep him alive. It may have been the table of the court, the church, the rich man wishing to adorn his residence, the statesman hoping to perpetuate his glory. But one way or another, the arts and artists have survived.

There are all sorts of theories to explain this persistence. It may be, as Plato thought, that the poet is the victim of a divine frenzy; it may be that the creation of art results from an inner drive that cannot be resisted by certain individuals; it may be that such persistence is one of society's ways of staying alive. Technology is one way of staying alive; art is another. Technology gives power to utilize energy of the environment so as to maintain human energy; art uses imagination to keep the past significant and the future promising. Since a civilization cannot persist without a significant past and a promising future, art has survival value.

In addition to the relaxing, amusing, celebrative uses to which art is put, it has a premonitory role that is more important still. Some insects have antennae wherewith to sense danger, and

I am told that some fierce animals—the rhinoceros is an example
—tolerate birds on their backs because they will signal danger.
Prophets, madmen, and artists have been cast in the same role.
Signs, omens, portents—tips on the shape of things to come—are
always important, and what computers and tank thinkers now
try to do scientifically, the artist has done through perfecting an
awareness of what in others is unconscious.

It is as if the artist, by being out of tune with his times, senses
earlier than others what might be wrong with them. This is his
redemptive force. Sensations that remain well below the thresh-
old of the conventional, well-adjusted consciousness impinge on
him vividly. Yet the vividness does not carry with it the kind of
definiteness about states of affairs that a scientific analysis pur-
ports to give. The image the artist projects may be sharp and
clear but not its import.

Long before Marshall McLuhan's disparagement of linear
logical discourse as a means of communication, long before the
problems of communicating solely by rational means overwhelmed the youth of the sixties, the Imagist poets had experi-
mented with the effect of showering the reader with vivid
images of feeling that formed an affective whole, although not a
logical one. The Joycean stream of language utilized connections
within conscious and unconscious experience. Before the conventional social forms of Victorianism broke up, the artist had
intimations that they would have to break up. He then imagined
a world in which they had broken up, or he imagined characters
for whom it had already broken up.

The impact of technology on society has been steady and
relentless, as Lewis Mumford, for one, has shown, but only in
the past few years have the people at large come to realize its
aesthetic consequences. Yet, by the end of the nineteenth century, Georges Seurat, Paul Signac, and other Impressionist paint-
ers were perceiving the world with a microscopic rather than a
naked eye. For the naked eye does not perceive separate dots of
color, even though the retina may so register the visual stimulus.
Pointillisme is the artist's rather gross version of the scientific
view that the truth of things is to be found by burrowing be-
neath the ordinary modes of perception. And the same sort of
intimation is found in the Cubists' rendering of the world in

more geometrico, not in Spinoza's sense of a deductive argument, but rather in the structural logic of space and matter in motion.

Technology revealed to the artists new modes of rendering images—from the motion picture to junk sculpture, not to speak of the innovations in architecture. But the artist has not used these new resources merely to celebrate science and technology. As one aesthetician has noted, the order of nature, which so closely controls the work of the scientist and the technologist, has been abandoned by the *avant-garde* artist, who uses the devices that modern technology has made possible. He uses them as a means of personal expression, and that often has meant the rejection of all externally imposed collective rules of order. He has used them even to abolish the conventions that separated the art object from the observer, so that one can now walk through sculptures and not merely around them. The audience is part of the play; the film is made by those about whom the film is. In other words, the clean, functional efficiency of the technological machine is satirized by the instruments it has devised. And contrariwise, there is a hard-edge type of painting that is developed with mathematical precision from the shape of a curve or the slope of a line or a systematic gradation of points. This has been interpreted as a kind of romanticizing of the efficiency of the industrial world masking its irregularities, goofs, and inefficiencies in practice. *

If one social role of the artist is to divine the future, then in a benign technological society he should be so regarded and valued. And this would mean that his freedom to create and to experiment is not restricted. It may also mean that he can never be fully liberated from the conflict with his social surround. A fat, complacent set of artists won't do.

But if society is to profit from the premonitory function of the artist, it cannot afford the great time lag in taking his warnings to heart. We waited too long to heed his admonitions about effects of technology on the aesthetic qualities of the environ-

---

* Don Denny discusses this conjecture at length in "Geometric Art and Romantic Vision," *Journal of Aesthetics and Art Criticism* 39, no. 2 (Winter 1970): 175–80. In the same issue is another apposite article, "Aesthetics and the Contemporary Arts," by Arnold Berleant, pp. 155–68.

ment. Serious art takes a long time to trickle down into the popular arts and thence into the consciousness of the public at large. So does serious science, for that matter. The length of these lags is the real indictment of our schools, and not that they are too slow in freeing every child and adult to do their thing. It is not from lack of freedom that we suffer but from a lack of self-cultivation to use freedom. A people well grounded in the intellectual disciplines and in the humanities would not be so backward in sensing what is going on about them and imagining the consequences. Although we have raised the general level of sophistication through schooling, the level is not yet sufficiently high to cope with the problems of living a civilized life even in a benign technological society. The impatience with study, with mastery, with induction into the cultural heritage, with structure and order of any kind; the rush to immediate gratification, the instant job, the heightening of any and every experience—these do not get the young ready for the demands of modern life.

Much has been written about the traumatic effects of rapid social and technological change, what Alvin Toffler has referred to as future shock. One gets the impression that the proper response to rapid change is to speed up the changes within the individual—to synchronize him with the social machinery, so to speak. As a means to synchronization, education readies the individual for change. What is the possible meaning of an education that would get the individual ready for change? What sorts of changes really upset us? And how does one get ready to match strides with change?

The unsettling changes are the unanticipated ones and especially the changes for which no reasons can be discerned, the capricious, arbitrary shifts that move us to say the world is crazy. If change were really random, the best way to prepare oneself for coping with it would be to follow one's impulse, that is, by becoming capricious—by countering disorder with disorder, chance with chance. Education for capricious living sounds odd, because one ordinarily does not think of capriciousness as requiring encouragement or tuition. Yet today the notion of education for capriciousness, for following impulse, is taken with utter seriousness. I refer to the spate of literature condemning the inhibitions imposed by the middle-class society. The Puritan ethic does discourage acting on impulse, whereas the counterculture, with true romantic insight, places its faith in the strength and intensity of impulse. Especially pure are the impulses of the young. Whatever the school can do to remove obstacles from impulse, the neohumanists argue, it should do forthwith. Hence the emphasis on cryptotherapy of various kinds, ranging from role playing to the staging of happenings in which everything is improvised. Let us hasten to join the lament about inhibitions and hang-ups. Indeed, if wisdom means anything, it is the ability to distinguish good from bad hang-ups; necessary from unnecessary inhibitions. The humanist tradition is no more and no less the search for that wisdom; giving up the search in favor of mere impulse is a rejection of that tradition.

The feeling of impotence in the face of great complexity either discourages action altogether or it encourages random action. For example, to the layman, the gyrations of the stock market are beyond understanding. He may own a few shares of stock, but to understand what makes them behave as they do would require as much reading and study as if he were obliged to manage thousands of shares. If this seems more bother than it is worth, he can make his decisions by ignoring the daily value of stock altogether and letting the market move where it listeth; or he can take the advice of a stockbroker or a friend; or he can follow hunches. Taking advice from a stockbroker is the most reasonable of these alternatives, but if our man makes very few transactions, he may regard consulting a broker as impractical. Or he may hit the jackpot in one of these transactions and attribute prescience to the broker, which—if the broker had it—would have made him a billionaire long ago.

Let us grant that there is a strong gambling component in the stock market, but there is a skill component also. A colleague of mine, upon retiring from teaching, studied the market faithfully and then, with a capital of $50,000, began to visit a brokerage house for several hours each trading day. Being conservative, he took small profits regularly, spread his losses, and kept his ears open. He didn't make a fortune, nor did he lose the $50,000. Between 1955 and 1967 he supplemented his retirement pension handsomely. He minimized the chance elements by as much knowledge as he could acquire. Form players at the race track try to minimize the hazards of chance in the same way. Of course, if the events do really occur by chance, as in the throw of dice or the turn of the card, knowledge—even of the laws of probability—is of little advantage in the short run.

However, not all change is purely random, and much of it follows patterns that can be discerned, are discerned, written about, discussed, and argued. One need not forever react in surprise. That the future does not replicate the past does not mean that one cannot learn something from the past with which to face the future. And once it is realized that the rate of change has been speeded up, should we be subject to future shock? And do we have to accelerate changes within ourselves in order to adjust to the increased rate of change?

In some ways the pace of life must be synchronized with the pace of events; if the world operates on the premise that one can fly from coast to coast in five hours, one cannot be successfully involved in certain enterprises and persist in using much slower forms of transportation. But the kind and degree of involvement permit some choice, and surely part of what is meant by self-development is a value hierarchy that helps us decide what we shall try to keep up with and what we shall allow to pass us by.

Change becomes manageable if there are principles that do not change—or change very slowly compared to the flux of events to which they are relevant. Education that facilitates adjustment to change is a search for general truths about nature, man, and society. Educational doctrines that condition pupils to believe that such general truths are myths leave them with nothing to confront change with except caprice and chance.

The most potent defense against future shock, therefore, is general education, a mastery of the sciences and humanities sufficient for the understanding of change. A benign technology, insofar as it has a rationale, can be understood and, within the limits of our intelligence and good will, can be controlled in behalf of the good life. Rational social institutions are one way of controlling it, but even with the best of institutions it will be left to the individual to negotiate the terms on which he will participate in the social order. The most benign technology will constrain him at many points and force him into collectivities for which he may have no taste, but with the resources of a general education, like a judo expert, he can often use the opponent's momentum to his own advantage.

I realize that the talk about a single-class benign technological society is open to misunderstanding. It may be construed as another utopia where men live in a kind of pre-established harmony dictated by the logic of mass production. To prevent such misunderstanding, may I note that, strictly speaking, a single-class society is a self-contradiction, for there is no point in talking about classes if there is only one of them. Quite properly, therefore, Marx used the term "classless" society for the happy state that was to follow the successful overthrow of the capitalistic system.

Perhaps a single-ladder society is a better designation for the society I am describing, and such a society is far from being a peaceful utopia. The traffic up and down a single ladder can be heavy and rough, more so than when it moves on a number of fairly distinct tracks. The struggle for money and power is no less ruthless for being carried on by people who differ in degree rather than in kind.

Nonetheless, in a single-ladder society, the relation between the competing individuals and groups is different from that which obtained between serfs and their masters or between the workingmen and the owners of the means of production in early modern times. In a multiclass society, the classes have different forms of consciousness and different ways of perceiving their natures, destinies, and relations to other classes and to the system as a whole. In a single-ladder society with many rungs there is competition and struggle, but there is also some unity of outlook, some integration of the value system, and for this reason I have argued that the same kind of schooling—however differing in amount and depth—will have to be provided for all citizens, on whatever rung of the ladder they happen to perch.

CHAPTER VIII

The Fallacy of Misplaced Relevance

The demand of a modern technological society on education is the implicit pivot around which controversies about schooling revolve. This is true even though the talk is often about something else. Much of the current controversy is bewildering because it is not clear whether the technological society is being rejected (as by some of the communes), or whether it is being accepted subject to certain changes in social arrangements (as by many of the political activists). Nor is it clear what changes are being urged. Are we being asked to make the social order more egalitarian or more elitist; more socialistic in its economics, more capitalistic, or more mixed? Above all, it is far from clear whether the parties to the controversies think of the new society as operating with the forms of consciousness—intellectual, moral, aesthetic—to which we have become accustomed for the last century, or with radically different ones.

But these questions are not the only ones that turn debates about education into general melees in which every combatant strikes out at any other who happens to get in his way. When, for example, we hear that the schools have failed, there are at least two lines of complaint that are presupposed, though not necessarily by the same plaintiffs.

Failure may mean that the schools have not produced in their pupils, or in some segment of the school population, like the children of the inner city, the learnings that they promised to produce. For example, regardless of the pronouncements of the philetics (those who believe that where schooling is concerned, love of children is all), children are expected to learn to read, compute, and write in a legible and, if possible, an intelligible fashion. These are the minimal expectations; accountability and performance contracts usually have to do with these expectations. Failure here means failure in didactics, that is, in imparting a given level of knowledge, skill, and attitude.

At a somewhat different level, failure means that the schools have not taught children how to think, or how to think critically, or how to think creatively. This is not necessarily a failure in didactics, but in heuristics. That is to say, the pupil has not acquired the habits of learning by discovery from situations designed to foster such discovery. Let us pass by, for the moment, the puzzle over what these kinds of thinking are and how one would test for their presence or absence. Let us also reserve the question as to whether heuristics can take the place of didactics, whether a form of thinking can take the place of learning content as such.

Currently a type of failure somewhat different from failures in didactics or heuristics is receiving attention from the critics. It is the failure of the school to instill joy into school children. First of all, just how many classrooms are joyless, and how many joyless classrooms are prisons? Statistics are dreary, but here they would help put the situation in perspective so that we could estimate its importance. But, for the sake of the argument, let it be granted that in many a classroom, from the elementary grades through college, one can see pupils drowsy and apathetic, or fidgety and restless. Now where is the failure in such class situations? It must be in the task, the teacher, the pupil, or in some combination of these.

As to the task, it must be admitted that not all school tasks are interesting, but some, like practicing the skills of the three Rs and getting facts straight, are important. Not only is it important to acquire the skill or the fact, but it is even more important to learn that drudgery diminishes with mastery. If the task is not beyond the pupil altogether, that he is not joyous when asked to perform it is no ground for declaring a crisis in the classroom.

Conversely, activities that pupils hail with glee may be more appropriate to the playground than to the classroom. Unfortunately, pleasure is not a reliable index either of the educational value of the activity or of the learning that accrues from it. Adolescents engaged in titillating encounters with the opposite sex in school will truthfully report that school is fun, but so may a good student who is doing well in physics. So whether or not joyousness is an appropriate criterion of schooling depends on what is generating the joy. As an accompaniment to growth in mastery, fun is fine; as delight with something other than mastery, perhaps not so fine.

The disciples of joy in the classroom, however, are less interested in the school task than in the teacher's pedagogy. Joylessness is blamed on the teacher's lack of imagination, creativity, sympathy, and intelligence. Little wonder, therefore, that many teachers themselves equate excitement in pupils with success in learning. The art of teaching, accordingly, is to excite the pupil. On one theory, the good teacher is expected to watch a pupil for any sign of a correct response (such as giving the right answer, looking at a book, or sharing his candy) and reinforce it on the spot with praise or money or whatever else he values. This is the Skinnerian method of operant conditioning, by which any task can be made rewarding to virtually any pupil. Another way of making school life joyous and exciting is for the teacher to allow pupils to do what comes naturally. While they are doing it, the teacher may join in as one of the group and be equally natural, or he may sneak in some "nonnatural" learning task.

The younger the child chronologically and mentally, the more this strategy is prescribed, but I find it hard to believe that any considerable number of schoolteachers would be ignorant of it. To use the strategy, however, a teacher has to know what pupils do "naturally." If ghetto children and suburban children do radically different things naturally, then teachers have to know this. If they do not, the resort to repression of what they regard as highly unnatural activities is almost inevitable.*

This conclusion holds at all levels of instruction. Pedagogy, as

---

* Aside from some physiological functions, what does a person do "naturally"? If natural does not mean "common to all members of the species," then it must mean whatever a child does without urging.

distinct from deep therapy, presupposes a common set of values about what is natural (wholesome, right, appropriate). Much of the joylessness in classrooms results when this commonality no longer exists.

A special form of this dissonance is registered in the cry for relevance. Like the words "relation" and "relating," "relevance" excludes virtually nothing, for everything mentionable is relevant in some sense to everything else that is mentionable.

As used in the criticism of schools, relevance is the degree of usefulness a course or an activity has for (1) the student's concerns about probable vocation, the community, the state of the world in general; and (2) his concerns about adjustment to peers, the opposite sex, drugs, parents, identity, and the like.

The assertion that X is not relevant may be mistaken, but when the charge is made by the student, there is a sense in which he cannot be mistaken. Or, to put it more accurately, if he cannot see the connection between X and whatever he wants it to be relevant to, then he is not seeing it, even though a thousand others may see it as clearly as a fly in the soup. It is like telling the hypochondriac that his ailments are imaginary; imaginary illnesses are accompanied by genuine pains. It takes psychic therapy to get rid of psychic pain, and considerable pedagogical ingenuity is needed to rid the student of his mistaken sense of irrelevance.

A college student enrolled in a fairly typical introductory course on the principles of economics complained that the course was irrelevant.

Question: How can economics be irrelevant?

Student: All he [the instructor] talks about are supply and demand, gross national product, marginal utility, and stuff like that.

Question: Don't you think these ideas are relevant?

Student: No.

Question: What sorts of things in such a course would you regard as relevant?

Student: We ought to be talking about the poverty in the black community or about Ralph Nader's fight for the consumer.

Now surely the student has a point. An economics course in which these subjects were not mentioned would be a strange one, to say the least, especially a course designed for undergraduates. But how should they be talked about in the course? One can "rap" about the Nader movement and black poverty, and one might take a position with respect to them. The instructor might supplement the discussions on these topics by supplying information gleaned from experts, and he might give the class interpretations that are more probable and subtle than the students could think up on their own.

Yet something is still missing, and it is precisely the element that the instructor is likely to think of the first importance, and that the student is likely to regard as irrelevant. It is the set of concepts and relationships, the generalizations and systems, that analytic economics has developed. Gross national product, supply-and-demand models, concepts of measurement of diverse variables—these constitute the cognitive skeleton that girds the dismal science. The instructor is likely to believe that these abstractions are the most useful part of the course and of what the student will learn. The student waits patiently or impatiently until these abstractions are out of the way so that he can get down to the black poverty and Nader's raiders. What, to the instructor, are examples or useful illustrations of economic principles are, to the student, the substance of the course itself. For the economics instructor, the appropriate learnings are not established until the student can analyze problems in terms of the principles; he assigns exercises to develop this ability, and he gives tests to determine whether the ability has been established. For the impatient student, such exercises are irrelevant to his own criteria of what is important, namely, an ability to become indignant about black poverty and enthusiastic about Nader's crusades. Little wonder, therefore, that such students resent examinations and grades that test their knowledge of principles rather than the depth of their indignation.

The student used as an example defined irrelevance as talking about X instead of talking about particular economic phenomena of interest to him. But a more militant student defines irrelevance as a paralyzing discrepancy between talk and action. For such a student, the irrelevance of the economics course lies not in talking about the wrong things, but rather in the fact that students and instructors are not involved in some project to relieve the poverty of the blacks or are not marching on a particular picket line to protest a particular abuse. For this type of student and his counterpart on the faculty, the university, to be relevant, must remove all army and business recruiters from the campus, abolish ROTC, withdraw its endowment investments from all corporations that are involved in any activity related to war or pollution, and cancel all research contracts that in any way further the ends of the military establishment.

An interesting variant of this complaint is what Myron M. Miller, product manager with the Singer Company, called the 55–45 Syndrome. Responding to Sterling Livingston's "The Myth of the Well-Educated Manager" (*Harvard Business Review,* January–February, 1971), Mr. Miller notes in that same periodical (May–June, 1971) that the analytically oriented graduate of a business school, imbued with management science, is admirably equipped to break down the positive and negative factors involved in a decision-making situation, say, 55 per cent positive and 45 per cent negative. Says Miller, "The 55–45 Syndrome is that characteristic of a person which prevents him from acting effectively" once he knows that the balance in favor is only 10 per cent. The man who overcomes the syndrome can make a decision with conviction and then "not look over his shoulder to agonize over his decision, or to do everything in his power to cover himself in case the decision is wrong."

These two views of relevance present more than a pedagogical difficulty. They reflect a difference in the concept of formal schooling, especially in the secondary, collegiate, and graduate years. The view of the academic guild is that the knowledge most worth studying is of principles having great generalizability. The opposite view ascribes most worth to experiences that resemble the tasks the student will frequently encounter outside school. According to the first view, for example, understanding thermodynamic principles is essential to the thorough understanding of a world in which automobiles and airplanes have a significant role; according to the second view, the ability to tune one's own automobile or adjust the carburetor is the most worth-while knowledge. Ideally, we all want both principles and skills; practically, there is never sufficient time for both. So we either elicit the principles as a by-product of perfecting the skills, or we practice the skills as an illustration of the principles. The results of the two different types of instruction are not the same. If one stresses principles, skill development is skimped; while from skill development a full elicitation of principles is unlikely.

There is much to be said on both sides of the controversy. The ability to deal with abstractions develops later than the ability to manipulate particular things and the names of things. And whatever else intelligence tests measure, they do seem to assay the aptitude of those tested for dealing with abstractions, especially abstract relationships. Since the mathematical relationships are among the most abstract, there is an impregnable belief that intelligence and the ability to do mathematics are either synonymous or very nearly so. In this regard the general opinion has not wandered far from that of Plato. Furthermore, since language also involves abstraction, and the scientific and philosophical uses of language involve a very high order of abstraction, language and mathematical facility are regarded as the intellectual tools par excellence. Consequently, the first duty of formal schooling is taken to be the development of these tools in the service of thinking at high levels of abstraction. Our entire machinery of scholarship and graduate education operates on these premises. Membership in the scholarly guilds is offered only to those who accept these presuppositions and who are willing to devote their lives as teachers to persuading others to do so as well.

Accordingly, although the doctrine that the very young should be taught via particular concrete things and happenings has been generally accepted, it has been accepted at the secondary level only for those pupils whose lower scholastic aptitude makes it unprofitable for them to persist with abstractions. Practically, it comes down to putting the pupils who can deal with abstractions into the college-bound curriculum and those who cannot into something less respectable intellectually—the vocational curriculum or the general curriculum or some other track not designed to terminate in matriculation at a four-year college.

For years some mathematicians, physicists, and historians on college faculties have derided educationists for worrying so much about the scholastically inept pupil. Indeed, much of the opprobrium that has been flung at the educationist and at public school teachers comes as a result of their concern with the learning difficulties of those who do not operate well with abstractions. The college professor could turn up his nose at the non-bookish pupil because he did not have to teach him—or teach him for long. The public school teacher had no such option. As some secondary schooling became compulsory for virtually all American youth, this problem became more and more acute, and the breach between the college faculties and the educationist widened. The college faculty member made a curious mistake: he assumed that those who were interested in the pedagogical problems of the noncollege-bound must themselves lack the intelligence and scholarly interests of the college-bound; that they were interlopers in the academic community.

By a species of divine justice, college faculty most vociferous in their contempt for the educationist who struggled to make the curriculum "relevant" for pupils of mediocre scholastic aptitude are now confronted—and in the best universities—with students who blame them for not doing what the educationist has been trying to do. Coming from the intellectually superior student, the demand adds insult to injury; it manifests a betrayal of the values of academe. For although the college student is quite capable of dealing with abstract principles, he is now disinclined to do so, because his interest is focused on more concrete things. Traditionally, such adolescents were told to stop their nonsense and get on with their coursework, term papers, and final examinations. Currently, at least some of the students say that they will do nothing of the sort and demand the right to design their own curricula and shape their own education.

How much of this revolt against the guild is merely a phase of the generation gap and a desire to embarrass the establishment and how much of it symbolizes a rejection of the Platonic value system is not easy to determine. To keep campus peace, college administrators and the faculty, in their quasi-administrative role, have made some moves in the direction of reform. Most of these changes have been in the direction of loosening requirements for various programs or giving the student more choices among the course offerings of the institution. These are pretty much surface shifts and will satisfy only those whose complaints are against the bureaucratic logistics of college life.

These surface reforms will not satisfy the rebels who reject the ideology on which the academic guild is founded and nourished, in short, the twin ladders of knowledge and reality, which, for Plato, rose from concrete particulars to universals that rendered the particulars intelligible. This rejection is not peculiar to this generation; Platonism has always had its opponents among those who felt that the particularity of the human individual should not be dissolved in the sea of principles and theories. This anti-intellectualism challenges the star system of professorial recruitment, the place of basic research, the importance of graduate instruction, and the Ph.D. degree—the basic values of the academic guild, not merely the logistics of study. It goes beyond the relevance of the course and reaches into the *raison d'être* of the school as an institution.

Insofar as relevance is relevant to schooling, it has to do with the strategy and tactics of instruction: the tasks chosen for the pupil to work at and the way these tasks engage the pupil and teacher. Bringing the abstraction level of the task into congruence with the abstraction potential of the pupil is the key to the strategy of instruction. The differences in abstraction potential of pupils in the elementary, secondary, and collegiate schools seem to require different mixes of what I have called didactics, heuristics, and philetics.

In the elementary school the strategy of instruction could be:

1. Didactics for certain skills in language, writing, and computation.

2. Heuristics, or the method of learning by discovery, for a varied assortment of items in history, mathematics, geography, and science.

3. Philetics to provide a psychologically healthy relationship between teacher and pupil, between pupil and pupil, as well as to promote conditions favorable to school attendance and learning.

This perspective represents a fairly broad consensus among educational theorists, if the extremists are left off, namely, the traditionalists, who regard all but didactics as a betrayal of the school, on one end, and the acute philetics, who regard nothing but love of children as relevant to instruction, on the other.

Given this strategy of instruction for the elementary years, that of the secondary school, grades seven through twelve, might be as follows:

1. Didactics for the key concepts of the basic disciplines: in mathematics, science, and the humanities.

2. Heuristics for discovering the ingredients of the dominant social problems of the culture, including the skills of collective deliberation about these problems.

3. Philetics for coping with the difficulties of adolescent adjustment to problems of schooling and personal development.

This general design makes didactics the central mode of instruction in the secondary school, and it does so on the supposition that at this level all adolescents will master—to their individual optimum capacity—the basic, key concepts of the intellectual and humanistic disciplines that supply the categorical maps that we call the human heritage.

This design has as its justification the fact that for a fairly large minority of the population high school will be the terminal of formal schooling, and, if the categorical system we call the cultural heritage is to be taught to all of our citizens, it had better be done in the secondary school. On the other hand, the emphasis on the discipline-centered curriculum in the secondary school presupposes that a highly differentiated system of vocational training will be available to all graduates of high school.

At the postsecondary level the instructional design might be as follows:

1. Didactics for those disciplines not studied in high school and for special skills needed in preprofessional or professional training.

2. Heuristics for synthesis of various disciplinary studies and for the study of the dominant social problems.

3. Philetics in the tutorial relationship between professor and students.

This pattern assumes that for the college student the amount of didactics can be reduced, and that what is needed can be supplied in part by means other than formal courses. For example, one might acquire information and skills by computer-aided instruction, by correspondence or independent study in the library, by laboratory experimentation, or by work "in the field." Many of the "alternatives" now being suggested are alternatives to didactics in general or to formal classwork in didactics.

As for the philetic component, it is generally agreed that a fairly long-term intellectual relationship between a faculty member and the individual student is desirable. It is further agreed that most college students do not ordinarily experience this desirable relationship in our large institutions. Some do in honors tutorial programs, but these are, as they say, statistically insignificant.

Unlike the buddy relationship, the tutorial bond is not between age peers, and unlike the teacher-pupil relationship, it is not that of imparter to impartee in a classroom setting. It is characterized by the intimate concern of the tutor for the personal intellectual development of the tutee. The tutor would ideally be thoroughly familiar with the tutee's reading, his attitudes toward intellectual and social problems, his progress in his various fields of study, his career plans. Because this type of relationship is so individualized, it is extraordinarily expensive. If, for example, a tutor's total academic load were to minister to fifteen tutees, meeting each one an hour a week, it would cost the university or college $1,000 per student per year (assuming that the $15,000 salary of the tutor was the only cost involved).

Compare this to the following costs when instructors teach classes of 100 students:

If a $15,000-per-year professor teaches four such classes each semester, he generates 24-times-100 student instructional hours in the course of a year (assuming each class meets three hours a week). This cuts the cost of each student hour to $6.25, and, if each student receives 30 such hours in the course of a year, the instruction costs less than $200. Multiplying the instructional cost by five is precisely what higher education cannot do in the light of other ancillary costs and their inflated prices. This means that the heuristic type of instruction abetted by tutorial philetics can be bought only if the amount of didactics is drastically reduced.

By drastic one must mean reducing the years spent on the campus by as much as 50 per cent or the amount of instruction by that proportion—without a corresponding reduction in the instructional staff. Since most of the nondidactic instruction in the sciences involves expensive laboratory facilities, not much savings can be anticipated in that quarter. However, some economies might be effected in space requirements, if the student body were reduced in size and if space for tutorial instruction could be combined with living and office space.

The new scheme would virtually eliminate from formal coursework all introductory and survey courses, the relatively inexpensive forms of instruction. Seminars, laboratory work, tutorials—the more expensive ones—would take their place.

The development becomes all the more plausible if it is the case that the improved high school curricula—largely in the didactics of the sciences—have absorbed much of what traditionally has been taught in the first two years of college. Is it the case? The answer is yes for a growing number of high school graduates who are admitted to college with as much as nine semester hours of advanced standing. Moreover, credit for many of the required introductory courses in college can be acquired by passing proficiency examinations. Finally, it is possible in many institutions to fill many requirements by independent reading plus a proficiency examination.

But there is an even more relevant fact to be considered, namely, that the average adolescent—and certainly the middle-class youth—absorbs a large volume of information from the communications media, from travel, and from books other than those supplied by the school. Even the advertisements, despite their obvious motives, willy-nilly inform the consumer of products and of the world in which they are to be used. One cannot advertise travel without informing the customer about geography and foreign cultures; one cannot extol the virtues of new building materials without introducing technological topics.

This mélange of information, generalization, principle, and theory is not well organized, but it is broad and varied. The school is asked to refine this agglomerate into orderly modes of thinking and feeling; to transform the un-co-ordinated mass of thought and attitude into retrieval systems that enable the thinker to put every sort of life situation into the appropriate perspective. For example, the average adolescent knows something about atomic fission and fusion, the supersonic speeds of aircraft and ballistic missiles. But if he is to think critically about the SALT talks on the limitations of strategic weapons, he will need an interpretive use of knowledge that, on the one hand, is far more organized than what he has, but, on the other hand, nowhere so detailed and complete as that of the specialist in nuclear weaponry. Acquiring a conceptual schema that enables the individual to use the various domains of knowledge interpretively, it seems to me, should be the goal of general education.

Given these factors and the rationale that I have tried to sketch in, one might argue that some such general scheme as the following would provide the kind of relevance that legitimately could be demanded of formal schooling.

1. Kindergarten and preschool: heuristics (learning by discovery) for everything and everyone; philetics (love) for everyone in all situations.

2. Elementary grades one through six: didactics for certain symbolic skills; heuristics for such knowledge as seems necessary to supplement that acquired informally through the media and the milieu; philetics for motivation.

3. Secondary school grades seven through twelve: didactics for the key concepts of the basic intellectual disciplines and the humanities; heuristics for the collective deliberation on social problems that require interdisciplinary or multidisciplinary thinking; philetics for emotional adjustment of adolescents to their peers, to society, and to themselves.

4. Higher education A (general education): heuristics to synthesize previous departmentalized study; philetics for rapport between faculty and student, and between student and student.

Higher education B (professional and preprofessional): didactics for specific knowledge and skill; heuristics and practical experience for everything else; philetics for acute maladjustment.

Should this scheme become the normal one, much of the just criticism of the educational system as a whole could be obviated. Rote learning and recall constitute most of the drudgery of schoolwork, but a legitimate reduction—never a complete elimination—is now possible and justifiable. Didactics could be concentrated in the secondary school but only for the *key* concepts and relations. Elsewhere necessary didactics could be relegated to computer-aided instruction or some variant of programmed instruction. The importance of this shift from didactics to heuristics cannot be overestimated, because the educational system has been erected on the supposition that if the school did not stock the minds of the young with retrievable skills and knowledge, nothing else would. This assumption is no longer needed—at least not in the simple form in which we have held it. And yet the degree to which we continue to operate on that assumption is revealed if one examines the routine of a typical college student.

Housed in huge complexes with thousands of other students, he spends a massive block of time in the logistics of grooming, feeding, sleeping, going to and from parts of the campus, waiting in lines for every sort of service.

Allowing some time for socializing, fooling around, and exercise, let us assume that the remainder of his time is spent in study. But what does he do when he studies? He goes to classes and listens and takes notes—if he cannot make arrangements to borrow a classmate's notes. Absenteeism from class can be as high as 25 per cent. He reads assignments in books and magazines. With the help of the ubiquitous Xerox, he obtains private copies of the assigned materials—to be read later. Instead of having to digest the material so that it can be encased in a few notes, he now either does not read it at all, or he underlines a few passages—hence much of what outside reading is supposed to accomplish is not accomplished at all.

The professor or lecturer is told politely but pointedly that if he could put his lecture on a mimeograph, it would save several hundred students from having to listen to him.

"But what will I do if my lectures are all mimeographed?" he asks.

"You can then use the class time to *comment* on the lectures."

"But why can't the comments also be mimeographed?"

"Well and good; then you can use the time to *discuss* the lecture with students."

"That sounds sensible, but what if a student says to another student, 'I can't come to class Tuesday. Will you take down the discussion and let me have it?' Couldn't the discussion be taped and then mimeographed and thus save everybody even more time?"

Two points are noteworthy in this colloquy. One is that college students spend most of their study time in didactics—gathering information from books or lectures; the other is that all heuristics tend to be degraded into didactics. The professor spends his lifetime producing things to read; students read what they must, take notes, take exams on what they are supposed to have read and heard.

The encounter in which the professor and his students mesh minds and personalities is rare. This encounter is the act of inquiry, with all the drama and uncertainty to which any real inquiry is subject. Insights as well as mistakes and false starts are unique events. The happy phrase, the clever turn of the argument, the indignations, the satisfactions—these constitute the living process of becoming educated. This, I suspect, is what high school students anticipate in higher education, and they are understandably disappointed when they find that they are expected to spend 90 per cent of their time continuing the didactics of high school.

Two factors militate against abolishing didactics as a major part of higher education. One is that the productivity of the encounter presupposes a mastery of content that comes only through didactics. The thrill and spontaneity of the football game do not betray the long hours of practice during the week, but this does not mean they can be eliminated. The spectacular vocal gymnastics displayed by the coloratura soprano were not improvised on the evening of the performance. One cannot blame students for wishing that the drudgery of rehearsals, practice, and didactics could be bypassed and that one could improvise the play, the game, and the educative process from moment to moment. In recent years some instructors have succumbed to this fantasy, and with undisciplined students they "rap" for hours under the illusion that they are being educated. It may be good therapy, and it is a heady sort of socialization; it may even result in good campus demonstrations, but it may not be education at all, for it does not necessarily or even usually enlarge the understanding or the imagination or the self-mastery of the participants. Education is accomplished when under the tutelage of the cultivated mind the less cultivated one achieves new insights or is provoked by a Socrates to make its own ideas clear and its own passions coherent with reality and with each other.

But there is another factor that keeps us from relegating didactics to its necessary and proper place—especially in higher education. It is the mistaken conviction that schooling must be a police action in which the student is frequently brought to trial to see whether he has spent his time profitably. How can one test this? By asking him to recall and recount what he has been asked to learn. We do this by tests and examinations, by term papers and assignments. In this game, faculty and students have no alternative but to convert all instruction to didactics. The professor must employ didactics or he cannot apply the required test. The student must reduce everything—from the simplest statement of a rule to the most brilliant class discussion—to something he can put down, study, and recall on cue or he cannot pass the test. Both faculty and student therefore unwillingly but inevitably conspire to transform the process into a product.

And what perpetuates this tragicomic act are the moral and social implications of schooling, not the educational ones at all. Why must we test and police the student? Because society has accorded him temporary freedom from toil; it is investing its hard-earned dollars, as the saying goes, in his future service to society, and in doing so, it is withholding this investment from others. Social justice demands that the student do his part and be made *accountable* for having done it. The undergoing of drudgery is taken as a proof of moral rectitude, and for this reason the system continues to operate on the principle of didactics.

Let me reiterate the absolute indispensability of didactics somewhere in schooling, and let me swear by the gods that grading and testing are not bad in themselves. But didactics can be tested (as in computer-aided instruction) automatically by the student himself and without the moral implications of a police action. Even the heuristic encounter can be judged, but not in a trial with courtroom overtones. As a matter of fact, the genuine heuristic encounter eliminates quickly and effectively those who cannot participate.

As long as our society cannot afford to give everyone as much schooling as he might wish, some selection will be not only necessary but socially just. Once we get rid of the dominance of didactic tests, the educational tests may be allowed to help with the selection and elimination of those who cannot profit from the educational process. It may also herald the day when the putative certification of people by artificial standards can be eliminated. In professional education, real work samples can be used as tests; general education will not be used for vocational certification at all, and it should not be, because if general education is successful, it will be its own reward and witness. General education results in thinking and feeling with the resources of the learned and the wise. The generally educated person provides his own test by self-cultivation; the test of the process is the process itself.

The reform of the educational system, or, if you like, the system of schooling, can be viewed more profitably as the redistribution of didactics, philetics, and heuristics in the various segments of the system rather than as a battle between the bad guys of the Old Establishment and the white knights of the counterculture. There is reason to believe that the amount of time allotted to didactics in the schools will be decreased, and that heuristics and philetics will be increased. For one thing, when appropriate hardware is perfected and mass-produced, much of the didactics can be done at home through the television set, especially if video cassettes fulfill their promise. Reading, writing, simple computation, history, and literature, as well as music and painting, may be so interwoven with the viewing of variants of Sesame Street that the child will acquire much of what the school now tries to achieve formally as unwittingly and informally as he does the use of his native tongue.

We can also expect that developments in drug therapy and neurosurgery, including brain stimulation, may be used to control the emotional factors that figure so largely and yet so darkly in learning. Drugs are already being used to sedate hyperkinetic children. Whatever else may be the aftermath of the drug binge of the sixties and seventies, the mind-modifying potentialities of drugs will not be forgotten. Early childhood education may well become a specialty in pediatrics.

We need not confine this science fiction tale to young children. One wonders whether the FBI and the other governmental agencies can refrain from using these and similar tools as opiates of the people. And all this without recourse to genetic tampering, which cannot be ruled out, although we are told that possibility is still decades away. So there is plenty of danger as well as opportunity in doing the rational and technological "thing" with didactics and in leaving more and more didactics to the mercies of the media and the milieu in general.

When one does consider these possible consequences, remote as some of them may seem, what is to be said about genuine relevance in education? Superficially it has something to do with vocational success and social issues, but that is not where the relevance problem lies. It lies in effecting a congruence between the entire school system and the social order in which the young of today will spend their adult lives. Relevance means the power to think and feel appropriately in a highly interdependent, all-embracing technological society, a technomeritocracy, which creates untold potentialities for good and evil, which provides the necessary conditions for any life at all on this planet, but not the sufficient conditions for the good life.

What knowledge, what skill, what forms of thought and feeling will the individual need to cope with these potentialities? What resources of character and competence will he need to wrest from this system that freedom and individuality without which we cannot and perhaps would not want to define humanity? My own answer, reiterated at various points in this book, is a simple, although not an easy, one. If I repeat it once more, it is only because there is a widespread expectation that only a cataclysmic revolution can make the system relevant.

Let us take, for example, the fact that although our population has been increasing at the rate of about 1 per cent a year, our energy consumption has been growing six times that fast. If, as is generally conceded, fossil-fuel resources will not be adequate to such a growing demand, and if nuclear power may have to be utilized, there will be ecological and economic side effects that cannot be fully adumbrated, but that, we can be sure, will only add to the ecological troubles now plaguing us.

Clearly, one possible solution is to reduce our energy uses by cutting out the use of electricity for all sorts of gadgets (including toothbrushes, can openers, and the like) or by restricting the use of the automobile. Laws can be written that will nudge us in these directions. If electricity prices are allowed to rise and if automobiles are heavily taxed, consumer habits may change. This may, to be sure, create new problems.

However, if we ask the schools to do something about this behavioral adjustment or readjustment, it seems we are asking them to create a public whose intellectual competence will enable them to understand the alternatives and their consequences. This is no mean order in itself, and the schools are very far from filling it. But, in addition, the task calls for a change in the value hierarchy of the American people, and in a way this change is far more important than the cognitive one.

But what can the schools do to change a way of life that is centered on uses of energy at ever-greater rates? They cannot compete with the mass media in producing short-range changes of taste; they cannot compete very well with fashion, either. If they can do anything, it is to make available to the young exemplars of the good life as they have developed through the ages. Inasmuch as each age projects its value problems into its religion, philosophy, and art as well as into its politics and economics, the study of cultural history is the most relevant of all school activities insofar as formation of attitude is concerned.

In studying the history or the products of a culture, one finds oneself running through experiment after experiment with diverse forms of the good life. In the arts these experiments achieve vividness by virtue of their aesthetic form; in history and philosophy they are given clarity by the intellect. In time the student comes to "perceive with" these categories of feeling and value, just as in time the student comes to think about the physical world with the categories of the sciences.

He may, indeed, as do many intellectuals, like Leslie Fiedler (*New York Times Book Review*, May 23, 1971), consciously try "to disavow all vestiges of the humanistic tradition that persist in my thinking." But persist in his thinking it will, and, if Fiedler succeeds in rejecting the tradition, it will be a far different denial from that of one who never participated in it.

Thinking and feeling *with* these products of the living tradition is the unique contribution of the school to the value crisis of our time—and perhaps of every time. I cannot summon the kind of evidence that will convince either the methodological skeptic or the authentic Philistine of the value of studying this tradition, and perhaps it is a mistake even to try. For the methodological skeptic does not act on his skepticism (as Hume admitted), and the true Philistine, being beyond tuition, can only be endured. Where, for example, are the merits of the materialistic and spiritualistic ways of life explored, compared, and contrasted? What epoch in civilization has not produced reflections on this theme? What is civilization, if not the reflection on the sort of life that in the long run gives men the greatest satisfaction? There is merit in discovering some of these judgments for one-self, but a world in which each one of us would have to redis-cover these principles for himself anew would be like one in which each one has to rediscover the corpus of science before he can use machinery. Certainly it would be a world in which schooling would be superfluous. Much of the soul searching over the work of the school that goes on today is little more than the shock of rediscovering that once upon a time an institution was invented in which young people learned *vicariously* to live as civilized human beings, so that they would not have to redis-cover everything for themselves. The attempt to reduce school-ing to reality—whatever that is taken to mean—is about as far as one can get from progressive education; it is regression at its worst.

The issue is pretty well summed up in Cardinal Newman's claim for a liberal education, namely, that it aims at

raising the intellectual tone of society, at cultivating the public mind, at purifying the national taste, at supplying the true principle to popular enthusiasm and fixed aims to popular aspirations, at giving enlargement and sobriety to the ideas of the age, at facilitating the exercise of political powers, and refining the intercourse of private life.*

Of course, the claim has never been made good so far as the public mind and national taste are concerned. It has been made good by individuals here and there, freed from the exigency of money-making and practical affairs. Yet, as Newman points out, this goal of education does not impugn the popular enthusiasm and popular aspiration. There is a faith—and, I believe, a justi-fied one—that the collective enthusiasms of men and their aspi-rations are valid; they define the human race and human nature.

---

* John Henry Cardinal Newman, *Idea of a University* (New York: Long-mans, Green & Co., 1927), pp. 177–78.

Education can only refine these enthusiasms and give them intellectual warrant. However, this does not make education otiose, any more than polishing rough diamonds or refining crude oil are otiose. True egalitarianism does not, therefore, mean a return to universal crudity on the grounds that all differences are hierarchical and invidious—but rather a faith in the benefit for all of the refining process that education constitutes.

I do not mean to play upon the truism that the new leisure for the masses makes it possible for them, for the first time in history, to choose the forms of thought and feeling for their own lives that the *aristoi* alone were privileged to do in other epochs. The truism is correct. A life of high quality is now possible for millions—if they choose to exert the effort to utilize the resources of education. It has always required effort—from the playboy as well as from the humble charity scholar.

Nevertheless, one can go beyond the truism to foresee the possibility of the education of the masses for another reason. For the decades to come may well confront us—as they are indeed now beginning to do—with the choice not between crudity and refinement, but between that measure of freedom we still associate with democratic societies and the utter slavishness that a technologically mature society in the hands of totalitarian governments virtually insures.

The saving faith for the future, one may conjecture, is that of the common human being who believes he can overcome the threat of automatization—the death of the self. Once this self is gone, once the will to preserve it is gone, nothing remains, for not only humanism but humanity itself will have become extinct.

I happen to believe that we shall not line up our schools with the social reality until we understand how the meanings of liberty, equality, and fraternity changed as our society moved from an agrarian, small-village, face-to-face community to a noncommunal urban complex. Freedom, equality, and fraternity are no less valid ideals today than they were in 1776 or 1789, but *real* equality, *real* fraternity, and *real* freedom imply equal access to knowledge and power that freeholders and small entrepreneurs once approximated but which characterize few communities in our time.

Today the image of the individual citizen with a musket defending his liberties, personal and political, is a tragic anachronism. Even the devices of the petition, the assembly, the mass demonstration, are anachronistic. Today, as Ralph Nader and others are saying, change comes through knowledgeable attacks on corporate and bureaucratic power through a collective counterpower. Many of our citizens are still bewildered by these new rules of democratic participation, and the schools are perhaps most bewildered of all, for in their proper veneration of the New England town meeting as the paradigm for democracy they have forgotten that New England villages are now outside the mainstream of our society.

I doubt that the public, general or sophisticated, realizes how deeply the small-group, face-to-face ideal of democracy is ingrained in the ideology of the public school. If John Dewey influenced American education, it was not through introducing a new way of learning the academic subjects, but rather in that he persuaded the most articulate educational theorists of the years between 1930 and 1960 that (1) learning academic subjects was not the primary goal of schooling; and (2) the method of problem solving so successful in the sciences could be adapted to group thinking about social problems. The first doctrine never really affected American school practice very much; ironically, it was not until the late sixties that it was revived as a protest against all formalism in education—at the college as well as at the kindergarten level. The second doctrine, however, was far-reaching in its influence, because the social studies curriculum became oriented to the discussion of social issues by pupils acting as a quasi-political decision-making group. The group was led to define the problem, to suggest hypotheses about diagnosis and remedy, and finally to "vote" on the solution. The teacher and books were resources for information and criticism relevant to the social issue under discussion.

Hence, the Deweyan notion of the school as the ideal community, the purified community, where the community of the small village, threatened by urbanization, would be preserved for the young. But, of course, that kind of small-group deliberation found little counterpart in the real world—a world in which the parties to a social problem were not even approximately equal in knowledge and power; where problems had technical dimensions that only experts could understand; where solutions had consequences so far-reaching that only disciplined minds could comprehend and assess them. In such situations, discussions by men and women of good will can go only so far: witness our well-intentioned but relatively impotent endless discussions of the problems of our day. For grass-roots, small-community democracy to amount to anything, the participants have to go well beyond their grass roots and local concerns. This the schools do not yet fully understand; their faith in face-to-face discussion —no matter by whom—is still very strong.

How relevant, then, is education? It is relevant at its deepest level only insofar as the exfoliation of the human potential—for humanity—is its goal. In this the new humanists are obviously right. They are wrong only in believing that crudity, raw feeling, and raw aspiration are the touchstones of true humanity. On the contrary, it is the refined versions of these feelings and aspirations that are the proper yardsticks for relevance.

Our salvation does not depend on finding "new values" or in founding new institutions. But it does depend on making most of our population sufficiently sophisticated to be clear about the promises and dangers of a mature technological society. Education is relevant if it enables us to wrest freedom from the interdependence of such a society; if it opens avenues for individuality in the rigid uniformities of mass production; if it reveals the moral dimension in the impersonality of system.

What are schooling's resources that will enable us to cope with this new society? What others are there besides the sciences and humanities?

CHAPTER IX

Paradoxes Come Home to Roost

If one could simply say that tomorrow will be something like today only more so, the future would be easy to foretell. It is tempting to assume that current trends will develop in the same direction: rising prices will continue to rise, a winning pitcher will continue to win, a bad boy will get worse. Sports writers are saved from being bored to death by upsets: the winning pitcher loses the crucial game; the favorite impoverishes his backers at the race track. The stockmarket takes a sudden drop, and the bad boy is elected mayor. In education this kind of extrapolation led us to expect that the rising school population of the fifties would continue to rise indefinitely; that the scarcity of Ph.D.s in the early sixties would continue through the seventies; that there would always be a teacher shortage.

There are just about enough upsets to warrant a fairly safe prediction that a trend will peter out or even reverse itself. For one thing, human needs do not always proliferate indefinitely. As the means for fulfilling them improve, urgent needs become mild itches. Some problems, moreover, are merely aggravated with every new step taken toward solving them; the solutions are self-defeating and become part of the problem. The increase of parking spaces and thruways merely adds to traffic congestion, while advances in medicine prolong old age and postpone its miseries. In a different domain, accelerated searches for novelty are almost sure to guarantee that nothing will remain new for very long. The *avant garde* has already committed suicide, according to some observers. For many trends, therefore, it is interesting and often safe to predict unexpected results.

In education, one example was mentioned in the previous chapter, namely, in the future egalitarianism in education may mean universal elitism. On the face of it, this is a self-contradiction, because elitism loses its meaning if everybody is elite. But, of course, paradoxes only seem to contradict received doctrine. That every educable child shall be given the chance to partake of the sort of schooling once reserved for the social elite is not only quite possible but, as was argued, may be necessary for the preservation of some semblance of democracy in a modern technological society.

Another paradox lurks in the analogy between the complexity of society and the complexity of education. It seems only common sense to predict that as our social order becomes more complex and interdependent, the schooling needed to cope with it will also become more complex and interrelated. The highest crime in educational circles is to "oversimplify," so that when the experts gather in conference, they have a happy time listing the factors that "cannot be overlooked." Because they overlook nothing, they see nothing, and their only solution is to confront complexity of phenomena with complexity of response: they confront confusion with confusion. The euphemism for such confusion is "cultural pluralism" or "alternatives." This argument rests on the abiding faith in the principle that like causes like. Of course, effects do not merely repeat their causes, for then nothing new would really happen. Even a new combination of old elements produces something new—if no more than the quality of the new whole, which is never identical with the qualities of its several ingredients.

The usefulness of formal education lies in the possibility of cognitive economy. Schooling obviates the need to deal separately with all the unique particulars that make up the real world. In educational theory, the possibility of cognitive economizing is called the problem of transfer. Baldly stated, it argues that learnings at time t in circumstances c can be utilized in circumstances c' at times t', t'' . . . t^n. To explain this possibility,

Edward L. Thorndike, a pioneer in educational measurement, asserted that the transfer was possible insofar as c and c' had elements in common. Thus, learning to spell "babies" would transfer to the spelling of "ladies" and "rabies," but might lead also to the inference that the singular of "prairies" was "prary." Given enough identical elements in various situations, learnings would transfer. Because this explanation explained transfer away, Charles H. Judd advanced the theory that transfer takes place through generalization, that is, we react to c' as we do to c, if and only if c and c' are instances of the same law. Thus, knowing the law of oxidation, we can figure out why iron rusts and oily rags burst into flame.

These two interpretations of transfer reflect about as well as anything can the two poles from which the human mind and education are viewed. The Thorndike view envisions the mind as a computer; a vast bank of connections programmed from the outside by outsiders who presumably are also programmed from the outside. Education consists of programming the pupil with precisely those connections most likely to be encountered in nonschool life. Accordingly, under the Thorndike influence, studies were made to find the 10,000 or so words most frequently used by American citizens in their correspondence, and pupils were drilled on them. Teachers were urged not to teach English grammar, but rather to practice those locutions that were most likely to cause trouble. This was consistent with the Thorndike view of transfer, which is, that there wasn't any. If the connection is built in, it will function; if it is not, then the organism will have to go through trial and error to build a successful connection.

The Judd view regards the mind as a logician, although perhaps not a very rigorous one. A law or principle covers a multitude of instances that vary in many, but not in all, ways. The intellectual act is to see in what *relevant* sense they are alike—oily rags, rusting iron, and burning wood. It is the mind, as a whole, as an entity, that acts, and to the mind is attributed the ability to achieve insight into whatever ingredients had been programmed into consciousness by experience.

The mystique of the intellect, the veneration of abstraction, especially mathematics, rests on the Judd view of mind, which, in turn, is a version of the Platonic view of mind. The elegance of the mind's operations, combined with an admiration for this sort of elegance, made it precious and honorific. Only the divine inspiration of the poet or the prophet could compete with it, and, for Plato, such inspiration could not compete successfully as a guide to life.

The demystification of mind is itself an intellectual feat of no mean order, for it, too, is a theory invented by theorists. That the debunkers do not hesitate to ascribe their theoretical achievements to themselves rather than to their programmers is an inconsistency with which we must learn to live. At least 50 per cent of the intellectual enterprise is devoted to debunking itself; it would languish if this were not the case. The current revolt against the academy, against formal study, against schools adopts this devaluation of the intellect as a political program, not merely as theory. Taxpayers refuse to vote bond issues, and legislatures slash university budgets.

It would seem reasonable that as the complexity of life increased, the premium on principles would rise, for principles, like formulas, enable us to manage large quantities of particulars with the minimum of cognitive strain. Strangely enough, there is a good deal of resistance to this. I suppose men are either Platonists or foes of Platonism; either they plump for the forms of existence or for its particulars as the ultimate realities; or, as another dichotomy would have it, men tend to be realists or nominalists.

Most of the objections to abstractions (principles or forms or formulas) stem from the fact that we have to act with and on particulars and not with their conceptual equivalents. People do not suffer from arthritis, but from a particular discomfort in particular joints, and, of course, physicians have to treat those particular joints and pains and not the concept "arthritis." And because action is almost always confronted with predicaments that are too complex to fit into neat formulas, men of action are suspicious of doctrines and doctrinaire solutions. Hence politics has been defined as the art of the possible, and pragmatic thinking is essentially a way of deciding in a particular situation on that action that will generate the maximum good with the least resistance. This is in itself a principle of sorts, but it is the principle of least principle.

The dangers in this attitude toward principles are manifold. In the first place it would be horribly inconvenient to deal with every particular as if it were a unique individual, say, as a person or as a work of art. For example, a physician could not prescribe asprin for arthritis, only this tablet and that tablet. Indeed, since no two tablets would be identical, he would, in accordance with his loyalty to particulars, label each tablet and have it administered at a given time. The possibility of intelligent action lies in the permission generalizations give us to ignore certain features of particulars in certain situations. For example, we are told that in taking aspirin we can ignore the name of the maker on the tablet, since all aspirin has the same chemical properties. Further, this attitude toward general principles may lead to abandoning principle altogether or to acting from wrong principles, but the important point for education is that it engenders a suspicion of theory "on principle," in short, a suspicion of all intellectualism. The reasoning goes something like this: if life is too rich and complex for doctrinaire solutions, then should not the school stick as close to life as possible and thus not waste time with undue abstraction and formalism?

Many of the current cries for relevance amount to no more than a flight from formalism and a return to the concreteness of nonacademic life. Why not have *real* businessmen rather than professors of business administration teach prospective businessmen? Why teach analytic skills to managers who will "succeed" in their firms not by ideation but rather by the courage to make bold decisions in spite of statistical risks? What has the study of theology to do with a humane ministry? Why read books when the community cries for bread or for love? As one of the apostles of the counterculture puts it: "Do it."

Another form of deintellectualizing schooling is the move toward what is now referred to as affective learning. The evils of the world are traceable, according to this theory, to a lack of love and a lack of sensitivity. Thus, in 1970 the Ford Foundation granted nearly $500,000 to the Laboratory of Confluent Education, at Santa Barbara, and to the Center for Humanistic Education, at the University of Massachusetts, to experiment with ways of counteracting the alienation of students by engaging their feelings and attitudes in the learning process.

But is it obvious that alienation will be counteracted by fiddling with people's feelings? Is not some alienation a function of
being mistaken about the nature of the reality from which one is
alienated? One's judgment about a parent or spouse from whom
one has become alienated can be just plain wrong. And this
might also be true if the object of alienation were one's own self;
changing one's feeling about this self might not effect a reconcil-
iation with it. And is alienation per se necessarily bad? If one's
self is a mass of lazy, sloppy, unkind thoughts and feelings, it
might be wise to become alienated from it. Of course, this kind
of self-examination requires more than sensitivity training; it requires knowing the difference between what is worth keeping
and what is not. If we take some of the talk about sensitivity
training literally, such a distinction seems to have no place in it,
for salvation comes from "accepting" whatever one finds with a
healing cheerfulness.

Does the commitment of the school as an institution dedicated to theory separate the school from action altogether? No,
not altogether, but it does restrict the school to the principles of
action rather than to action itself. In vocational education, the
school supplies theory that can be applied directly to the classes
of future actions by the practitioner. In general education, however, the school supplies the sort of theory and principles that
enable their possessor to understand problems in order to recognize the sort of knowledge that would be relevant to them. This
sort of knowledge has been called interpretive or perspectival
knowledge, and, although it may make action more intelligent, it
may also impede action insofar as it promotes reflection. This
type of paralysis is standard for the academic. He recognizes it
as a defect, but there is little he can do about it, except, of
course, analyze it properly.

Having said all this, we nevertheless are confronted with the
paradox that *the more complex the society and its problems, the
simpler the curriculum for general education must be.*

For what are the alternatives?

One could particularize the school so that it trained people
only for the particular tasks they were likely to encounter in life.
In a complex social order the number of such tasks is so large
that no school could hope to do more than sample a few of

them. But no less important is the impossible burden of choice particularization would impose on the school. Take consumerism. Surely this constitutes a basket of real tasks that confront the citizen. Suppose the school were to train children to be good consumers by using real-life situations. What tasks shall we select, and what texts shall the school use? Those issued by the U. S. Chamber of Commerce or by Ralph Nader's associates? Shall the schools habituate the young to buy new autos annually or to keep the same model until it disintegrates or even to renounce automobiles altogether? Teaching the young to be good consumers means advocating that they trust one source of information rather than another, but which source is trustworthy is a matter of theory, a theory about what is the good life and the proper priorities to set in our spending habits. So either the school commits itself to principle, to abstractions, to formulas or it brings its role as an educational agency into question. This is not only a theoretical dilemma, but a very practical predicament as well.

Or one could say that the school should merely inculcate habits of inquiry or attitudes that will generalize to a wide variety of particular tasks. This, however, means simplifying the curriculum, although not necessarily intellectualizing it. Encounter "group thinks" and "group feels" could be concrete, immediate, and nonintellectual and yet might transfer to other phases of life. This seems to be the alternative for which the new humanists in education are opting. Whether or not it is adequate to the stresses generated by a technological society is another matter; I do not think that it is for reasons that cannot be repeated too often, or at least as often as they are overlooked or simply forgotten.

Not only is the realm of particular existents too vast and complex for our minds to manage, but knowledge itself is proliferating so rapidly that no man can be at home in more than one of its compartments. So it is knowledge about knowledge that provides the only good handle to it. But knowledge about knowledge comes to what? Well, the objects of that knowledge are the structures of the various disciplines and especially the structures of the basic disciplines; they constitute the principles of inquiry in these disciplines. Not all specifics can be avoided, not all facts can be evaded, but some facts and concepts support more knowledge than others. In this sense, physics is more basic than thermodynamics; chemistry is more basic than the applied science of nutrition. Further, the total number of *indispensable* concepts must be kept as small as possible. Educators and the masters of the diverse disciplines (especially philosophers of science) have the job of judging which concepts, which structures, which analyses, are most fruitful for generalization. And if the academics who should have been collaborating on this task had not dissipated their energies in fighting for control of teacher education, for publicity, for research-and-development grants in the past decade, we would not now be trying to reform our school systems by grant-inspired trial and error.

The point is, however, that such a consensus would make possible a fairly simple curriculum—simple in principle and general design, yet rich in the diversity of materials and methods by which it is readied for instruction. Once the consensus in principle is achieved among educators, the public will breathe a sigh of relief. Citizens are tired of having to educate educators; of being asked to decide in committees and P-TAs what their children should study. Their unhappiness with the public school, shared by pupils and teachers, is caused less by the school's authoritarian "oppression" than by its lack of intellectual authority, its failure of nerve, its attempts to be all possible things to all possible children. What is one to do with a school system that at one and the same time justifies its procedures by such diverse reasons as teaching children to read, teaching them to love their fellow men, teaching them to hate those of their fellow men who presumably hate them, teaching them to think as little scientists, teaching them to think as little statesmen, teaching them to question everything; and yet teaches them "sound values" that presumably are not to be questioned—at least not by them? On what is the pupil evaluated? Knowledge, skill, an exhibition of excitement, creativity, serenity; on how well he adjusts to the middle-class culture; on how well he accepts the counterculture?

Understandably this diversity of expectations, goals, ploys, and strategies contributes to the insecurity of pupils, teachers, parents, and administrators, while exasperation waxes in school boards and legislatures. Yet it is not diversity as such, but rather *mere* diversity, a congeries of doings without a unifying design, that causes the mischief. And, as one might expect, such mindless diversity reduces flexibility, for mere diversity ties us to unrelated particulars demanding unrelated responses to each. Experience accumulates but is not cumulative.

Consensus on the key concepts in the sciences and the humanities, on the symbolic skills needed to acquire and manage information, on the strategies for using knowledge in the understanding of life is not impossible to achieve. It already exists latently in the designs of the intellectual disciplines, and it can be the unifying form of the curriculum for general education. Within this form heuristics, didactics, and philetics can be adapted to a wide variety of particulars.

All of which may serve as a reminder of the thesis that the complexity of the world does not always necessitate a corresponding complexity in our schools.

Let us turn now to another instance of the dangers of simple extrapolation on a current trend. A technological society inevitably depersonalizes many of its activities. For many societal purposes, we *are* our Social Security numbers. Doubtless Saint Peter will have our dossiers within seconds after the last breath. Mass production methods fragment our jobs so that they no longer bear *our* mark, not even our Social Security numbers. Our privacy is now shielded by a very permeable membrane; some say that privacy is a myth, that credit bureaus and the FBI know all. The fight to maintain individual rights becomes awkward, because it is becoming increasingly difficult to say what is individual about any of us—except, of course, our Social Security numbers.

The pleas for leaving individuals free to do their "thing" and the exhortations to be concerned with our fellow human beings collide. Liberals have always been embarrassed when asked to draw the line between these equally human and humane impulses, and the counterculturists, although they are not especially embarrassed by logical inconsistency, cannot escape its consequences. The paradox is mitigated somewhat if we look at individuality as an achievement, not as a given. Part of genuine individuality is a style of relationship with our fellow men. This can be the result of reflection and cultivation, or it can be the result of stereotyped responses. It can, of course, be the result of caprice, impulse, and spontaneous sentiment. What education can do for individuality depends on how one wants to go about building it. The same may be said about the fate of individuality in a technological society in which there is a steady pressure for collective uniformity.

If we now posit the continuance of this trend, where will it end? Orwell and others have pictured us becoming proles in a society of robots, governed by a totalitarian apparatus of Big Brothers or Big Fathers who can control thought, feeling, and action and who can make us like it in the bargain.

There is enough probability in the continuance of this trend to disturb even the fully jelled complacency, but what if the trend reversed itself? Suppose, for example, that as a man's work becomes more and more depersonalized there comes a time when he no longer identifies what he is with his work—when he is literally only a hired *hand*. His mind and soul are free to wander elsewhere. But at that point, would it not be better to have a robot doing a robot's work? So now there are no robotlike men workers; there are only machines. Hence, the depersonalization of work is halted—a trend is changed. Or if the worker remains on the job, the fact that it asks no more of him than his hand and a few reflexes *frees* him from his work and *for* other things.

Take another example. The strength of mass production depends on one model being replicated thousands and thousands of times. But a mass technological society also depends on mass demand, and unlimited uniformity of product will dampen demand. So variety is needed to perk up demand. But variety puts a premium on imagination and creativity, hence mass production can be a great stimulus to creativity. Although I make no claim of profundity for these dialectical exercises, I believe that the development of mass production in Russia and in the Western countries offers some interesting comparisons on these points. The different effects of technology in these countries is not a function of the technology, but rather of the political and economic manipulations of that technology. Or we might put it this way: the inherent logic of a technological society depersonalizes the human ingredients in the name of and for the sake of efficiency. This, I believe, is inevitable, efficiency being the prime and perhaps the only virtue of technology. But the more perfect the technology becomes, the less it utilizes persons as its source of power, the less it needs their muscles, and the more it needs their minds. So the system tends to dispense with persons, and to that extent it no longer depersonalizes them.

This was foreshadowed in Karl Marx's image of the classless society, about which everyone is so curious and about which he said so little. He said that in that society—which presumably had taken over the modes and means of large-scale machine production—people would not work at one job but would vary their jobs to their interests and talents. This follows, in a way, from the notion that in the classless society workers would not be exploited by the capitalists and, therefore, would not be alienated from their work. Yet, to make this kind of occupational happiness the privilege of all means that drudgery—the work that produces sweat and boredom—can be left unchosen by all. But this would be possible only if that drudgery were performed by machines.

If one construes the future in this way, then we come upon the odd notion, almost a paradox, that for some of the children now in the early grades, adult work may come to be the most important expression of their selves, while for others, no expression at all.

For one group, by far the smaller one, the professions and the upper echelons of business, industry, and government will afford a perfectly satisfactory form of self-expression. The full powers of the person will be engaged in his occupational life. His social life and every other phase of existence will probably be tuned to the demands of occupation. For such persons their work will be everything, unless, of course, a good general education prevents or inhibits such a lopsided development. The technological society offers numerous opportunities for rewarding work; it has not been equally successful in enabling men to maintain a perspective in which one's work does not become everything.

But for those who cannot qualify for such work or who do not choose to qualify, there will be a sufficient demand for hands on jobs that do not express the selves of the workers in any significant way. Their jobs will tell us almost nothing worth knowing about them. This is the polarizing effect of a mature technological society so far as work—for which term read "gainful employment"—is concerned. The lower on the technomeritocratic scale one is or chooses to be, the less significant will his work be to himself, however necessary it is to the apparatus of production.

In highly routinized work, not only is the worker alienated from the work, but he is also alienated from the ultimate beneficiary of his work, so that he feels no responsibility to him. Or, to put it more realistically, it takes a considerable effort to envision responsibility to a nameless customer. To be sure, revenge on the unknown customer by poor workmanship on any component of the final product is possible. One hears stories of automobile workers on the assembly line of expensive cars taking malicious delight in having some small share in the ultimate malfunctioning of the product. The thought of a gasoline tank falling off or the air conditioning failing as the nabob uses the car phone to talk to his minions a thousand miles away gives some workmen unbounded delight. It is far easier for the malevolent worker to gloat in his revenge against the system than for the virtuous assembly line man to reflect that some unknown individual depends on him for a satisfactory product. It can be done, but to do it for every ball bearing or cam that one's machine turns out is asking for a degree of moral sensitivity that few possess.

The more insignificant the job is to the individual, the greater is the demand on the individual for moral sensitivity and imagination. So instead of saying, as we are likely to do, that the lower on the social scale a man's work is the less we are to demand of him, it would be more accurate to say that from those who have least the most shall be asked. Lest this sound merely paradoxical, consider some examples.

An accomplished physician finds that his patient has an incurable tumor. Forthwith he is confronted with a nestful of moral issues. What shall he tell the patient, tell his family? Suppose the patient pleads for a sufficient number of pills to save himself from the suffering that our mores and laws force on the dying. There is no evading these moral issues or the fact that they are moral.

Consider the corporation head whose plant is polluting the atmosphere; or the lawyer who knows his guilty client will wreak social havoc if he is acquitted; or the politician with many choices, all having solid consequences for his constitutents, for his country, and for his re-election.

There is little point in saying that these individuals should be sensitive to the moral import of their actions. Moral relevance is thrust upon them.

But no such obvious moral demands force themselves upon the assembly line worker or the garbage collector or even the ordinary repairman. He knows the job he is asked to do. He goes through the motions necessary to that job. He can point to the manual or to custom and prove to his own satisfaction and that of his peers that he went through an approved procedure. There his obligation ends. If the product is not satisfactory, he feels no guilt. If he is asked to redo the unsatisfactory job, he can repeat what he did before and in good conscience get paid for doing so. This double and even triple payment, of course, is what gives Ralph Nader his political potential. It should be clear why such workers must have unusual moral sensitivity if the bland tolerance of poor work is to be replaced with elementary responsibility to the consumer.

This may help to explain why an elitist education—that is, a high-grade general education—for all may not be so implausible and quixotic a notion after all. For it is the workman to whom his job is no more than a brute necessity who most urgently needs the schooling that will lead to a reflective capacity to expand the narrow margins of his life. It is he above all—because, by virtue of numbers, he exercises great political power—who must have the benefit of disciplined thought and feeling. The careerist scrambling to the upper rungs of the meritocracy has his work to keep him intellectually and morally alert (not necessarily morally good). He commands a salary that enables him, if he chooses, to enjoy a rich aesthetic environment. Not so the so-called workingman. For him these advantages—if they are to be so regarded—must come through an education that gives him a strong taste for these things, a will to seek them out in the public museum, lectures, libraries, concert halls, and the self-cultivation to enjoy them. Power to the people is monstrous unless education to the people goes with it.

If it is a rude shock to discover that reality does not match rhetoric, it is an even greater shock to find that it could. Although youth regularly is condemned to undergo the first sort of shock, the potentialities of the technological society for making the reality match the rhetoric of the enlightened democratic society add outraged indignation to the shock. In this sense we cannot blame the young for impatience with the middle-aged liberal who deep down does not believe that society is *ready* for his ideals. It is no longer merely a play on words to say that democracy—in a matured technological society—requires uncommon cultivation for its common men. This is now a necessity. However, serendipity has contributed an odd twist to the fate of the common man, namely, that only the well-paid workingman who can do his job in three or four days a week will have the leisure and freedom from status hunger to devote himself to the business of being a man and cultivating his powers to be a good one. He alone will have the time and the motivation for pursuing a liberal education.

This is more than a way of speaking and more than a taste for paradox. Ask any doctor, lawyer, accountant, business executive, what happened to the promises he made to himself during his college days about the reading he would do, once his career was secure. The books stand there shelf on shelf; the magazines lie there layer on layer. Perhaps next week there will be time to do some nonprofessional reading. As an undergraduate one was happy to get a standing-room-only ticket for the opera or the symphony or the ballet; today only the fact that one is a patron (contributors of $100 or more) makes attendance unavoidable. So months follow weeks, and years follow months, and books and magazines wait. Presumably their day will come when the busy and important man "retires," if he ever does.

Thus, to say that only the man whose work is *not* his life, the man who must create his significance *off* the job, is in a position to undergo liberal education is more than a piece of whimsy. For as Aristotle pointed out, education is liberal only insofar as it is undertaken for self-cultivation, not for the making of money or for the more efficient discharge of our duties civic and domestic. If, therefore, there is truth in the assertion that there is no room for liberal education in the American school system, it is not because the so-called liberal studies are not taught, but rather because there is neither room nor time for any studies that cannot demonstrate their relevance to employment value or civic competence. And this indictment applies to departments of humanities as well as to professional schools.

The developments that have brought the possibility of the masses' inheriting the cultural privileges of the classes are too complex to expound, even if I had the competence to do so. The Marxian thesis that sooner or later the relations of production must make their peace with the modes of production is persuasive. It will take a long time for the social implications of a technologically based economy to be worked out. The beginnings of such a change have been with us for some time now. Mature trade unionism and the growing role of government in every phase of life tend toward redistributing wealth, so that the capacity to consume the products of the industrial machine are maximized.

Belatedly but steadily, schooling has also worked in the same direction. Although much of the public school fervor of the nineteenth century can be interpreted as the bid of the middle-class family to rise in the economic and social scales, it did sweep some of the lower working class up as well. Compulsory schooling, now under attack, was precisely what its critics say it was—an ideological tool of the middle class. What they seem to forget, however, is that the middle class was already casting an eye on the values of the upper-class elite, and that the working classes were fermenting with middle-class ambition. And inasmuch as the elite of the new country were not always members of the loftiest birth castes, the values of the middle and upper classes were not radically discontinuous. The Protestant ethos of hard work, individual enterprise, and economic *laissez faire* characterized both upper and middle classes, so that the differences between them were seen merely as matters of time. In such a society, being a wage worker was perceived as but a transitory stage to becoming an entrepreneur and a member of the middle class. For those who accepted the workingman status as permanent, there was little left but the possibility of legislation to keep their wages and working conditions at a level that did not outrage the Christian sentiments of philanthropists. After years of effort, the labor movement and Franklin Roosevelt substituted collective bargaining for Christian sentiment.

Yet these wage-earning masses *had* to send their children to school. It is difficult to say how much compulsory schooling up to the age of fifteen and sixteen shaped the consciousness of the working-class child. Certainly it made him receptive to the ideas of labor leaders and politicians; certainly it imprinted him with that technological sense so badly needed in an industrial society. Certainly the rhetoric of democracy, so steadily enunciated by the school texts, must have seeped into something deeper than speech patterns.

I know that it is fashionable to sneer at the old civic education courses in the schools, at the study of the Constitution and the Declaration of Independence, while ward politicians infested Boards of Education and the schoolhouse. Yet, for most American children, it has become almost second nature to expect a voice in decisions that affect them. Fair play is a standard demand even by the very young. If it is true that the social milieu did not support such sentiments, then where did Americans get them? As previously noted, Gunnar Myrdal, in *An American Dilemma,* observed that there is such a thing as the American Creed to which young and old, rich and poor, Democrat and Republican, appeal as the ultimate justification. Moreover, as Myrdal noted, there is a loyalty to the higher-order evaluations with which we try to bring our legislation into some kind of congruity. Perhaps the American public school has been partly responsible for the gap between the values we profess and the conduct we tolerate, but who is more aware of this hypocrisy than Americans themselves? The school cannot create the social conditions for the realizations of ideals, but it can generate that strain for consistency that bothers the conscience and that, when the time is ripe, changes the social reality itself.

Nevertheless there is a sense is which Ivan Illich and his fellow advocates of deschooling are right. There is no point in schooling people to expectations that the social order cannot fulfill. Such schooling to such people in such a society is a debilitating fraud from which the blacks, especially, have suffered in our country, and which the populations of the developing countries may suffer in the decades to come. Illich's argument, however, does not hold for a social order that can and indeed, if I am right, *must* fulfill the expectations it arouses; it *must*, because it cannot compete with other advanced societies if it does not.

It is difficult, in the literature criticizing the public schools, to disentangle these complaints. Some blame the school itself for not fulfilling the expectations it arouses; some blame the social order for frustrating these expectations; and some deny the validity of the expectations themselves. But in a technologically mature society there is room for a variety of expectations. The Protestant ethos and middle-class ambition may well be the driving forces in such a society, but the system has made many jobs so insignificant to personal development, yet adequately remunerative, that one can "cop out" of the middle-class dynamic and at the same time use it as a base from which to pursue a quite different order of values. One can, therefore, use the school to play the achievement game or use it for other purposes. Neither the establishment nor the schools need be torn down or abandoned to do so.

The really important paradox, therefore, is that the American public school system, for all its chaos and ineptness, in taking the rhetoric of the Founding Fathers seriously, was anticipating a social order in which the rhetoric was turning into reality. To speak of an academically overqualified population, as Illich does, is itself a way of saying that the worth of life for everybody must be measured in occupational status, a language in which a workingman reading Proust or Plato is a freak, and a plumber participating in a debate over space exploration is an eccentric. In a society in which philosophical plumbers are not oddities, academic overqualification will have to mean something other than not getting the job that corresponds to so many years of schooling or a specific degree. It will mean failure to use schooling to determine one's life by the resources of the cultural heritage in a society where such fulfillment is not inexorably tied to a particular kind of job.

The new freedom in the fully matured technological society is liberation from the customary stigmata of success or failure. I think we are on the road to achieving this freedom. A recent survey of 1971 college graduates showed that 88 per cent hold that "being able to enjoy living is much more important than being a success in one's field." Yet, right as the new humanism is in stressing this attitude, it is, with the best of intentions, wrong in believing that authentic freedom is synonymous with anarchy. The freedom for which we all would want to fight, I take it, is not the freedom to do or be anything that at any given moment one might wish, but rather the freedom to be or do what reason and feeling make us want to be or do. This doctrine, of course, is the old standard brand of humanism, and I am arguing, I suppose, that the social reality of a mature technological society fits it better than did the historical epochs that gave it birth.

It is often said that the Aristotelian notion of the good life for the good man was a genuine potentiality only for the *aristoi*, the fortunate few who had the leisure and means to cultivate their distinctively human powers, and that even for them slave labor was necessary to provide the goods and services that made leisure possible. Hence this notion of the good life was held to be grossly inappropriate to a modern democratic society. Some, like John Dewey, even argued that the Aristotelian view of truth and goodness was itself a rationalziation of the social system that favored the *aristoi*.

Yet history has rendered this argument implausible. The better argument is that a social order is inadequate unless the good life, as characterized by Aristotle, is a possibility for all who choose to cultivate it. If Aristotle nodded, it was when he justified slavery rather than rejected the society that made it necessary for him to deny his own definition of man. History has provided the possibility of a society in which his definition is a practical guide to the good life. What could not have been true in Athens is quite plausible in New York, Indianapolis, and Peoria.

Plausible, yes; inevitable, no.

This trend, too, cannot be extrapolated too far. The forces and logic that yield the possibility of an elite form of life for the masses rather than—or as well as—for the classes, to use an old terminology, will not of themselves effect this transformation. The glory of technology lies in reducing cognitive strain for the users of its products, but it cannot be extended to realizing the potentialities for a truly liberal education and a truly liberal life. There is no ready, machine-tooled liberalism that one can just buy and use without an inkling of what makes it work, not that some people have not tried to manufacture such packages of instant culture. A mechanistic, technological system of production and a social order based upon it open an extraordinary realm of freedom replete with what William James called momentous options! This is a dialectical joke of the first water.

I say this because the common man—and in some sense, aside from our fields of specialization, we are all common men—need not choose between the good life that gets him into heaven and the evil one that leads him to hell. We do not face, as did the feudal serf, the choice between servitude and death or the choice confronting the early factory worker between long hours of drudgery and starvation.

On the contrary, our choice is between two modes of life. Neither will destroy their chooser or even make him miserable.

One style is that which the mass production system is so well designed to serve with a ready-made set of products and values. There is no need to repeat that packaged ideas, packaged foods, ready-made clothing, and appliances are relatively easy to obtain and use. By any standard, moreover, these mass products are not bad. The ready-made ideas that constitute the intellectual capital of the common man today are superior to the ideas the common man entertained a century ago. I am not sure that even the aesthetic and moral standards of today's common man are inferior to that of his counterpart in other times. For the design and production of the standard, mass-produced object—when it is not downright shoddy by intent—engages the best talent of our times. The simplest appliance embodies considerable intellectual resources. At the same time, the ready-made culture is by all reasonable measures pretty good; quite good, as a matter of fact. And it may well be a mark of ingratitude not to appreciate it wholeheartedly, as the apologists for the system do not fail to remind us.

The other style of life is characterized by self-determination, self-realization, and self-integration. This is not a ready-made life for a ready-made self. We do have the chance to remake our early experience and our environmental influences into a custom-made self and a custom-made life. What provides that chance? Leisure and education. These, in turn, are provided by a technologically mature society, not out of humanitarian motives but as necessary factors in its own development.

Here the determinism ends. The system does not provide a compelling force or reason for choosing one mode of life rather than another. That calculus of costs and benefits must take place in the individual. In that calculus a very heavy counter is the amount of effort the authentic tailor-made life demands, especially the educational effort. The good enough, the pretty good, as many have said, is the greatest enemy of the good. Far from demoralizing life, these options force all of us to make a moral choice between them. The elite in any domain take the hard alternative.

This is why the elite are minorities. The number of persons who will discipline themselves beyond the necessary minimum is always bound to be small compared to the total population, especially when the necessary minimum yields quite satisfactory results.

Accordingly, education for the highly individualized life encounters the resistance of the pupil who has not yet felt the peculiar satisfaction that self-cultivation affords. When the drudgery stage of learning ensues, one stays with it until the drudgery gives way to ease of performance, or one quits long before that state is achieved. This phenomenon is quite familiar to anyone learning a new skill. For the individual with unusual talent, the promise of high rewards for championship performance is a strong incentive to endure the drudgery, but what incentive can we hold out to the young if their interests do not lead them to crave mastery in a particular field of knowledge? Why perfect language usage beyond what the ordinary commerce with life makes necessary? Why think with precision in the various domains of learning? Won't several mumblings plus a few "Y' know what I mean" assurances do? To become a buff in any field—old automobiles, music boxes, dolls, stamps, batting averages—makes sense; that's a hobby, and a hobby is absorbing. But why become a buff with regard to the quality of one's own life?

At this stage, education gambles. It promises high intrinsic satisfaction to him who will exert the effort to cultivate his modes of feeling and thinking with the devotion of a buff. There is no hard evidence that the promise will be fulfilled. Aristotle believed that any human function when performed well would be accompanied by pleasure and malfunctioning by pain. Perhaps so, yet people who reason badly are not automatically pained, and when our liver works well, we do not notice how well our liver feels. In any event, even without education and undue cultivation, most of our human functions work well enough—common sense and common feeling will carry us a long way.

About the only way to give the skeptical learner a glimmer of what the rewards of self-cultivation will be is to appeal to his experience as a buff—if he has been or is a buff in any field. A buff, or, if you like, a connoisseur, is one to whom small differences make a big difference. The connoisseur learns the criteria by which the experts make their judgments, whether it is in wine or Colonial antiques or *bel canto* singing. No detail is too small, no refinement too esoteric, to be neglected by a buff.*

If you ask the buff what difference such small differences make—let us say between one wine and another—he will either refuse to have anything further to do with you, or he will plead with you to taste both wines and to note, just note, the difference. And dollars to doughnuts, if you do notice, you will feel a smidgen of satisfaction—with yourself. If you keep on this road, you will become a buff yourself and will be no more able to endure the Philistine than the connoisseur was able to endure you in your common-sense obtuseness.

Connoisseurship, therefore, is the road to self-cultivation. A really first-rate, authentic, free life today means becoming a connoisseur, or at least entering upon connoisseurship, in many fields of knowledge and in many modes of feeling. The cost and effort are more obvious than the benefits. How far down the road in connoisseurship one needs to go in general education is itself a matter of delicate judgment—of connoisseurship. Too far down the road leads one to overspecialization; too short an induction results in superficiality and a mere outward show that cheats the self.

Education has to persuade and often to coerce the young to

* A buff in a field that is socially unimportant or that means nothing to us is known, interestingly enough, as a "nut."

undertake the drudgery for which experience has not yet given them the incentive. Furthermore, education selects that portion of the cultural heritage that deserves cultivation and the degree to which the initial cultivation is to be carried. The experts within given intellectual disciplines are not competent to decide this matter of portion and degree. Beyond the initial cultivation, external pressure is inappropriate, for if it is not self-sustaining, it has failed.

Although the current revolt against establishments is a revolt against all forms of authority that the establishments embody, the rejection of the authority of the expert is the one that should cause the most apprehension—at least among educators. For the academicians are not unequivocally defenders of all authority. When the attack on authority is directed against prescriptions and proscriptions for which no reasonable grounds can be adduced, most of them are sympathetic and many of them applaud. That is why in the campus troubles university faculty and administrators responded so equivocally. But the authority of the expert, validated by study and special modes of inquiry, is to the academician the very essence of rationality. Once this is rejected, the university and its guilds are silenced. There is no more reasoning together or even arguing against each other, and, bidden or unbidden, the police arrive.*

But, as Bennett M. Berger noted in "Audiences, Art and Power" (*Trans-Action*, May, 1971), the current counterculture challenges all expertise and the right of the expert to expect deference, as defined in the formalities he interposes between himself and the layman. The revolt, he notes, is now directed at the last remaining bastions of elitism—the university professor and the professional artist.

The elitism of the university is centered in the academic guild system, and when students demand the right to design their own courses, to grade themselves or not to be graded at all, or to grade the professor, this elitism is challenged by an assertion of egalitarianism—that there is really no way of distinguishing the expert from the layman.

Similarly in the arts. Berger quotes Albert Goldman to the effect that

* Cf., for example, Eldon Johnson, *From Riot to Reason* (Urbana: University of Illinois Press, 1971).

these kids can't stand professionalism because it makes them feel inferior. The spectacle of someone exercising a hard-earned skill doesn't always inspire them with admiration.

In the arts, therefore, the audience is asked to participate; anybody can do it—make a film, create rock music, weld sculptures, paint murals.

From a slightly different perspective the revolt is against the seriousness of either knowledge or art. Hilton Kramer brought this out in commenting on the difference in our attitude toward the work of Cézanne.

Cézanne may still occupy a pivotal position, marking a significant transition—perhaps *the* significant transition—into the modernist epoch in which we find ourselves. But this is not the way Cézanne actually looks to us today. His art inhabits a moral universe totally different from our own. It exerts a moral pressure on our sensibilities that is inseparable from its esthetic revelations, and it is precisely this moral pressure that the new art repudiates.*

The new artist, Kramer observes, thinks of his work as a cheerful game of ideas and of himself as a "dispassionate broker in visual concepts and sensations." Gone is Cézanne's famous "anxiety."

Oddly enough, this rejection of the elitism of the expert runs counter not only to the premises of the technological society that subdivides its myriad functions among specialists, but also to what I believe is an even more important characteristic of that society. This is the fact that even the ordinary citizen must have a degree of expertise that nobody ever dreamed could reasonably be required of the common man. This is why, much as many of us sympathize with the revolt against "the establishment" and its entrenched guardians, most thoughtful surveyors of the present or the future cannot even imagine how a modern society can be run without the elitism of the expert.

The important elite of the future will be constituted by those who select the life style of self-cultivation, of connoisseurship. They may not be the ruling elite or even prominent among the nongoverning elite; they may be masters over nobody but them-

* New York *Times,* June 6, 1971.

selves; they may not be high on the occupational ladder; they are not likely to be celebrities, and they will not have to consult *Who's Who* to find out who they really are.

These possibilities, I repeat, are but a few that emerge when we think of trends not only as continuing on their present course, but as doubling back on themselves, as giving rise to side effects that will initiate new trends. When we view developments in this way, paradoxes do come home to roost: views that seemed implausible when first formulated become plausible to the point of inevitability. I believe the dialectics of social development are not to be despised in educational planning and educational criticism. Here especially, "Beware of the obvious" should be our caveat.

These paradoxes renew the hope that the development of a technologically mature society neither commits us to an unbridled, robotlike materialism nor consigns us to the desperate alternative or tearing the whole thing down, "dropping out," or resorting to bizarre behavior. The odd turns of history, however, reveal no royal road either to mathematics or to anything else that is really first-rate in education. Ready-made, instant, frictionless education is itself a ready-made illusion.

CHAPTER X

The Master Question

What has been written about education and schooling in these pages will not be dismissed, I trust, as defensive apologetics. In the first chapter, the careful reader will recall, doubts were raised about the possibility of banishing all bias from the discussion. To paraphrase Sören Kierkegaard, education without bias is like love without passion. There is scarcely a serious sentence about schools that does not carry some value judgment on its face or behind its back.

Surely my biases are obvious to the reader; there has been no attempt to conceal them. Not only do I favor a certain view of life and truth and reality, but I write from the perspective of an academic and with whatever vision the subclan of that tribe devoted to the study of education permits. Hence the reader should expect and perhaps discount a bias in favor of the guild, its traditions, and its values. Nevertheless, I would urge once more that the reader keep in mind the bias of the critics of the schools. Oversimplification, distortion, hasty generalizations, rampant utopianism—these are some of the limitations of that criticism. But more deceptive than these is the illusion that only the educationist has an ax to grind. The U.S. Office of Education, the foundations, the education industries, the academic guilds, the teachers' unions, the Colleges of Education—all push their mission in the name of the welfare of the child. Like other institutions, they use a rhetoric that justifies what they do as being in the public interest. But each of these institutions employs people who, besides sharing the righteousness of their cause, have careers and family fortunes to think about. No society has ever been able to separate concern for public and private welfare in its leaders without resort to the radical remedies proposed by Plato: the abolition of private fortunes and families.

The trite sally that education is too important to be left to the educationist—which could be paraphrased for every one of the professions—makes sense if it is taken to mean that all professionals become narrow in their specialization and that all institutions tend to become self-serving and self-perpetuating. Hence a broader perspective on their activities is always in order. But there is a sense in which schools specialize in inducting the young into the human heritage through instruction—the broadest and most general of all enterprises. Accordingly, not only is dissatisfaction with the schools socially justifiable but is the rule rather than the exception, because this induction affects every phase of life—every failure as well as every success.

However, the right to criticize the schools does not guarantee the justice or even the reasonableness of the criticism. If this book makes any contribution to the discussion of education, it is to show that the attacks on the schools, when taken in aggregate, reflect a maze of inconsistent motives and anomalous solutions. I have tried to show, for one example, that it is impossible for a school as an institution to respond simultaneously to two equally vociferous theses: one, that reading is no longer important and is a false criterion of being educated; and two, that the troubles of ghetto children can be attributed to the fact that they can't read as well as their middle-class schoolmates.

I shall now take the liberty of commenting on some of the major issues in education on the assumption that the reader has become familiar with some of the arguments and theses developed more fully in the previous chapters.

DO WE NEED PUBLIC SCHOOLS?

If the schools have "failed" as badly as the critics say they have, is it because they have outlived their usefulness? Outraged by the inefficiencies of the postal system, we did not urge the abolition of a unified system of mail delivery, but when the railroads collapsed as passenger carriers in 1971, there was some real doubt whether we really needed them for passenger traffic. That the criticism of the schools raises the latter sort of doubt is suggested by some of the proposed remedies: the voucher system, decentralized school districts, moves toward deschooling, a rash of legislation to give state aid to private schools, religious and otherwise. The financial and ideological support provided by the U.S. Office of Education for these moves would also indicate a doubt at the highest level that the nation needs a system of schools that reflect any unified goal.

Well, do we have national goals? Is there some sort of unity in American life that requires an analogous unity in the educational apparatus? Can we speak of an unspoken ethos of the American people as Gunnar Myrdal did in the 1940s when he discovered the American Creed? Wherever one turns for evidence, the answer seems to be negative. In politics, in economics, in national priorities, in the arts, one finds evidence of fragmentation, of demands for cultural and social pluralism. To be sure, there are clusters of consensus: large minorities and even sizable majorities agree on stopping the war in Vietnam, on cleaning up the environment, and on demanding truth in advertising, but these states of mind are more like moods than long-range commitments. Nobody knows how long they will last. In the space of five years, various forms of the counterculture blazed into prominence and subsided into boredom. Drugs alone seem to hold firmly the center of the stage. This faddism, this cynicism, this randomized pluralism, mark the overripeness of a culture and not its prime bloom. Yet, if this is the mood of the country, the schools will reflect it in a variety of *ad hoc* "innovations," which, if they do nothing else, relieve dullness. And dullness threatens any activity, including education, when no deep, strong current gives it direction and urgency. It is like peacetime barracks life, which, I am told, is the ultimate in dullness. When much of our fiction is antihero, antiplot, antiorder, then the social reality, one may well suspect, has lost its dramatic coherence.

This loss of purpose need not affect everybody at the same time and in the same degree. On any given issue, at any given time, the majority is likely to be silent. At the extremes of opinion the extremists are articulate and confront each other. Abbie Hoffman and Spiro Agnew spoke their pieces fiercely and loudly, but most of their partisans kept quiet. The silence of the majority, therefore, conceals much diversity and possible conflict. It includes all cautious souls regardless of political affiliations. The great virtue of the democratic process is that it culminates every so often in a vote that polarizes the silent ones into commitment. It would be surprising indeed if the schools did not exhibit the same ambiguities of silence. This ambiguity manifests itself in an exaggerated hospitality to diversity. There is, on the one hand, a respect for differences and doubt about one's own convictions. On the other hand, mere hospitality to diversity may indicate a contempt for differences—insignificant differences make no difference. Practically, a school can use a variety of programs and outlooks as a defense mechanism against the bellicose partisans of all the warring camps.

Pluralism is beneficial when a variety of members contribute to the over-all functioning of a single organism. The heart, liver, and brain differ from each other but, by their difference, strengthen the unity of the organism. In art, one theory holds that the test of success is the unification of variety. In other words, highly developed organisms exploit great complexities for unity of function.

However, when the diverse members of a collection do not contribute to a unified goal or function, they cannot claim significance as contributors. Each alternative must have significance on its own account, and there is no way to adjudicate a conflict between any of them. But must there be conflict? Are there not many roads to the same mountaintop? Ah, yes, if we agree that there is one mountaintop, we can still have creative diversity, because such agreement does regulate the character of the journey in some ways. But must there be conflict even if the various paths do not lead to the same mountaintop? No, not if they do not interfere with one another, not if one can travel his own path without giving thought to the others, when differences don't matter.

Pluralism becomes enervating when all differences become insignificant. When the difference between the Republican and

Democratic parties becomes insignificant, then politics will have lost its bite and political life will slacken. One way of insulting each other is to act as if the differences that distinguish us as individuals do not really matter.

For example, I can find no principled grounds on which to argue against the essential program of Women's Liberation, and yet it seems to ask at least one unreasonable thing, namely, that a male react to the beauty of a woman as if it were *not* significant. For, to react to her beauty as such, I am told, would be to treat her as nothing but a sex object, from which fate she desires to be liberated. A culture in which all differences are equally insignificant is well on the way to becoming an insignificant culture.

As opposed to Herbert Marcuse's "oppressive tolerance," there can be a tolerance born of indifference. This toleration becomes depressive when the only reason we can adduce for doing something or being something is "Why not?" The creative phase of a culture is positive in the sense that it tends to unite men's efforts in certain directions and to look with disfavor on expending effort in other directions. It is a phase marked by a certain exclusiveness that insures concentration.

If there is a unifying force in the American culture today, it is to be found in the silent logic of a technological industrial society. It is virtually impossible to find any aspect of life that can be shaken loose from involvement with the system. I do not propose to remarshal the evidence for this, because it is all around us. Its ubiquity is witnessed equally by the plenitude of goods and services and our resentment against being deprived of a larger share in it. The fact that the mass production system is the source of both blessings and curses means that to fight it, one must use its resources and methods; it lays down the rules of its game, and it is virtually impossible to refuse to play the game.

For this reason, a public school system, rather than techno-idolatry, is mandatory in a modern society. The character of an industrial society, moreover, translates our ideals into new forms of behavior. Our loyalty to democracy has to be translated into democratic behavior suitable to a technologically mature society. Even if one subscribes to an unchanging human essence, that essence has to be externalized under the conditions dictated by the nature of a technologically mature society. If the children of Arizona and Maine, of Alaska and Hawaii, are all subject to the nature of this system, then it makes sense to say that all American children need certain kinds of schooling in order to live in that system. And to the extent that one can say this, the ethnic differences between Hawaiians and Eskimos will not be decisive for education.

America, on these premises, does need a public school system or a system of public schools. That the demands of the technological society could, in principle, be met by a variety of patterns of school support I do not deny; indeed, some private schools have met them better than some public schools. The question is whether we can leave this duty safely to the discretion of private families going shopping for educational goods. Every effort to do this in other areas of the common good has failed. Social Security, Medicare, the postal system,* have had to be taken over by the federal government; so will welfare and mental health—and political socialism has nothing to do with it. Failure of a plurality of enterprises to solve a truly national problem forces the federal government into centralization. Left to the states, divorce, taxation policies, education, have created gross inequities that affect the whole nation, not merely the inhabitants of the several states. Left to individual discretion, these enterprises would generate even greater inequities. The voucher system, for example, unless hedged in by the sort of "public" controls the situation requires, will make the present inequities of the schools seem trivial by comparison.

The impact of the mass media, the mobility of the population, the technical demands of the economic system—all militate for significant uniformity in schooling. The current revolts against these deep currents in our society are minor flurries that will not affect the main line of development. If we are headed for a single-ladder society, then we shall move toward a single-ladder system of schooling. Whether this uniformity is deadening depends on our creativeness in finding variations on a theme. I happen to believe that we can be creative in utilizing the resources of a technological society if we give all our people access to the resources of our cultural heritage.

* The postal system in its present guise as a public corporation is, in truth, no less a national or federal operation than it has always been.

I have tried to give reasons for believing that the future will favor a simplified, highly generalizable curriculum pursued through the elementary and secondary grades, and that higher education will gradually confine itself to specialized work of a professional or preprofessional nature. These, it seems to me, are the large swells of the future; the current fiddling around with decentralized systems of control, alternatives in curriculum, vouchers for religious and other private schools, are transitional moves designed to preserve differences that are vestiges of a dual system of society and of schooling. Parochiaid (state aid to religious schools) has about as much religious significance today as has spending public money for medieval Christian art to be displayed in a city museum. I still believe that the effort to help religious schools violates the spirit of the Constitutional intent to prevent public support of an establishment of religion, and thus it ought to be opposed, but religious schools sealed their doom when they accepted public funds for the secular part of their curriculum. If the whole enterprise is not religiously justifiable, then the part that is secular will gradually paint the religious part into an insignificant corner—hardly worth maintaining separate schools for.

Further, the more ecumenical churches become, the less reason is there for separate religious schools. If God is dead, if doctrinal differences are to be overcome, then parochial and private schools represent little more than school space, which in hard times ought to be utilized rather than lost. Most of the parochiaid legislation is sponsored and passed in a fiscal rather than in a religious spirit. It does not represent a victory for sectarian schools, but an acceleration of their demise, in which those who attach significance to organized religion might be well advised not to collaborate.

The same may be said for the moves to give public funds to private colleges. The virtues of their privateness seem not to outweigh the disadvantages of their high tuition fees. Academic excellence is no longer the exclusive privilege of private institutions. Indeed much of the prestige of these institutions derives from the quality of the students rather than from the quality of instruction. Since good schooling always means deficit spending, only the state can undertake it on any large scale, and with half or more of the high school graduates in the nation feeling they ought to be given an opportunity for postsecondary schooling, only the state can possibly meet the demand. Even the prestigious large private universities cannot endure without governmental grants. Whatever elitism these universities enjoy is not by virtue of the uniqueness of their programs, goals, or faculty. They are all of a piece with those found in the large public universities.

Private colleges, like private schools of any sort, represent educational resources. It may be cheaper to subsidize them than to let them wither on the vine, but their long-run prospects are not bright. This has nothing to do with their quality or lack of it. Rather it is a consequence of a highly interdependent society dominated by the requirements of sophisticated technology. To the degree that schooling is a necessary condition for maintaining that system, it will become more centralized, more bureaucratized, more uniform.

Can such a centralized, bureaucratized system of education be a liberating force? Yes, it can be, if it can stake out for itself a unique domain in which its autonomy can be legitimated. It probably cannot, if it tries to imitate the complexity and confusion of the community at large, if it fails to concentrate on the liberating power of knowledge.

The special domain of the school has been knowledge, truth as certified by those expert in its discovery, defense, preservation, and promulgation. The autonomy of schools needs no other or more ultimate legitimation. This is the knowledge that can make men free, if they are willing to validate their life commitments by appeals to it and faith in it. Schools, on this view, would have a bias—a well-publicized bias—in favor of knowledge and of the traditions in which knowledge has been fostered. In general education, the school would induct every pupil into the vestibules of connoisseurship in all phases of human life. It would preach openly that not only is the unexamined life not worth living, but that the cultivation of one's power for living well is a duty as well as a high privilege.

This faith is muted in the country today. It is regarded as conservative by the academic activists, and utopian by the conservatives, both of whom respect knowledge only when it coincides with their ideology. It is not for nothing that the image of the ivory tower has been identified with the intellectual and condemned as an escape from partisanship. Yet, if being outside the fray is forbidden, the claims of the intellectual to dispassionate judgment are vain. Once in the fray as an active partisan, the peculiar authority of truth is dispelled. The sacrifice might be justified if academicians were good in politics, but with few notable exceptions, they are more fit to discuss issues than to resolve them—a solved problem has no further interest to the intellectual.

Intellectual competence in our time has been equated with glib skepticism, a challenging of every assertion on the grounds that it "ain't *necessarily* so." This is easy because no existential truth is "necessarily" so, and to conceive its falsity is always possible. This is a species of low intellectual gymnastics and has its place in logical games, but it is not the kind of intellectualism to which education can be committed. For education summons knowledge as a justification for life, and methodological skepticism has never done very well as a way of life for any man. Intellectual autonomy in the school, therefore, is based not on propositions that are "necessarily" so, but on those that are highly warrantable in terms of evidence for which the intellectual disciplines themselves provide the canons. It is in terms of such knowledge that the school can both transmit and criticize the culture.

There is plenty of room for even trivial and irresponsible criticism in an open society. The mass media, columnists, book reviewers, the arts, are and should remain free to criticize without first furnishing the censor with their moral and intellectual credentials. Such criticism keeps the cultural pot boiling and prevents thought and feeling from jelling prematurely into stereotypes. It keeps institutions on their toes and, in general, is necessary for a vital and active society, especially a technologically mature society.

Schools, however, have a somewhat different mission. They have the task of furnishing a knowledge base for both commitment and criticism. What the pupil does with this knowledge outside school is his business; that he receives every opportunity to appropriate this knowledge is the school's business. The calls to political activism by the university itself (as distinguished from such calls addressed to—or even issued by—individual faculty members), the downgrading of the study of the disciplines, the rejection of the authority of the faculty to design and evaluate instruction—all of these in their own ways erode the most clearly defensible function of the school. I can only conclude once more that in a culture characterized by a division of labor, a school without a special task has no place. If it does have a special mission, then to that extent all schools will have a core of common tasks and responsibilities, regardless of how they are supported and the ethnic peculiarities of the populations they serve.

MODES OF INSTRUCTION AND CLASSROOM CLIMATES

Much of the recent criticism of the schools has had to do with the lack of happiness in the classroom. The American public school has been charged as systematically producing misery in ghetto children by imposing upon them the middle-class attitudes of teachers. Rigid rules of behavior, rote learning, and drill, we are told, kill the spontaneity and creativity of pupils, young and old. Children come to dislike learning in general and school learning in particular. What can be done about this? A return to permissiveness, open classrooms, self-selection of school tasks—all have had their advocates in recent years.

The complaint has two versions. One is that children are being asked to learn what is not worth learning; the other is that what is to be learned could be learned more effectively if the children were happy during the process, and they would be happy if they were free from domination of teachers who were not sympathetic with the disabilities of ghetto children. However, even middle-class children, it is argued, are oppressed by an establishment that cannot brook freedom for pupils. The public schools are, therefore, to be regarded as the enemy of the youth cult, the new consciousness, of peace, kindliness, and all humane impulses.

It is not easy to respond to such a welter of arguments by any general disclaimer. Whether what is being taught to children is worth learning cannot be decided by whether it makes them happy or not. Whether children are happy if every action is left to their choice is not obvious, either; most children clamor for somebody to tell them what to do. That children left to their own devices would become spontaneous, happy, naturally gifted learners is a conjecture that has never been proved, since no such environment has ever been available for the experiment. Nor is it clear that the current experiments in communal living, returns to nature, drugs, bohemianism, and other ventures in anarchic hedonism have proved their efficacy in producing happiness.

A more promising approach to liberate schooling from misery is to ask what sorts of learnings are now being taught in school that could be achieved outside schools and perhaps informally. The drudgery of schooling for both the pupil and the teacher comes in what we have called didactics, *i.e.*, the formation of specific skills and the imparting of information. If the information can be accumulated through television, comic books, travel, and other means, the burden of teaching it in the schools could and should be lightened.

The more class time that can be released from didactics, the more can be devoted to what we have called the heuristics and philetics of teaching, or, in less technical language, helping the pupil discover for himself not only knowledge but the import of thinking and judging for himself. In such desirable circumstances more time will be available for that psychological rapport between pupils and teacher that is now considered to be so crucial, especially in the teaching of disadvantaged children.

For the future we can look to a preschool and an elementary school that will serve primarily as a day-care center, but one that will provide a stimulating intellectual and aesthetic atmosphere as well as custodial care. This is fairly sure to happen if the nuclear family cannot survive the understandable rebellion of women against child care and household chores, because it is difficult to envision an economic system in our society in which men and women share household tasks equally. This, of course, may happen with the advent of the four-day week, but whether it will decrease the demands on the school is doubtful.

If the school does assume custodial care of young children as its primary function, it can and will shift its emphasis from didactical exercises in reading, writing, and arithmetic to personality development. The open classroom, self-selected curriculum, learning by heuristic methods, and encounters of all sorts fit in very well with the growth problems of children. The classroom today is still laboring under the impression that child-rearing is taking place in the family, and that didactics is the business of the school. When we no longer assume this, we can avoid bitter recriminations against both the family and the school.

How muddled the situation is can be seen from the attacks on the elementary school by (1) the romantics on both coasts; and (2) by ghetto parents. The former have homes in which the intellectual growth of the child can proceed far better than it can in most classrooms. A plethora of good reading, good talk, and stimulating people make ordinary schoolwork very literally child's play for the youngster.* So this group bemoans the didactical drudgery and stodginess of the schoolroom. But the ghetto parent knows that his home and neighborhood are not conducive to intellectual development (in the scholastic sense) and so wants the public school to stop fooling around and start teaching his children to read.

Much of what will happen in the school depends on the shape of the home and family in the future decades. Strong pressures are testing the nuclear family. The response may be the emergence of a new form of the extended family, a commune of some sort, or several generations living together in an apartment complex. We ought not to discount these possibilities as a counterdevelopment to the ever-mounting cost of welfare for dependent children and mothers who are unable to take jobs. If this comes about, much of the instruction now given in school could be given within the extended family compound or in some neighborhood combination of compounds. Or, if the extended family fails to emerge, then the school may have to furnish the total environment for many children from infancy to puberty, in which eventuality the school will take on many of the present characteristics of the family. But these transitions proceed at an obscure and leisurely pace. As a consequence, we can expect the controversy about the atmosphere, the curriculum, and the teaching styles of the elementary schools to continue.

The formal study of the key concepts of the basic sciences

* Yet children from such homes do not always escape reading difficulties, or, as someone has said, "It almost seems that the other side of deprivation is intimidation."

and the humanities will have to be done sometime during the school life of the young. I believe that the secondary school (grades seven through twelve) is the most appropriate time and place for doing it. One might expect that general education would be completed during this period so that it need not be continued in higher education. With the pedagogical resources that should be available, there is no reason for not being able to adapt this general (and fairly simple) curriculum to a wide spectrum of ability. I would not concentrate on meeting a wide variety of adolescent interests, however, because the need for general education transcends individual needs, and because general education will make it possible for individuals in their post-secondary years to achieve their individual life goals.

The big problem of the adolescent years is social, not scholastic.

Adolescents present a special problem in our society because they can do some of the things adults can do. They can, for example, kill people by reckless driving and by spontaneous, random violence; and, sexually, they can create life. They cannot be treated like younger children, because the consequences of their acts are very real and socially significant.

Unfortunately, except for military service, the adolescent has no indispensable role in the social order. Like younger children and retirees, he is not needed on the labor market. Apparently all the productive labor can be performed—with the aid of automated machinery—by the cohorts between the ages of twenty and fifty in less than a forty-hour week. The increasing proportion of women in the labor force will further reduce the need for whatever work the young and old might do. In an economically fixated society, all nonproductive members are an embarrassment and are themselves embarrassed. They are not part of the productive public, although they remain as part of the consuming public.

In our country the grades seven through twelve have been chosen to serve as the holding area for the young during this period, but recent years have demonstrated what many have long feared, namely, that a school is a dubious holding area for the young adolescent, and the university has severe limitations as a place to complete adolescence.

The single outstanding, contemporary fact about the relation of parents to the young is the breakdown of communal supervision. It is difficult to overestimate how much the whole enterprise of child rearing and education depends on communal supervision; or at least one does not realize it until such supervision breaks down.

In my youth, I was rarely out of sight of someone who knew me and my parents. It might be a neighbor, a member of the religious community to which my family belonged, a friend of the family, one of the relatives or their children. I did not have the mobility to escape surveillance, informal though it was. If I visited the pool hall—then the epitome of youthful vice—my parents knew about it before I came home. Secret romances were virtually impossible—one was lucky if he could escape with a few unobserved or unsuspected escapades. Without planning or even a committee meeting, the neighborhood—whether in town, village, or city—constituted a surveillance apparatus that had few rivals for efficiency. Part of it was the desire for gossip and a natural curiosity about everybody's business, but I think now that a good deal of it was simply the unspoken assumption of responsibility for the behavior of the community's young. Everybody minded the other fellow's children and felt an obligation to do so.

In this connection it may be pertinent to note how this limitation of privacy helped the police to cope with local crime. In the community of which I speak there were very few unsolved crimes, especially crimes involving theft. A venerable police sergeant every morning would march down Central Street, which led to one of the larger elementary schools in the less prosperous district of the town. On the way he would greet his many little friends on their way to school, and as he walked with them, he would listen for such tidbits as "My big brother got a new pair of fancy shoes," or "My father wasn't home last night," or "Jimmy's brother had a big bandage on his head." Or he might ask certain children what their big brothers were doing these days. It took time, but an amazingly large number of big brothers, fathers, and uncles found their way to the prisoners' dock. So long as the mobility of the delinquent was limited, crime did not go undetected too often. Indeed, certain criminal acts were almost immediately charged to a well-known individual or a well-identified group of cronies and even to certain families. Once the automobile enabled the delinquent to operate far from home, detection became much more difficult, because the community-based surveillance apparatus had broken down.

Both physical and psychological mobility have been responsible for the breakdown in the supervision of the young. Physically, the young can be transported by automobile far from any region in which they are known; the small community no longer has any absolute advantage in this regard. If a youngster is denied the use of the family car, he travels in a friend's family car or even the friend's own car. Given such mobility, alcohol and drugs are easy to consume in relative privacy. The adolescent determined to do what his parents disapprove of needs only mobility and a willingness to lie. If their children want to deceive them, there is no practical way that parents, however determined, can really know what they are up to or where they are.

Even when parents catch children in their delinquency or quasi delinquency, the punitive alternatives open to parents are few and of doubtful efficacy. One can forbid the offender to leave the house, but for how long? And after the period in the penalty box is over, what has been achieved other than a resolve to be more cautious or more subtle the next time? Physical punishment may or may not work; it can lead as easily to revenge as to obedience. Leaving aside the parents who are too busy to be concerned about their children, what, as the vernacular has it, is a parent to do?

The ultimate weapon, especially as far as the middle-class adolescent is concerned, is running away altogether. What in *Penrod and Sam* or *Huckleberry Finn* was an accepted episode in the life of most preadolescent boys—rarely in girls, who probably indulged more in retributive fantasies of suicide—is now a real possibility. The number of runaways—from middle-class homes—is substantial. The flight of the young from the draft to foreign countries still shocks most middle-class Americans—even when the parents share the sentiments of their fleeing sons toward war and especially toward our Asian misadventures. Running away from home is a far more lethal weapon than attacking the establishment with bombs and stones. It inflicts a deep and lasting wound. The hurt is more than shame at the reflection it casts on the home in the eyes of the community. I have seen the anguish in the faces of intelligent, modern, well-meaning parents as they cry, "What have we done wrong?"

If the nuclear family is increasingly unable to cope with the young child, I doubt that the school should try to be a home substitute, for a home of any kind is precisely what hampers the adolescent. He craves peer environment in which to experiment with adulthood. The old boarding school might be revived for this purpose; so might labor or service camps. The mobility of the young would argue for a more nomadic type of existence, something like that of gypsies. Some have urged a two-year period of military or social service, but this is usually suggested for the postsecondary years. Trying to combine formal study with the restless urges of the body and spirit so characteristic of early adolescence has always been a thankless task. There may be merit in trying to alternate a year of highly disciplined life with one that is relatively free and unstructured. If the expectations of the family discipline are weakened, if the pressures of social class are diluted—as I think they will be—if the demands of a job do not exist, then youth may be destroyed, for it cannot—by the very fact of its youth—discipline itself into ordered thought and feeling. And reliance on trial and error is too risky. Hence the discipline of intellectual work is necessary for the young, but there must be outlets for peer urges and peer life. To institutionalize these also seems to be self-defeating somehow, like overorganized play or love or art.

Perhaps we have been too eager to abolish generation gaps. Perhaps we are expecting the young to mature too quickly, and perhaps we have been unduly impressed by the evidence that the young are mature in so many ways. Certainly when eighteen-year-olds are called upon to fight war after war and are permitted to vote, it is difficult to defend a sharp gap between the generations. And yet youth still needs a special environment in which to come to full maturity, intellectually and emotionally.

It has to be a special environment, because the real community is too harsh in its punishment of mistakes—*e.g.*, the brutality, by and large, with which drug addiction, serious delinquency, even chronic truancy are treated—and yet, while punitive, it does not follow through and also exert a steady convincing demand for achievement and responsibility. The community is too dangerous an environment; the home too bland, too restrictive, too protective. The special environment must mark out areas of delinquency in which certain real offenses against the mores and even against property are conventionalized so that the rules of the game limit the damage and the punishments. These societal devices have been attenuated in our time. Our logic may be sound in these matters, but not our social sense. It is futile to legislate against the specific delinquencies of the young, and the fact that we need so many specific legal barriers shows that we have not devised a social arrangement in which the young can be themselves, that is, neither childish nor adult.

When all delinquency is regarded as equally real, we deprive youth of the chance to experiment safely with life, but if all errors are shrugged off without penalties, then experimentation loses its zest and its educative influence. In the sixties the young trapped us into regarding all their actions as adult, and they made adults look foolish both when they failed to suppress the young and when they succeeded. It is a wise and happy society that can invent rituals that can make it possible for youth to grow into adulthood with excitement devoid of terror. War that forces the evils of the old on the young is a complete betrayal of youth; an economy that keeps them helpless and dependent is no less a betrayal.

We should do more to exploit the aesthetic or artistic potentials of adolescence—a period in which the imagination plays with reality and possibility in a fascinating drama. It is no accident that this period of life is so prominent in the arts.

Folk art or popular art in our culture is pre-eminently adolescent art, both in the sense that it is for adolescents and about adolescence—the golden period of life for Americans of all ages. Youth uses "pop" music, poetry, drama, film, to objectify its troubles and aspirations. Participatory art, like participatory democracy, has figured prominently in the counterculture or youth cult. And there is also evidence that this youth art has affected adult art, just as the sentiments of youth have affected the feelings of the adult generation. Adult males, for example, do look shaggier; their clothes are more colorful, more varied, more informal.

In this connection, the school's role is no different from what it is in intellectual development. Just as popular science needs no formal tuition, so popular art needs little in the way of formal instruction. If the more serious arts are to function profitably for youth, however, they require the same refinement as do the sciences, and this necessarily means instruction in due course.

By the time of early adolescence, the aesthetic spontaneity of childhood has evaporated. The uninhibited poetizing, music making, dancing, and acting of the young give way to self-consciousness about technique. The adolescent confines his expression to the medium of ordinary language laced with slang. Even on the receptive side he is at home only in the most popular music, film, and literature. There is nothing wrong with that, except that by definition popular art is highly stereotyped and conservative. This may sound odd, but the popular arts celebrate what has been accepted and validated by the most recent fashion, although the fashions change rapidly. It is in the probings of the serious imaginative artist that the expansive and originative powers of art are manifested.

But the adolescent who is critical of common-sense science because his earlier schooling has made him familiar with sophisticated science has no such preparation for distinguishing between serious and popular art. In this he mimics his culture, of course, in which serious art is regarded as an esoteric interest or as a genteel hobby for the wives of the rich.

COLLEGE TEACHING

If philetics and casual heuristics constitute the dominant (but not exclusive) modes of instruction in the elementary school, and didactics, with some practice in problem solving (heuristics), is to be stressed in the secondary school, what mode of instruction can be anticipated in college or higher education?

Here there is no uniform style. In postsecondary schooling designed for vocational training, some combination of didactics and apprenticeship will continue. For the preprofessional curricula in the four-year institutions, heuristics would seem to be the answer to the complaints of students and professors. This would make sense if the secondary school had laid the proper didactical foundation for it. It is difficult to persuade university professors to teach undergraduates if they are asked to do didactics. The discussion, the seminar, the interdisciplinary course—all of these are heuristic in that they lead the student to some activity of discovery. I find that faculty members, even very distinguished senior ones, have no aversion to heuristic teaching. Indeed, as they will tell you, that is precisely what they do so well with their more promising doctoral advisees.

The numerous alternatives proposed to reform undergraduate higher education depend on the possibility that by means of a highly developed technology, proficiency examinations, and independent study the didactics of general education can be done with a minimal use of formal class time. Since this makes up the bulk of undergraduate study, it drains off huge amounts of time and money both for the student and staff. If we could be relieved of this burden, or if it could be accomplished by more economical means, we might recoup resources for the heuristics that everyone agrees ought to prevail in higher education. And although didactics may have to be the prime style of the secondary school, even there whatever can be done by machine, programmed instruction, and electronic devices should be done that way. For throughout the entire school system only didactics lends itself to mass production economies, and without these the hope of providing quality education on a mass scale is vain. I should reiterate that giving over didactics to machines or machinelike methods does not in the least diminish its indispensability in the total schooling process. Reformers who inveigh quite rightly against the drudgery of rote learning and the systematic study of a discipline are mistaken if they think that they can dispense with it. They cannot, but didactics need not be done by teachers who try to act like machines and end by performing like very imperfect ones. Heuristics, stimulating as it is, can never take the place of didactics.

As for philetics, or love, that, too, can go a long way. A recent winner of the best-teacher-of-the-year award, when interviewed on television, said that the secret of her success was just plain "love of children." I am sure she had some other pedagogical assets, but she was reluctant to take anything away from the power of love.

At the college level philetics is a sticky problem for a number of reasons. It is all too easy and all too hard to establish personal relationships between faculty and students. It is easy for young staff members to talk with students at coffee houses and in each other's lodgings. Many teaching assistants are themselves still graduate students and share their students' antipathy to establishments in general and to that of the university in particular. In such circumstances student-staff friendships can bud and blossom, and this is no doubt a satisfying part of college life.

There are some difficulties, of course, with philetics as a style of teaching. One is that there is no intrinsic relationship between learning X and loving the teacher of X. Hence motivation is even more extrinsic than in didactics, which comes out when the teacher-friend gives out poor grades to student-friend. This outcome is likely to ruin a beautiful friendship. For another matter, the psychic needs of students vary even more than their intellectual ones, and to treat any more than a handful of them as persons in any serious sense of that word is probably beyond the capacity of most instructors.

The love of students is manifested in many ways. Generally it expresses itself in a teacher's willingness to spend considerable time outside class talking with them about their problems, educational and personal. There is an old saw to the effect that teaching keeps one young, because one is renewed by the youth of the students. Perhaps one has to remain young to maintain a genuine fondness for the young; a sense of duty alone will take the teacher only so far; as a rule, not far enough.

In recent years the complaint has become endemic that students do not have access to faculty for the kind of personal relationships they want. A multitude of schemes for counseling and advising have not satisfied the complainants, perhaps because formal procedures cannot take the place of a genuine desire to be with students and to become involved in their problems. I suppose that American undergraduates yearn for something comparable to the tutor available to the Oxbridge undergraduate— an intellectual mentor who not only knows the academic ropes but who, to some extent, also becomes identified with the tutee's academic career.

Formal interviews with professional counselors, interviews with the professor during his stated office hours, and even informal beer sessions at the faculty member's home or in one of the academic pubs—these do not add up to the tutor's continuing concern for the tutee. For the few that have one, the tutor does know what the tutee is reading and writing. There is discussion about books and authors and whatever else may stir student interest. Nobody knows as much about a student as his tutor does. A few American schools provide some version of this tutorial relation, but it is a relatively rare phenomenon. Whether the rarity is caused solely by its expensiveness I do not know, but there is no doubt that it is a very expensive form of instruction.

A teacher whom students rate highly is likely to be one who is around the office a lot and whom they do not need an appointment to see. But this means spending one's time on something other than writing an article or doing research in the laboratory or jetting all over the country for conventions and consultations. The latter activities contribute to the faculty member's guild visibility, something that impresses the dean much more than it does the undergraduate. Accordingly, when students complain that faculty are inaccessible, it will not do to retort that one has office hours or that one occasionally invites students to his home, for what students have in mind is a personal concern for their academic and personal welfare.

At the American university something like the tutorial relationship is available to the good doctoral student from his advisor. The latter often regards the student as an embryonic junior colleague in his field of study. The advisor takes the student's personal and domestic problems very seriously and identifies with his career. The undergraduate, especially if he has no field of specialization, cannot generate this sort of interest in a faculty member, but something like it, I believe, is what he craves.

Many of the so-called cluster colleges and residential colleges try to recruit staff who feel about undergraduates as university professors feel about their promising doctoral students. The more expensive independent secondary schools were able to find such faculty, and no doubt there are still some small liberal arts colleges with a sizable complement of Messrs. Chips. In the modern large university, faculty attracted to the young tend to fall into three groups: first, the younger faculty members who are political activists and who find allies among students; second, those who are not drawn to research or scholarly work as such; and third, those who would like to get away from conventionalized teaching—especially didactics.

By and large, the first two sorts listed above do not have a bright future in the better university, for they are not going to rise very high in the guild status system. The third is more promising—if we can relieve the professoriate as a whole of the burden of didactics. The move toward cluster and residential colleges on the university campus is an acknowledgment of a genuine need of adolescent students who not only want to further their education, but who also want to solve the problem of completing their adolescence. But the cluster college is at best an oasis for a relatively small portion of the student body, and one must still conclude that the better the university academically, the less likely will it be a good place for living through the storms and stresses of adolescence.

Whether the large university can provide its undergraduates, or some of them, with the proper philetics—that is, collegiate staff interested as much in students as in research, consultation, and other high-status guild activities—remains to be seen. I doubt it. Perhaps a more viable solution is to begin induction into the guild earlier, during the freshman and sophomore years, but this would mean the virtual elimination of general or liberal undergraduate education. Nevertheless, there is some reason to believe that we shall be moving in that direction, at least in the university. Professional and preprofessional curricula (such as engineering and agriculture) have no special problems in this regard; and the pattern they have established may well become the dominant one.

THE TEACHER

I have tried in previous chapters to describe a type of professional teacher who, one might hope, would constitute about 10 to 15 per cent of the instructional staff in our public schools. I repeat that teachers at this level of training and competence now constitute a far smaller proportion of the classroom teacher population, although the word "professional" is freely misused to designate their status. Only well-trained professionals could be expected to be adept at didactics, heuristics, and philetics, and even they are unlikely to be equally adept in all three. In the face of an insufficiency of professional teachers we are tempted to rely on the love of children to take the place of expertise. We are tempted to attribute the failure of schools to the philetic deficiencies of teachers. This justifies the reiteration of what has been noted in these pages about the nature of the love relation appropriate between a professional and his client.

Now the love appropriate to the professional is not fleshly love or fleshly love sublimated into a love of mankind in general. It is concern for the welfare of the client with respect to the service to be rendered. Woe to the patient whose doctor is repelled by sight of diseased tissues or who so identifies with the pain of the patient that he writhes and moans as does the patient himself.

Of course, the patient, the client, the pupil, crave more than depersonalized professional concern. The client naturally is preoccupied by his pain or his needs, and he might indeed welcome tears in the eyes of his physician or lawyer or priest. But these tears, so appropriate in the eyes of the spouse, the parent, the sibling, the lover, are grossly out of place in the professional eye. However, the parent who may forgive the pediatrician who does not love her child will not forgive a teacher who can remain coolly impersonal toward that child, and, conversely, parents of children who love their teachers cannot find it in their hearts to pass a negative judgment on such a teacher, regardless of what the child does or does not learn. Natural as these sentiments and judgments are, they are peripheral to love as a professional concern.

As human beings, pupils create an obligation in all other human beings to treat them as persons, or, as Immanuel Kant put it, never as "means merely." The teacher's duty to pupils is to their potentiality for development. It is the development of the pupil—not the salary of the teacher or the ambitions of the administrator, not the structure of the school system or the state of the nation—that must come first for the professional teacher. Insofar as teachers forget this obligation or find plausible reasons for subordinating this concern to others, they are guilty of a breach of professional ethics.

I would much rather place my faith on such professional

morality and professional expertise for the welfare of pupils—including the retarded, the dull, the handicapped, the unlovely, and often unlovable ones—than on romantic sentiments about individual children or mankind in general.* The attempts of some of the reformers to put romantic notions of love into the classroom attest to their own warmheartedness but do not augur well for the welfare of pupils as pupils. School can never serve *in loco parentis* as far as personal affection is concerned.

I believe that the American people will continue to be committed to a system of public schools that serves the needs of all its children for vocation, citizenship, and self-development *in a modern technological society,* and I believe that as this society matures, its demands will become more and more uniform for everybody. We shall continue to play the achievement game in one form or another, continually struggling to maintain civil probity and individual integrity in that system. The American public would like to see that system staffed by real professionals. But the number of professionals needed would be so great that only an extraordinary financial effort on the part of the American people could satisfy that need. That the people will exert that effort is doubtful. A comparable effort now being contemplated in the health services has met with dismaying results. Our experiments with Medicare have shown what adequately distributed medical services cost. And the public, it must be said, will be less likely to tax itself as heavily for education as for health.

Accordingly, paraprofessionals in all professional fields—medicine, law, education—are probable. In schooling the area most amenable to machinelike operation and therefore most easily assigned to paraprofessionals is didactics. Hence we may

---

* Among the blessings conferred on mankind is the fact that no task is so distasteful but that routinization can make it tolerable and theory can render it respectable. Surgery, garbage disposal, burial of the dead, care of the sick, and scores of other jobs that are not aesthetically attractive get done because we can devise routines for depersonalizing them and thereby disinfecting them from the emotional overtones that make them repulsive. Professionalism carries this routinization forward into areas of critical concern—health, salvation, freedom—and bases the routine on theory. Hence emptying bedpans is revolting to the ordinary civilian, tolerable to the nurse, and a very professional task for the laboratory analysts of fecal materials.

have to settle for a relatively small cadre of, let us say, 300,000 to 350,000 teachers trained to the fully professional level, who will prescribe and monitor the work of paraprofessionals.

I believe that colleges of education should devote their energies to training this professional cadre, leaving the training of paraprofessionals to other postsecondary institutions.

Much, therefore, as I sympathize with the sentiments and applaud the zeal of those who have smoked out the evils of our establishments—to an old liberal, institutional evil hardly comes as a surprise—I regret to have to conclude that the effect of the new humanism—the Kozol-Holt-Friedenberg-Illich-Silberman kind of thing—is not constructive, and not even constructively destructive. Like the Bestors and Rickovers of the previous decade, the new humanists are strangely blind to the multiple demands of the social order that the school struggles to serve. To say that we shall merely maintain the elitism inherent in the old humanism or that we shall throw over all the establishments in favor of some romantic return to nature are exercises in nostalgia rather than sober visions that will change our stubborn social reality for the better.

I differ from these critics of the right and left not because they are extremist and not because they are either revolutionary or overly conservative. Extremists are educative in themselves, although they are almost never right. I differ with them for two major reasons: One is that, without belief in some inherent or at least a highly stable form of human nature, it is fruitless to argue what men "ought" to do or refrain from doing; without it all controversies about education are reduced to self-serving partisanship. Fighting may get you somewhere in such confrontations; argument will not. Nevertheless, the justification for an open society and an education for membership in such a society lies in the possibility of a great range of behavioral forms by which the human essence can be expressed and manifested. This form or essence acts as a limit and criterion by which some possibilities are precluded as nonhuman or inhuman. Only hard reflection can help us decide in individual instances what our final judgment will be. We think by means of the categories of thought and feeling that the living tradition has preserved. Induction into this tradition as a participating active member is the inescapable content and ground of formal education. The critics who would destroy this tradition by ignoring it or downgrading it, at any level of schooling, are regressive, not progressive. They are not revolutionary in any honorific sense of that badly battered term; moreover, in their anguish they have missed the nature of the revolution that is going on.

I do not preach a faith that somehow we shall respond creatively or successfully to our time of troubles. Such optimism is itself a misunderstanding of the true nature of the revolution. The real dialectical joke being played on man is that the technological revolution is laying the groundwork for a new moral order—if individual men will exert the intelligence and effort to use the resources that technology is liberating. But we are not compelled to exert that effort; indeed there will be every temptation not to exert it. We can go just so far with corporate arrangements to provide justice and to provide collective insurance against injustice. But the greatest import of the technological revolution is that, properly exploited, it will enable the individual —if he so wills—to take an individual stance toward it and to define himself against it as well as being a part of it.

The moral, intellectual, aesthetic armamentarium for this eventuality is the sort of education I have tried to describe. Seen in this perspective, the schools, like our other social institutions, can scarcely qualify for unqualified veneration, but the prescription for their reform may be quite different from what many people believe.

On this there is room for debate. My premises may be unwarranted and the conclusions mistaken. This kind of debate, like the debate over the state of the union, is the business and duty of every citizen. Indeed, one measure of good education is the ability and willingness to engage in such discourse. But if teaching and schooling are genuine arts, then professional expertise also has a valid voice in the debate. Great as is my distaste for journalists who pose as experts in education, my greater distress is that the professionals (the educationists) take their doctrine from the journalists.

And this distress is not self-serving, certainly not entirely so. Rather it is occasioned by the realization that a profession in charge of so great an enterprise as education has achieved so little autonomy, so little faith in its own research and study, that it makes a virtue of taking its directions not only in policy but in tactics from whatever group pays its salary.

The American people should be worried if this is the case, and I believe that to a great extent it is. The major factors in determining educational strategy in our country are not the professionals—whether administrative or instructional. As far as elementary and secondary schools are concerned, the major influences now are the Ford and Carnegie foundations, the U.S. Office of Education, the embryonic education industries, and the teachers' unions or associations. The professionals cheerfully serve any or all of these who have money to contribute for salaries, consultation, and research. The foundations and the U.S. Office of Education exert their influence through money for various projects and the publicity these efforts receive. The actual effect on practice is far less than the publicity would indicate, but the publicity is important in providing bait for the professionals and in launching bandwagons that school superintendents find it tempting to board—especially if there are some financial incentives for the ride.

The lines of influence, of course, flow to and fro between the U.S. Office of Education, the foundations, and the education industries, and these constitute an establishment of great power. This power is diluted by the fact that most of their innovations are *ad hoc* improvisations and very often last only as long as the pump is being primed.

The very lack of a body of authoritative expertise among the educationists allows these innovations to go directly to the consumer, and since neither the consumer nor the producer has theoretical criteria wherewith to judge these proposals, the results are predictably erratic and spasmodic.

The influence of teachers' organizations is that of any group that can withhold a service. Even if schools give little more than custodial care (which is far from true), the public is panicked at the thought of closing the schools. The administrators are too busy to think about the instructional process because they are occupied fully in manipulating school boards and their constituencies to secure sufficient funds to run the schools in one way or another. The teachers, realizing that they are members of the proletariat after all, are determined to fight for better wages and conditions of work by negotiating directly with their employers, the school boards. As union leaders achieve power, they use that power in an attempt to become determiners of educational policy. So in the Sunday New York *Times* we find columns side by side—the first a feature, the second a paid advertisement—by the education editor and the head of the city teachers' union, simultaneously giving the public and the professionals their pronouncements on education.

This, then, is the disordered state of American schools, and to this mix of pressures and counterpressures the schools respond by doing on any Tuesday just about what they did on the previous Tuesday. This inertial momentum is the great stabilizing factor, and understandably it is not particularly progressive or imaginative. It is difficult to suggest any other course the schools might take, because they alone remain on the firing line day after day. The foundation representatives, the researchers, the revolutionaries, make their noise and go away to make noise some other day in some other place. The problems are left with the teachers. Their proper leaders—the professional corps, the guild, the gatekeepers—exist only in name. There is no doctrine to unite them, no body of scholarship to legitimate them, no long investment in the preparation for teaching to command their dedication. Given such a situation, it is not surprising that teachers do what they can; that they wish they could get more solid on-the-job training with which to cope; that they haggle over salaries and seniorities; that they quit as soon as something better opens up or as wives move to where their husbands' careers lead. The nation's schools and children deserve something much better. It is not too late to give them what they deserve and what society needs.

If better public education in better public schools is to be provided, however, the whole enterprise of education will have to be taken with greater seriousness than American society is now taking it. If it is to work as we think it must, then it will demand not only more money but also more respect and discipline. There are teachers everywhere who would welcome such responsible rigor. There are pupils everywhere who would respond to it. It can be done. The question is how to set such change going at a sufficient depth and on a sufficient scale to make a difference in the system as a whole. To this question—the master question in American education—there is a babble of prophecy and dissent, but there is no current program that offers a coherent answer. If this book has set out the issues so that the true nature of the question is clear, then perhaps—no stronger term is possible—it may help clear the way for the beginning of the change itself.

A Brief Bibliography
Briefly Annotated

For the most part, and with some notable exceptions, the books listed in this short bibliography date from the sixties and have had some impact on the thinking and politics of education. Most of the titles cited have influenced both the educationists and the general public through the attention accorded them by the popular press. Even in this category no attempt has been made to list all the important works. For example, relatively few of the tremendous output of books in the last decade on higher education are included, and also missing is the vast literature on the miseries of the technological culture. However, the books that are listed do document the sources of the criticisms of the schools around which this book has been built.

Much of the material that has affected the schools is dispersed in reports of conferences, foundations, and commissions. For example, there is a great to-do now about behavioral objectives, performance-based approaches to teacher education, and accountability. The sources of these doctrines are to be found in fairly old behavioristic learning theories, but their impact derives from the fact that they have been picked up and embodied in projects financed by the U.S. Office of Education and some of the education industries. I have not listed these reports or the more technical works on humanistic psychology that take issue with the behaviorists and the efficiency advocates. The effects of these writings can be discerned in many of the books that have been listed.

Finally, may I ask the forgiveness of the many educationists whose writings are eminently worth reading but which I have not listed because they have not created sufficient furor either in the literary or academic establishments. I shall not even mention examples, because to do so would do grave injustice to the scores left unmentioned. For those who are curious about who these writers might be and what they have contributed to the philosophical discussions of education, I

253

suggest a perusal of *Philosophy of Education: An Organization of Topics and Selected Sources* (Harry S. Broudy et al., 1967) and the Supplement to it (Christiana M. Smith and Harry S. Broudy, eds., 1969), both published by the University of Illinois Press. This work is the result of a project, funded by the U.S. Office of Education, that exhibits the structure and content of a field that Mr. Conant, Mr. Koerner, and other critics of teacher education curricula either denied existed or the existence of which they deplored. If any of these critics ever read this rebuttal of their arguments, I have never had any evidence of it.

Barzun, Jacques. *The American University.* New York: Harper & Row, 1968.
> A penetrating and witty dissection of higher education by an urbane old-line humanist with strong elitist predilections.

Berg, Ivar. *Education and Jobs: The Great Training Robbery.* New York: Praeger Publishers, 1970.
> Discusses the lack of correlation between people's performance as employees and as students. The main interest of the book lies in the subtitle.

Bloom, Benjamin S. *Stability and Change in Human Characteristics.* New York: John Wiley & Sons, 1964.
> An influential study of a large mass of data on the shaping of human beings from infancy to adulthood. In general, and in classical modern fashion, the findings reveal the tremendous importance of the first few years of life for everything thereafter.

Bronfenbrenner, Urie, and Condry, J. C. *Two Worlds of Childhood: U.S. and U.S.S.R.* New York: Russell Sage Foundation, 1970.
> Report of interesting experimental research on child development in contrasting cultures. Excellent, pertinent illustrations.

Bruner, Jerome S. *Process of Education.* Cambridge, Mass.: Harvard University Press, 1960.
> Perhaps the most influential book to come out during the curriculum reform movement of the sixties. Stresses the structure of knowledge and Jean Piaget's account of the pupil's affinity for it; in latter days Bruner has confessed to doubting the primacy of the intellect in schooling.

Clark, Kenneth B. *Dark Ghetto.* New York: Harper & Row, 1965.
> Argues that black children do not learn because they are not taught. He is critical of white, middle-class teachers who are waging socio-economic and racial warfare against hopelessly outclassed working-class youngsters. Clark is more than half right but not perhaps for the reasons he adduces.

Cole, Stephen. *The Unionization of Teachers: A Case Study of the U.F.T.* New York: Praeger Publishers, 1969.
A study of the development and in-fighting that attended teacher unionization.

Coleman, James S., *et al. Equality of Educational Opportunity.* Washington, D.C.: U.S. Government Printing Office, 1966.
A prestigious $1.25 million study, which proved that racial segregation in the schools existed, but that poor schools were not the exclusive possession of blacks. As to whether black schools were poorer than white schools, the study concluded that "it depends."

Conant, James B. *Slums and Suburbs.* New York: McGraw-Hill Book Co., 1961.
One of the early warnings that something serious was on the boil in schools of the inner city.

————. *The Education of American Teachers.* New York: McGraw-Hill Book Co., McGraw-Hill Paperbacks, 1963.
This book, done with the blessing and financial help of the Carnegie Foundation, did a great deal to discredit "professional education" courses and curricula in the training of public school teachers. It was influential in reducing teacher education to a form of apprentice training that would supplement a liberal arts degree.

Coons, John E., Clune, William H., III, and Sugarman, Stephen D. *Private Wealth and Public Education.* Cambridge, Mass.: Harvard University Press, Belknap Press, 1970.
This is largely a lawyers' view of the problems of financing public schools. Especially interesting in the light of the 1971 California Supreme Court ruling in the *Serrano v. Priest* case.

Deutsch, Martin, *et al. The Disadvantaged Child.* New York: Basic Books, 1967.
Argues that lower-class children fail in school because of the conditions in school as well as in the home and community environment.

Drucker, Peter F. *Technology, Management and Society.* New York: Harper & Row, 1970.
Business management attitudes and methods are spreading rapidly to agencies such as schools. The book has some important implications for the sort of schooling that life in a mature technological society will require.

Engelmann, Siegfried. *Preventing Failure in the Primary Grades.* Chicago: Science Research Associates, 1969.
"Hard-nosed" engineering approach to learning disabilities. Techniques for reinforcement and behavior modification are described and unblushingly prescribed.

Fantini, Mario D., and Weinstein, Gerald. *The Disadvantaged: Challenge to Education.* New York: Harper & Row, 1968.
Typical of the vast literature of the late sixties in search of the villain responsible for the plight of disadvantaged children—especially in the inner city. In this book and the one below the villains are the school and the hang-ups of the white middle-class teacher.

————, Gittell, Marilyn, and Magat, Richard. *Community Control and the Urban School.* New York: Praeger Publishers, 1970.
Advocates school decentralization. Traces the development of the concepts now guiding public education and surveys growth of bureaucratization. Discusses effects of decentralization on integration and urban structures. Presumably the disadvantaged communities are the best judges of what will be to their advantage.

Featherstone, Joseph. *Schools Where Children Learn.* New York: Liveright, 1971.
Shows how the informal approach of the British primary schools has enabled ordinary teachers to achieve impressive results. The open classroom is one of the popular bandwagons launched in imitation of the British model. Lately some doubts about the way the imitation is being carried out have been voiced by Featherstone and others.

————. *Informal Schools in Britain Today.* New York: Scholastic Book Services, Citation Press, 1971.
More of the same.

Friedenberg, Edgar Z. *Coming of Age in America.* New York: Random House, 1965.
Deplores the atmosphere in schools. Students are forbidden to smoke. Passes, tight scheduling, the reliance on threats of detention or suspensions, are modes of social control; tight dress regulations are universal. Adolescence, Friedenberg tells us, is too good to waste in classrooms like that.

Galbraith, John Kenneth. *Economic Development in Perspective.* Cambridge, Mass.: Harvard University Press, 1962.
Good for an insight into the part played by education in a modern technological society.

Gardner, John W. *Excellence.* New York: Harper & Brothers, 1961.
An influential book by an influential man, it was consonant with the curriculum reform of the early sixties as well as the Kennedy spirit in Washington. Gardner was a major figure in the new educational establishment through his position as Secretary of the Department of Health, Education, and Welfare, and through his prior connections with the Carnegie Foundation for the Advancement of Teaching, of which he was president.

Goodlad, John I., and Anderson, Robert H. *The Nongraded Elementary School.* New York: Harcourt, Brace & World, 1963.
The nongraded school is a device whereby children are grouped for instruction by criteria other than age and grade. Like other devices, it has received fairly wide adoption, but the authors are not happy with the superficiality of much of what is done in the name of nongradedness.

Goodman, Paul. *Compulsory Mis-Education.* New York: Horizon Press, 1964.
Goodman is one of the culture heroes of the disaffected young who appreciate his indictment of formalized, institutionalized schooling. Like Friedenberg and others who discuss these themes, Goodman knows what adolescents do not like.

Harrington, Michael. *The Other America: Poverty in the United States.* New York: Macmillan Co., 1962.
————. *The Politics of Poverty.* New York: League For Industrial Democracy, 1965.
Although not dealing directly with schools, these books were influential in the rediscovery of poverty in America and helped change the pressures on the public schools in the late sixties.

Holt, John. *How Children Fail.* New York: Pitman Publishing Corp., 1964.
One of the earliest screams in the sixties against public schools. Holt is impressed, as everybody has been since Plato, with how much children learn on their own without instruction before entering school.

Hunt, J. McVicker. *The Challenge of Incompetence and Poverty.* Urbana, Ill.: University of Illinois Press, 1970.
A scholarly formulation of the thesis that the child's interaction with the environment is the only determiner of cognitive development. Hunt has been an important figure in the new push for the study of childhood education.

Illich, Ivan D. *Celebration of Awareness—A Call for Institutional Revolution.* New York: Doubleday & Co., Anchor Books, 1971.
Illich is one of the more consistent advocates of deschooling, especially for children of the poor, for whom, he believes, conventional formal education cannot be a means of social mobility.

Jackson, Philip W. *Life in Classrooms.* New York: Holt, Rinehart & Winston, 1968.
See Kozol, Holt, Friedenberg, *et al.*

Jencks, Christopher, and Riesman, David. *The Academic Revolution.* New York: Doubleday & Co., 1968.
A widely read account of turmoil in academe.

Jensen, Arthur R. "How Much Can We Boost IQ and Scholastic Achievement?" *Harvard Educational Review*, Winter, 1969.
An influential article because it aroused the fury of the environmentalists, who took it to be a slur on the native intelligence of black children.

Kahn, Herman, and Wiener, Anthony J. *The Year 2000: A Framework for Speculation on the Next Thirty-Three Years*. New York: Macmillan Co., 1967.
A primer for futurists.

Katz, Michael B. *The Irony of Early School Reform: Educational Innovation in Mid-Nineteenth-Century Massachusetts*. Cambridge, Mass.: Harvard University Press, 1968.
Katz disputes the notion that popular education was the result of idealistic humanitarianism's victory over the wealthy elite and orthodox religionists. He attributes the origin of the free school movement to a coalition of social leaders, status-anxious parents, and status-hungry educators. This book is in line with the current debunking movement of the evangelical fervor of the public school advocates of the previous century and helps support the charge that the public schools are the tools of the middle class in its drive for money and status.

Keniston, Kenneth. *The Uncommitted: Alienated Youth in American Society*. New York: Harcourt, Brace & World, 1965.
————. *Young Radicals: Notes on Commited Youth*. New York: Harcourt, Brace & World, 1968.
Representative of the new humanism. Popular on campuses.

Kerr, Clark. *The Uses of the University*. Cambridge, Mass.: Harvard University Press, 1963.
A statement by the controversial president of the University of California, whose analysis of the modern multiversity is the basis for most of the agonizing in and outside academe about higher education.

Koerner, James D. *The Miseducation of American Teachers*. Boston: Houghton Mifflin Co., 1963.
Unlike most of the critics of teachers and teacher education, who meant it but didn't come right out and say it, Koerner blamed all educational evils on the inferior intellectual quality of the education faculty. Whereupon Koerner was invited to address conventions of educators. Whether this proved or disproved his estimates of their intellectual caliber is hard to say.

Kohl, Herbert. *36 Children*. New York: New American Library, 1968.
See Friedenberg, Kozol, Holt, *et al.*

Kozol, Jonathan. *Death at an Early Age*. Boston: Houghton Mifflin Co., 1967.
Argues that racism is rampant in the school system. Quotes school of-

ficials as saying that there was no *de facto* segregation, that "we gave them everything they asked for," and "we had a hard time, so why shouldn't they?"

Leonard, George B. *Education and Ecstasy*. New York: Dell Publishing Co., Dial Press, 1968.
Another of the odes to joy in the classrooms.

Marcuse, Herbert. *One Dimensional Man: Studies in the Ideology of Advanced Industrial Society*. Boston: Beacon Press, 1966.
Influential among undergraduate left-wing activists; not very hopeful about possibilities of a benign technological society.

McLuhan, Marshall. *Understanding Media*. New York: New American Library, 1964.
———, and Fiore, Quentin. *The Medium Is the Massage*. New York: Random House, 1967.
The McLuhan thesis is that modern man has become accustomed to getting his information from print, word following word, according to the rules of a given language. But in the electronic media we are assailed with an instantaneous mosaic of simultaneous messages, and so we are caught between the diverse demands of the different media. In education, this thesis has helped to play down the traditional emphasis on linguistic skills and boosted the popularity of turning on all the sensory batteries. Since all conventional curricula and even "intelligence" tests are solidly anchored in aptness to acquire linguistic skill, the McLuhan notion is more radical for schooling than all the other "innovations" combined.

Myrdal, Gunnar. *The Challenge of World Poverty*. New York: Random House, Pantheon Books, 1970.
The internationally eminent Swedish economist, author of *An American Dilemma*, makes recommendations for the reform of society, agriculture, education, and politics in developing countries and points out the responsibility that the industrially advanced countries share for their development. Teachers, parents, and those who make a good thing out of denouncing the schools need to put the school as an institution into this kind of context.

Neill, A. S. *Summerhill*. New York: Hart Publishing Co., 1960.
A bible for advocates of informal education by one of its archbishops.

Oettinger, Anthony G., and Marks, Sema. *Run, Computer, Run*. Cambridge, Mass.: Harvard University Press, 1969.
One of the workers within the field of educational technology expresses some reservations about the virtues claimed for it.

Postman, Neil, and Weingartner, Charles. *Teaching as a Subversive Activity*. New York: Dell Publishing Co., Delacorte Press, 1969.

The "new education" is to be student-centered, a "crap detecting and relevance business." The content for every lesson can be nothing more than student responses and cannot consist in anything else.

Rathbone, Charles H., ed. *Open Education: The Informal Classroom.* New York: Scholastic Book Services, Citation Press, 1970.
A collection of twelve essays examining the principles and practices of informal education as they are being applied within the British primary schools and their counterparts in the United States. Contains excerpts from the *Plowden Report*, with a "thoughtful introduction" by "noted educational critic" John Holt.

Raywid, Mary Anne. *The Ax-Grinders.* New York: Macmillan Co., 1962.
Documents the sundry causes in behalf of which sundry interest groups try to use the public schools.

Schaefer, Robert J. *The School as a Center of Inquiry.* New York: Harper & Row, 1967.
One of the few voices protesting the arrogance of liberal scholars in the curriculum reform movement of the early sixties. The contempt of the scholars for the teacher was manifested in the attempt to produce teacher-proof curricula.

Sexton, Patricia C. *Spanish Harlem.* New York: Harper & Row, 1965.
Demands a total reorganization of the educational system in deprived communities. Not only the curriculum but also the power structure of the schools need to be changed through community arousal. The author foresees the power and pride such change can provide for impoverished citizens.

Silberman, Charles. *Crisis in the Classroom.* New York: Random House, 1970.
Another Carnegie-inspired and -financed exposé of the public schools, "researched" with the help and advice of choice spirits at Columbia Teachers College. Blames almost everything on the mindless teachers who are trained by mindless educationists. Belongs with the radical-chic literature on the schools. Much touted "best seller."

Skinner, B. F. *The Technology of Teaching.* New York: Appleton-Century-Crofts, 1968.
Skinner is the father of the education industries, at least as far as theory is concerned. His theory of operant conditioning, supported by his brilliant accomplishments with teaching pigeons to do extraordinarily sophisticated tasks, is the most promising basis for a "science" of teaching, as well as for the management of society. A society conditioned by Skinner might not be a bad society, because Skinner, after all, was brought up by non-Skinnerian methods, but give a barbarian Skinner's methods, and Skinner's program is as frightening as it is plausible.

Smith, Mortimer, ed. *A Decade of Comment on Education, 1956–1966*. Washington, D.C.: Council for Basic Education, 1966.
Staunch defenders of intellectual quality in education speak out against the educationists of whom the editor remarked, "It has been a happy experience to discover over the years that not all educationists are anti-intellectual clods. . . ." Smith is "apprehensive of the new establishment, that rather amorphous body made up roughly of some of the large philanthropic foundations, the 'new' faces in the U.S. Office of Education, the commercial producers of school materials, and those who devise 'new curricula' with governmental funds."

Stephens, J. M. *The Process of Schooling*. New York: Holt, Rinehart & Winston, 1967.
This book, which deflates the efforts to relate educational results with class size, school size, administrative organization, teacher's ability and personality, teaching methods, and kindred variables, should have cooled off the scientific pretensions of the efficiency lads, but it didn't.

Taylor, Harold. *The World and the American Teacher*. Washington, D.C.: American Association of Colleges for Teacher Education, 1968.
Taylor says, "Preparing to become a teacher is like preparing to become a poet. The preparation begins in a decision to become something, a commitment made about one's own life and the purpose of it." Taylor is one of the more wholesome romantics in education, but this description of how and why young people go into public school teaching is more romantic than reliable.

Wees, W. R. *Nobody Can Teach Anyone Anything*. Garden City, N.Y.: Doubleday & Co., 1971.
Sharp indictment of modern education. Before the child came to school, he had taught himself many things; but schools snuff out the spark of learning. Touches on "humanistic" elements of education and calls for a reinstatement of the notion of the "whole child." Wees is a Canadian educator but apparently has been overwhelmed by the influence of the big noise to the south.

Weinstein, Gerald, and Fantini, Mario, eds. *Toward Humanistic Education—A Curriculum of Affect*. Ford Foundation Report. New York: Praeger Publishers, 1970.
Calls for involving the child in the learning process through a "curriculum of affect" based on the child's own concerns and responses. This book is fairly typical of what might be called the new humanism, which locates the human essence in the autonomic nervous system.

Index